BLENHEIMS
OVER GREECE
AND CRETE
1940-1941

BULGARIA

Durazzo • Tirana
Brindisi • Berat
L.Ochrida
Valona • Monastir
Tepelene
Argyrokastron Salonica
Corfu
Olympus
R Kalamas • Yanina
Paramythia • Larissa

Thermopylae Euboea

Corinth • Menidi
Argos • Athens
Kalamata Eleusis
• Sparta
Giorgio

Cape Matapan
Kythera
○ Anti-Kythera

Canea
Maleme Candia
Heraklion
Crete Rho

MEDITERRANEAN

BLENHEIMS OVER GREECE AND CRETE 1940-1941

BRIAN CULL

WITH

SIMON LORD, THEMIS SERBIS, IAN CARTER,
ALEKS OGNJEVIĆ & LUDOVICO SLONGO

FONTHILL

Learn more about Fonthill Media. Join our mailing list to find out about our latest titles and special offers at: www.fonthillmedia.com

Fonthill Media Limited
Fonthill Media LLC
www.fonthillmedia.com
office@fonthillmedia.com

First published in the United Kingdom and the Unitess States of America 2014

British Library Cataloguing in Publication Data:
A catalogue record for this book is available from the British Library

First published in hardback in 2014
This paperback edition published 2017

ISBN 978-1-78155-280-3 (hardback)
ISBN 978-1-78155-631-3 (paperback)

Typeset in 10pt on 13pt Minion Pro
Printed and bound by CPI Group (UK) Ltd, Croydon, CR0 4YY

Contents

Introduction

When Simon Lord contacted me a couple of years ago about the hoard of documents he had amassed relating to 30 Squadron's Blenheim operations during the early days of the Second World War, we initially discussed the possibility of writing an account of his Grandfather Bert's involvement as a Wireless Operator/Air-Gunner with the Squadron, both pre-war and up to the fall of Crete in May 1941. But, when I had the opportunity to see for myself the mass of documents including copies of logbooks, the possibility then existed of writing about the 30 Squadron's activities during the fighting in Greece and eventually Crete, not just Bert's participation.

I had a personal interest in the subject since I was co-author of *Air War for Yugoslavia, Greece and Crete* published way back in 1987, a book that includes stories and accounts of Blenheim operations during the campaign, including those of 30 Squadron. Further research revealed that access to surviving records and accounts of the other RAF Blenheim squadrons involved was feasible, and thus the project was expanded to include all relevant Blenheim units. These include much information made available on 211 Squadron via the auspices of Ian Carter and Don Clark, both specialists in the activities of that unit, made famous by the writings of RAF Press Officer Sqn Ldr Tommy Wisdom in *Wings over Olympus*.

Once underway, Themis Serbis, a young Greek graduate who lives in Ioannina but originally from the beautiful part of Greece known as the 'Valley of Fairy Tales'—Paramythia—joined the team, and via his efforts came the story of the Greek Air Force's only Blenheim squadron, 32 Mira. Contact was then made with Aleks Ognjević, a Serbian aviation historian/author, who is writing a book on the Blenheim in Yugoslav service, and who has generously extracted information from his research for inclusion in *Blenheims over Greece and Crete*. Last but not least, my good Italian friend Ludovico Slongo has provided much previously unpublished material regarding the Regia Aeronautic pilots who confronted the RAF and Greek Blenheims during their forays over Albania.

Thanks guys for your contributions.

Brian Cull

Foreword
by Simon Lord

Grandson of 30 Squadron's Herbert *Lofty* Lord DFC

In February 1988, I swore allegiance to Queen and country and in doing so continued the family tradition of serving in the Royal Air Force. I was joining my brother, Andy, as the third generation to serve after my father Alan and his father Bert. Only my mother Wendy and sister Karen did not join the RAF; however it can be argued that they both served, Karen being born at RAF Wegberg, Germany and my mother raising us kids whilst my father was sent here there and everywhere, as is the RAF way. We were a typical RAF family and despite all the moves we loved every minute of being part of the wider family that is the RAF. My joining the RAF came less than a year after the death of my Grandfather Bert, in Australia, where he had emigrated when I was ten years old.

Fifty years prior to my signing on the dotted line, in May 1938, my Grandfather Bert, better known as *Lofty*, arrived at RAF Habbaniya, Iraq, to join his first unit, 30 Squadron which had recently become the first overseas squadron to receive the Blenheim MkI (see Appendix II).

Throughout my childhood I knew little of my Grandfather's service in the RAF and even less of his exploits during the war. My abiding memory of Grandpa was that he used to tell us he'd had his tongue shot off during the war and he used to chase us round the house showing us the black mark across his tongue where it had been sewn back on. I'm certain he took a secret delight in scaring us but I never believed he had actually had his tongue shot off.

It was not until I had left the RAF that I took a keen interest in Grandpa's war years. During a visit to my parents I first saw the medals and logbooks that he had bequeathed to my father. Whilst looking through the logbooks I was astounded at how much he had done in his aviation career. I came to realise I knew nothing of the man himself so I decided to try and research as much information about him as possible starting with his time in the RAF.

I decided the best way to get to know more about my Grandfather would be to understand what hardships he and his colleagues had to endure. This involved attempting to trace any living members of 30 Squadron and/or their relatives. I became adept at tracing the relatives of those names in the logbook that had flown with *Lofty*. Mostly I was a little too late to speak to the aircrew themselves but relatives were a mine of information, with logbooks, photo albums, diaries and other items that built the picture of life on 30 Squadron and flying the Blenheim. I generally found that I could provide information and sometimes photographs to people I contacted, which helped them understand their relatives' time and what they had to endure at the beginning of the war. In one instance I was able to help bring closure to the daughter of a 30 Squadron pilot who was killed in 1940. She knew nothing of how and where her father had been killed and it brought her great comfort to finally have all the facts. It was those instances that made all my work worthwhile.

Over the years I compiled a large collection of copies of logbooks as well as photos and general information about 30 Squadron, their Blenheims and the crews that flew in them. Trips to the National Archives at Kew were an exciting outing for me as each visit uncovered more nuggets of information that helped piece together the big picture. I was lucky in the fact that 30 Squadron was still an active unit, based at RAF Lyneham flying Hercules (it has since moved to RAF Brize Norton). I must give special thanks to the Squadron and its Association for all the help given me including access to the Squadron history room, and the freedom to borrow anything I so wished.

It was during a trip to a 30 Squadron reunion that I had the pleasure of meeting a Blenheim Wireless Operator/Air-Gunner by the name of Johnny Vellacott. When I introduced myself to him as Simon Lord he replied "Not *Lofty* Lord's grandson?" As it turned out Johnny had been my Grandfather's best friend from 1938 through to the end of their time with the Squadron. The photograph albums I had contained numerous photos of Johnny and *Lofty* together and now here I was, talking to the same man 70 years later. Johnny was full of stories and gave me a real insight into my Grandfather's character. It was a very surreal and emotional experience and one that was to bring about a great friendship between us for the few short years before Johnny passed on.

After a number of years of researching I had amassed a great deal of material and I felt closer to my Grandfather than when he was alive. I had achieved my goal of getting to know the man, but now I had all this extra material regarding 30 Squadron and it was my secret desire to have it published; however I hadn't a clue how to go about it nor the time (or capability) to write a book using it. After a couple of false leads I was lucky enough to be chatting to a fellow Blenheim enthusiast Ian Carter, who is the editor of the *Blenheim Society Journal*. We were discussing my research and my desire to have it published when he mentioned that a friend of his happened to be a respected and widely published aviation author Brian Cull. I already owned a couple of Brian's books and was flabbergasted to think that he may possibly be interested in my research let alone agree to using it in one of his books.

Ian kindly made introductions via e-mail and one afternoon I gave Brian a ring. We spent over an hour on the phone talking through all aspects of life and

Brian agreed to take on my research. I was thrilled to say the least. An amount of my research has gone into *Blenheims Over Greece and Crete*, which is my little dedication, not just to my Grandfather, but to the whole of 30 Squadron and to all the other 'Blenheim Boys' who fought so courageously in all theatres of the second world war.

Hope you will enjoy reading it as much as I did.

Simon Lord

A Word from Ian Carter
Editor of the *Blenheim Society Journal*

The significance of the Greek campaign and events surrounding it have long been overlooked within the history of the Second World War. The publication of this book is a valuable insight into those events of 74 years ago.

Brian Cull is a well-respected author who understands the 'people' as much as writing about the events, while in Simon Lord and Themis Serbis we have two enthusiasts that, although separated by country and age, have direct links to the campaign. Simon's grandfather fought with 30 Squadron as a Wop/AG and Themis was born in Paramythia, the beautiful valley in Greece that years before had been an RAF forward airfield, while the contributions from Ludovico Slongo and Aleks Ognjević have greatly enhanced the account.

In May 1941, the evacuated allied forces were still in large numbers on Crete when the Germans invaded, and this mix, including Greek and Cretan civilians, fought a fierce and in many cases, hand-to-hand battle with the paratroops. The defenders included a large number of airmen from the Blenheim squadrons. These airmen fought with incredible courage and sacrifice as the memorial to 30 Squadron at Maleme shows. As Tom Henderson, armourer with 211 Squadron recalled, "it was raining blood—we were shooting that many out of the sky."

Before this point was arrived at however, the Blenheims had fought difficult odds, not only with the Italian fighters, but more importantly the weather. This was some of the worst anywhere in the world—an air-gunner commented that his aircraft had been flying along quite happily when the Blenheim suddenly dropped 300 feet and he hit his head on the the top of the gun turret! The valleys were another hazard and clearance was extremely tight. Often an imaginary plumb line would be dropped down each side of the aircraft to check they could squeeze through, and this was before the target appeared! One other thing, in terms of aircraft performance; the Blenheims did not have the advantage of 100 octane fuel as in Europe, hence they would be down on engine performance before they had even got going. And, if you were shot down and injured, the chance of medical attention was slim, and some aircrew died in very difficult circumstances.

Blenheims over Greece and Crete is likely to be a final and fitting tribute to the Blenheim air and ground crews of the RAF that achieved so much, but that has been largely forgotten.

Ian Carter (see Appendix III)

Requiem for the Blenheim Crew

The solemn march of these immortal few
Is beating in the skies;
From silent ranks there gleams the steadfast light
Of triumph in their eyes;
They know the ecstasy of battle's thrill,
And victories finest prize.

Though they were few, too few, who fought in Greece,
They waged a constant fight;
A new mythology of glorious deeds
Their mountain tombstones write;
So tell their lasting honour to the world.
And keep their torch alight!

Air-Vice Marshal James Gordon-Finlayson DSO DFC Greek DFC
Commanding Officer 211 Squadron, 1940-41

Preamble

Blenheims in the Middle East & Greece 1940

When Italy entered the war in June 1940, the RAF Middle East order of battle included nine Blenheim squadrons, of which five were based in Egypt: 30 Squadron (Mk.I and IF) at Ismailia, 45 Squadron (Mk.I) at Fuka, 55 Squadron (Mk.I) at Fuka, 113 Squadron (Mk.IV) at Ma'atan Bagush, and 211 Squadron (Mk. I) at El Daba. In addition, 84 Squadron was currently in Iraq with Mk.Is, while 8, 11 and 39 were in Aden also with Mk.Is.

At dawn on the first day of the war (11 June), six Blenheims from 211 Squadron flew an armed reconnaissance over the frontier, followed two hours later by eight of 45 Squadron that carried out a low level attack against an airfield at El Adem, with disastrous results. Meeting AA fire and CR.32s, three were shot down and two more damaged. Later, Blenheims from 55 and 113 Squadrons were in action, the former unit having one aircraft damaged while the latter lost one. An inauspicious start for the Blenheim in the Middle East war.

During the remainder of the month, daily small-scale raids against Italian Army bases and airfields in Libya were made in rotation by aircraft of the four Egyptian-based Blenheim squadrons so that each squadron operated only every fourth day. However, 45 Squadron soon ceased operations and from 15 June was released from active service and placed in reserve at Helwan, as a measure of the severity of the losses suffered by the unit during the first four days of war (three complete crews). The Blenheims of all the squadrons had been dispersed to satellite landing grounds to avoid the frequent bombing of their main airfields by the Italians. It was not possible to launch any larger-scale raids, as fewer serviceable aircraft remained available. At the end of the month, 45 Squadron sent a flight of four aircraft to 211 Squadron at El Daba and three aircrews to 113 Squadron at Ma'aten Bagush.

Meanwhile, 30 Squadron had begun fitting packs containing four forward-firing Brownings under the fuselage of B and C Flight Blenheims, converting the aircraft into Mk.IF fighters. These fighter Blenheims had in the meantime been joined by one Mk.IF from 211 Squadron and two from 11 Squadron, so that the strength of the former unit by 15 June was twelve Mk.IFs and six standard Mk.Is. Several detachments from 30 Squadron were temporarily sent to Amiriya,

Helwan, Qasaba, Gerawla and Mersa Matruh during the first weeks of the war, but no action was recorded. One of the first duties assigned to the Squadron was that of 'Shadow Patrols', shadowing the Italian bombers after they had bombed Amriya and Helwan and to follow them to their home bases to discover where these airstrips were. This type of mission was very dangerous and of dubious utility, and thus was quickly cancelled.

Throughout the summer months of 1940, operations for the Blenheim squadrons continued unabated, with some success but also with many losses to both fighters and ground fire. However, replacement crews and aircraft were available to fill the gaps. Many of the survivors of the summer battles would find themselves in Greece before the year was out.

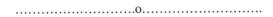

Meanwhile, in Greece, 32 Mira (Squadron) was one of the three bomber squadrons of the Royal Hellenic Air Force (RHAF) in 1940 and the only squadron flying Blenheims. Negotiations between the Greek government and the Bristol Aeroplane Company had begun in 1937 and as a result the Greeks ordered 24 Blenheim Mk.IVs. The first twelve aircraft arrived via Hungary between April and May 1940, flying to Greece with British civil registrations (G-AFXD to G-AFXO), painted with the classic RAF temperate colours, carrying Greek roundels and serial numbers B251 to B262 on the fuselage, and void of any equipment except machine-guns. The reason for this lack of equipment was that the deal for the purchase of these aircraft covered only the aircraft itself.

When the first Blenheims arrived, 32 Mira, under the command of Major Charalambos Potamianos, was based at Eleusis (pronounced 'Elefsis') airfield, just outside Athens, which in mid-1940 turned to be one of the best organised air bases in Greece. As this type of aircraft was something absolutely new for Greek pilots and engineers, it took many days with hard work until the crews were ready to fly safely. The problems, however, did not stop there. These brand-new aircraft arrived without bomb sights, radios, intercommunication system, photographic cameras and bomb holders. 32 Mira, as with all RHAF units, also lacked experienced aircrew: there were no trained machine- gunners, bombardiers, radio operators or navigators.

On 1 June, the Mira was ordered to move to the airfield of Nea Aghialos, outside Volos city, which was intended to be its new base. Two days later, in the morning of 3 June, the first four aircraft were already airborne as the fifth was preparing its take-off from Eleusis. At that moment the Blenheim flown by Major Potamianos returned with the news that Nea Aghialos was flooded due to heavy rainfall and was unsuitable for landing. However, one of the three other aircraft did land on the muddy and flooded airfield, while the second landed at Larissa airfield, which was in better condition. The third aircraft, though, had a much worse luck. Lost in bad weather, it crashed in the water of Pagasitikos Gulf, east of Nea Aghialos. The three crew members, 2/Lt Michael Davakis, Flt Sgt Michael Gakas and Sgt Spyrou were instantly killed on impact. Wt Off Georgios Sakkis wrote on this tragic event:

> I do not know if the meteorological service did its job correctly that day. But, since the movement of the Mira was ordered, our leader, Ch. Potamianos, who took off first in row, ordered the rest of the airborne aircraft to return to their base, as he did himself, if there were communication systems among the aircraft.[1]

After this tragic event, the transfer of 32 Mira to Nea Aghialos was cancelled and all aircraft and the crew remained at Eleusis.

During their stay at Eleusis in the summer of 1940, the crews undertook an intensive training course with all available means on the ground and in the air in order to gain experience. While many of the crewmen were not even airmen, the training task became even more difficult as they were transferred to the Mira from infantry army schools. These men were rapidly trained as gunners and bombardiers and, thus, the gap regarding these positions was, theoretically, filled.

From the first days of June 1940, 32 Mira began flying long navigational sorties all over Greece, to let the crews become familiar with the aircraft, the country and other airfields; and to practice various tasks, such as virtual target reconnaissance, virtual bombing (using small training bombs), and formation flying, machine-gun and instrument training. Lack of equipment was soon rectified by ingenious local modifications, but the Mira still faced many problems due to the deficiencies of the aircraft. Not only was there no radio contact with ground control, there was no means of communication between the crew members. Therefore, on approaching the target, the pilot was required to keep an eye on the bombardier in order to follow his hand instructions, in addition to what was happening outside. The problem was temporarily solved by a string attached on the right arm of the pilot to the right leg of the gunner in his turret, as described by Wt Off Georgios Sakkis:

> If I pulled once this meant enemy fighters, twice meant anti-aircraft, while three times meant we have to bale out. We added nothing more as there was a big possibility of making mistakes, which would probably have cost us our lives.[2]

In addition, the gunner had to be very careful as his gun would not stop automatically firing in the line of the rudder. A number of Blenheims returned having had their rudders damaged by their own bullets.

On 23 August, 32 Mira received orders to move northwards to Niamata, an ancillary airfield—actually nothing more than a large, flat field—near Larissa. After their arrival, the crews passed the night in tents and only in the next morning did they realise that the area was inappropriate for the establishment of the unit as it was full of mosquitoes! They suffered so many mosquito bites that they decided to move immediately the next day, to another auxiliary airfield, at Vasiliki, near Trikkala. In the morning Major Potamianos and his crew, flying the first aircraft, B260, to arrive at Vasiliki, were surprised to see flocks of sheep grazing around the airfield. The living conditions at Vasiliki were primitive and crewmen remained living in tents, under continuous alert, without electricity, lighting, water or any buildings. A move back to Eleusis followed in due course.

CHAPTER 1

Another Greek Tragedy

*With faith in God and the destiny of the Race, the Nation, united and disciplined
as one man, will fight in the defence of hearth and home until final victory.*
King George II of the Hellenes

Italian forces invaded Greece via Albania on the morning of **28 October
1940**, following years of tension between the two countries. There followed a
Proclamation of War by Prime Minister Joannis Metaxas:

> The moment has come for us to fight for the independence, for the integrity, and
> for the honour of Greece. Although we have observed the strictest neutrality,
> with absolute impartiality towards all, Italy, denying us the right to live the life
> of free Hellenes, demanded from me at 3 o'clock this morning the surrender of
> positions of the national territory, to be chosen by herself, and informed me
> that her troops would move forward at 6am in order to take possession.
>
> I replied to the Italian Minister that I considered both the demand itself
> and the manner of delivery as a declaration of war on the part of Italy against
> Greece.
>
> It is now for us to show whether we are indeed worthy of our ancestors and
> of the freedom won for us by our forefathers. Let the entire nation rise as one
> man. Fight for your country, your wives, for your children, and for our sacred
> traditions. Now the struggle is for very existence.

The Greek military could offer little in the way of defence apart from blood
and guts. It was potentially outnumbered by a well-equipped Italian army, navy
and air force. The Greek air force comprised a motley collection of mainly
obsolete fighters (three squadrons of PZL-24 and one of Bloch MB.151s) and
three squadrons of light bombers, the most modern of which were the Blenheim
IVs.

Italy's air force in Albania, *Comando Aeronautica Albania*, was in fact not
much better equipped but was more numerous and with greater reserves. Its
main fighter aircraft was the CR.42 biplane—roughly equivalent to the RAF's

Gladiator—(393ª Squadriglia with eight aircraft was based at Koritza) although G.50s were coming into service, 395ª Squadriglia being based at Berat. Within days of war breaking out, three more squadriglie of G.50s (354ª, 355ª and 361ª) arrived at Tirana, and three squadriglie of CR.42s (363ª, 364ª and 365ª) flew into Tirana, Valona and Argyrokastron, respectively. On arrival at Tirana, 361ª and 395ª Squadriglie were detached from their parent units to form 154° Gruppo Aut.CT. There were also eight bomber squadriglie equipped with SM.79 and S.81 trimotors available to *Comando Aeronautica Albania,* together with a number of Ro.37 reconnaissance machines and Z.506B floatplanes.

The initial Italian aerial incursion over Greece came on the first day of the invasion, SM.79s and S.81s operating from Valona and Tirana, plus Z.1007bis and BR20s from Lecce and Grottaglie on the Italian mainland, carrying out bombing raids on the Doliana-Kalpaki road during the early afternoon. One S.81 was hit by AA over Patras and subsequently force-landed near Otranto. The Italian General HQ published its first communiqué of the war the following day:

> Yesterday at dawn our troops in Albania crossed the Greek frontier and penetrated enemy territory at several points. The advance continues. Our air force, in spite of unfavourable atmospheric conditions, had repeatedly bombed the military objectives assigned to it, obtaining hits on the buildings and platforms of the railway station at the port of Patras and starting fires. It has also bombed installations along the Corinth Canal, the naval base at Preveza, and installations at the Tatoï airport near Athens. All our planes have returned to their bases.

The Italian plan was to strike at the heart of Epirus, and by seizing Yannina and Metsovo, to make fullest use of the Albanian port of Santi Quaranta, which was linked to Yannina by road. Yannina and Metsovo were they keys to Larissa and the Plain of Thessaly and ultimately to Athens. At first the Italian advance proceeded smoothly and soon Italian cavalry patrols were reported in the neighbourhood of Yannina. While this was happening, more units had crossed the wooded heights of Grammos and Smolika on the northerly slopes of the Pindus and had penetrated as far as Samarina and Distrato to within striking distance of Metsovo. The Greek units fell back at the onslaught and could only fight delaying actions to allow the main Greek forces to mobilise and concentrate.

32 Mira flew its first war sortie on **31 October**, when B260 in the hands of Lt Alexander Papaioannou took off from Vasilki/Trikkala for a reconnaissance of the Italian-occupied airfield of Koritza, in the south-west of Albania. The mission was successfully completed with no interference from Italian fighters or AA fire. Towards the evening of **1 November**, three Blenheims made their first raid, an attack on the two airfields at Koritza. One of these, Drenova, escaped damage,

but Koritza itself was hard hit, fifteen personnel being killed and 20 wounded. The raid caused heavy damage to the airstrip and buildings. The Greek aircrews believed that they had destroyed many aircraft on the ground, but none in fact had suffered damage during the bombing. However, soon after the attacks, a CR.42 and a CR.32, arriving from Tirana, crashed into bomb craters and were both damaged.

During the return flight one of the Blenheims became lost in the dark, but soon fires were spotted on the ground, which the pilot, Lt Photius Maravelias, assumed to be an improvised flare path at his base, set up to aid his landing. In fact, he landed in a field where peasants had been burning old grass. The bomber was undamaged, but the crew was confronted by peasants who believed them to be Greek-speaking Italians. At first, nothing would persuade them otherwise, not even the national markings on the Blenheim. The peasants stated repeatedly that the Italians were displaying duplicates on their own aircraft. This fallacy stemmed from the fact that at a distance the white cross painted on the rudders of Italian aircraft did indeed look like a Greek flag, while the press and radio had stated that Italian bombers displaying a Greek flag had bombed Patras, Salonika and Corfu. Finally, in desperation, Lt Maravelias sang and danced a Greek folksong, which at last convinced the peasants, who joined in.

A friendly fire incident occurred during the morning of **2 November**, when three PZL-24 fighters engaged an unidentified aircraft, which turned out to be a civilian Ju 52/3m of the Greek airline *EEES*. It force-landed on the bank of the Pineios River fortunately without casualties, but two of the fighter pilots involved were killed later that afternoon, north of Yannina, by Italian fighters. Meanwhile, seven 32 Mira Blenheims again raided the Koritza airfields. As they attacked, two CR.42s tried to scramble piloted by Sottoten. Franco Fatigati and Serg. Ardesio Pippo of 393ª Squadriglia, but the aircraft of Pippo (MM4302) was caught in the blast of the bombs and was destroyed, the pilot being killed. According to Italian records, the raid comprised six bombers only. Three attacked Koritza and three Drenova, damaging both airstrips. At Drenova there was one dead (presumably Pippo) and four wounded. One Blenheim, B260, was hit by AA fire and was obliged to force-land just short of Visiliki/Trikkala, without injury to the crew. On **3 November,** shortly before the arrival of the first RAF Blenheims at Eleusis, 32 Mira again transferred to Larissa/Ampelonas airfield, which remained little more than a flat field susceptible to becoming waterlogged.

While the British had been quick to secure Crete when the Italians declared war on Greece, initial reaction had not brought a similar despatch of aid to the mainland. On 30 October, the British Minister in Athens sent a telegram to General Wavell indicating that, while Greek morale remained high, the need for direct and observable aid was critical if their resistance was to be sustained. Wavell turned to the AOC ME, Air Chief Marshal Sir Arthur Longmore, who at once allocated 30 Squadron for immediate movement to Greece.

30 Squadron was to be followed as swiftly as possible by two more squadrons of Blenheim bombers (211 and 84) and one of Gladiators (80 Squadron), the latter unit to be reinforced with Hurricanes as soon as they became available. A squadron of Wellingtons (70 Squadron) was also allocated for operations over Greece and Albania. At the same time Air Commodore J. H. D'Albiac, AOC Palestine and Transjordan, was ordered to Greece to take command of the air contingent.

Before 30 Squadron departed for the new theatre of war, Flt Lt Ron LeDieu, senior pilot and adjutant, was ordered to travel to Greece and make the necessary preparations:

> I was flown over to Piraeus in a Sunderland with a senior army officer who was apparently on the same sort of job as I. I enjoyed the trip. I was even allowed to take the controls of the Sunderland for a little while. I was told I would be put in touch with the Greek air force, who were the only ones who knew where we should be based, get all the information about the size of the field and facilities available, and signal them back so the Squadron could make their plans.
>
> When we got there I was met by the air attaché from the Embassy and taken to the *Gran Bretagne Hotel*. I went out to Eleusis, a Greek air force station about 20 or so miles out of Athens, which we were to have as our base. I had a long chat with the station commander and got all the information I needed. Of course, I had to wait until I got back to Athens before I could send it back to Egypt.
>
> While talking to the station commander at Eleusis, he asked me if we had any equipment for tracing radio transmitters. He was sure, he said, that there was one or perhaps more transmitters operating close round the base which acted as beacons for Italian aircraft to follow when they made raids on Eleusis or Athens. He also said they knew when to expect a raid because, as it got dark, fires were lit on the tops of all the hills that surrounded the base, almost like a flare path to guide the attackers[1].

Sgt Johnny Vellacott (a 30 Squadron air-gunner who arrived shortly thereafter) added:

> A little quiet work by our Greek friends revealed that a man with a radio was hiding just outside the village of Eleusis, and from his vantage point could be aware of much of our flying and the direction in which we proceeded. He was caught red-handed and quietly dealt with.[2]

Study of the situation in Greece had already demonstrated that the main problem associated with a sustained air effort would be the lack of all-weather airfields. It seems that Wg Cdr Lord Arthur Forbes[3]—former Air Attaché in Bucharest (Romania)—who had been despatched in his official capacity as Air Advisor to the Minister of State for the Middle East, to various regions of Greece in search of suitable landing sites, had only negatives to report. He flew his personal twin-engined Percival Q.6 (G-AFMV) whilst engaged on this somewhat clandestine duty. His assessment was that only Eleusis/Athens and Tatoi/Menidi—from where the Blenheims were to operate—could be considered moderately suitable, but both were situated a considerably long distance from the targets to be attacked in Albania. The mountainous nature of much of Greece left few suitable sites for the construction of other airfields. However, the matter was partly solved by the decision to use Eleusis as a forward refuelling and rearmament base for the Wellingtons operating from Egypt.

CHAPTER 2

Arrival of the RAF

In a Blenheim to Valona
Every morning just at nine
Same old aircraft, same old target
Same old place and same old time

Oh Intelligence Department
Sitting coy at HQG
How I wish I could show you
Musso throwing things at me

How I wish I were at HQ
Drinking coffee by the score
And I'd send you out to go to
Our Valona more and more

30 Squadron thus transferred from Egypt to Eleusis airfield, 35-year-old New Zealander Sqn Ldr Ulic Shannon leading eight Blenheim IFs of C Flight to Eleusis on **3 November**, the very first British fighting unit to arrive in Greece, its priority task being the air defence of Athens. The Blenheims were accompanied by four 216 Squadron Bombay transports carrying equipment and kit. They were followed by B Flight's bombers led by Canadian Flt Lt Al Bocking DFC (awarded for operations in Palestine), who wrote:

> We didn't see Crete on the way to our destination. Cloud covered the whole of the area—low-lying stratus, almost a surface fog—out of which arose the tops of many small islands that increased in number as we neared the Greek coast. They looked for all the world like boats sailing on a strange milky-white sea.
>
> We had no 'alternate' and little fuel when we reached Athens by straight DR navigation, and I found myself hoping that in our case it really meant what it stood for, because the biggest snow-covered mountains that I'd seen for many years lay straight ahead in a vast crescent shape. As *Bud* Richardson aggrievedly put it, 'The gravy's getting mighty low!' But Dame Fortune was in a good mood that day, and she saved the lumps for later. We crossed the Corinth Canal, and there before us we saw the airfield at Eleusis. [1]

Although the accommodation at Eleusis for the NCOs was one room comprised of beds made of wooden boards and straw paillasses, it was luxurious compared to the 'dug in' tents they had been used to whilst in Egypt. The scenery of hills and mountains of Greece was a spectacular and welcome change to the drudgery of the Iraqi and Egyptian sand, as recalled by Sgt *Lofty* Lord, air-gunner aboard Canadian Flg Off. Harry Card's K7099:

My first impression of arriving in Greece, as part of the vanguard of the Squadron, was of partial delight on leaving the sand, flies and heat of the desert. Green scenery and pleasant autumn weather lulled one into a sense of false security, which was rudely awakened as week by week another aircraft and another crew of friendly faces disappeared and new ones gradually took their place.

He continued:

On arrival at Eleusis, A and B Flights were converted back to bombers, and C Flight (my Flight) remained as fighters to cover the defence of Athens—4 or 5 aircraft, 4 or 5 air-gunners and 6 or 7 pilots—so the air-gunners were in constant demand at this time. This seemed to me to be a period in which one just resigned oneself to day to day happenings as we were under Greek control, so to speak—we were never put in the picture as far as events.[2]

The weather surrounding the mountains could be as dangerous to the Blenheims as the enemy fighters would be. Flt Lt Bocking reminisced:

We were ill-equipped to cope with the Balkan winter. The gentle Etesian winds of the Greek summer had given way to the cold snow-laden Kashava winds that roared down out of Yugoslavia. Our accommodation was primitive. We were billeted in an unfinished terminal building on the airfield. Though I'd had a little experience of this kind of living before, there was a difference here. The rain was colder than the Palestine rain, and sometimes, rather disconcertingly, it turned into sleet.

He continued:

Maps were issued (in Greek, and of questionable reliability), with the heights marked in metres instead of feet. Bombs were provided by the Greeks. They were of local manufacture, square and yellow and reputedly filled with TNT, and weighed approximately 250 lbs. Their trail angle was unknown, but, as it turned out, this didn't really matter, as any use of the bombsight was purely cursory during those first few weeks. In the face of the weather and the heavy fighter opposition, we were lucky to get over the target and drop the bombs at all. The weather was, if anything, worse than the fighters. No meteorological facilities were available, and every flight was a gamble.[3]

Flt Sgt George Hartup, in charge of the Squadron's Inspection and Repair Flight, added:

> As we were relying on the Greek Air Force for rationing, and food was not readily available at any rate, all we got for breakfast was a totally insufficient amount of black bread roll with some sort of jam! We discovered a splendid mobile field kitchen which was not being used; this we commandeered and appointed one of our junior fitters to service it and nurse it back to healthy production.
>
> We also commandeered a mobile workshop lorry, which was beautifully appointed with every tool a tradesman could wish for, including a lathe. We made good use of these vehicles, both of which were of German manufacture, and equipment. Not far away there was a stores park, but it had little to offer in the way of spares for Blenheims. However, it was discovered that in an Athens workshop, run by an Englishman, the Blenheims being used by the Greek Air Force were being repaired, so the stock of spare parts was raided![4]

30 Squadron flew its first operational sorties the next day (**4 November**), three Blenheim IFs flying a patrol over Eleusis and sighting an Italian seaplane that evaded by entering heavy cloud. Six Wellingtons arrived at Eleusis next day, in preparation for a daylight raid on Valona—the Italians' main supply point on the Albanian coast, on the morning of **7 November**. On arriving over the port, a CR.42 and two G.50s (the latter being reported as Breda 65s by the crews) were already airborne. Two Wellingtons were promptly shot down and two others damaged, while a CR.42 was claimed in return. On the flight home, the survivors encountered three Z.506 floatplanes and shot down one, its crew being rescued by another.

The Blenheims of B Flight undertook their first offensive flight later in the day, their target also the port of Valona. The Blenheims would have to cross the Gulf of Corinth and then turn north and fly up the west coast of the Greek mainland. After passing Corfu on their left the Blenheims would gain height for the 'run up' on the target. Valona harbour was in a deep and narrow bay encircled by mountains with the island of Sazan, bristling with AA guns, at its entrance. Added to this the Blenheims faced the threat of Italian fighters as well as the atrocious weather over the mountains, so all in all Valona was a very dangerous target to attack.

Taking off at 11:20, Sqn Ldr Shannon (in L6672) led the other two, Flg Off. Derek Walker and Sgt George *Jock* Ratlidge (K7103), to Trikkala, where they refuelled and then, at 02:10, to Sarande, where two ships were bombed, without observed results, before flying to Valona. Here, many aircraft (identified as SM.79s, Bredas and CR.42s) were observed on the airfield. The crews believed very heavy damage had been inflicted by their bombing, but, in fact, only three S.81s of 38° Stormo BT were damaged.

As Sqn Ldr Shannon led the Blenheims down to strafe, three CR.42s of 364[a] Squadriglia were seen taking off (in fact there were four) and all three Blenheims were engaged and hit, Sgt Ratlidge's gunner, Sgt John Merifield, being killed. Cap. Nicola Magaldi, the leader of the CR.42s, followed the Blenheims for 20 minutes, as far as Corfu, and believed that he had succeeded in shooting down one and claimed a second as damaged (later upgraded to a probable). One CR.42 (most likely Magaldi's) was damaged by return fire, while the Blenheims managed to get back—with a considerable number of holes in each of them. The Press Bureau of the Greek Legation in London published its first communiqué, stating:

> We are informed authoritatively that a formation of bomber aircraft of the British air forces in Greece yesterday, 6 November, carried out a most successful raid on an enemy aerodrome at Valona on the Adriatic coast in Albania. Enemy aircraft on the ground were bombed and machine-gunned, and a large number of airmen standing on the tarmac were also attacked. A number of bombs were seen to obtain direct hits on aircraft which were completely destroyed and near misses severely damaged other aircraft.
>
> British aircraft were attacked by enemy fighters, all returning safely to their base. One air-gunner was killed by a stray bullet. The leader of the formation [Sqn Ldr Shannon] on returning to base reported, "We took the enemy completely by surprise and were able to make our runs over the target without interference. Our observers watched bombs bursting among the aircraft on the ground and very heavy damage was inflicted."

20-year-old Sgt John Merifield from Co. Durham was afforded a military funeral, attended by newly arrived Air Vice-Marshal D'Albiac, Prime Minister Metaxas, a representative of the King and several other high-ranking officers. One of the Greek newspapers reported:

> The coffin was covered with two crossed flags—the flags of Britain and Greece. The dead, a young English airman, the first to be killed on Greek soil, came down out of the blue sky wounded while chasing the assassin of Greek women and children—the Italian aviators. He was the first British eagle, his wings broken, to fall on the sacred soil of Attica, the first hero of the new generation of the Philhellenes of 1940.

Fellow air-gunner Johnny Vellacott recalled:

I only knew him very briefly. He came to us as a replacement and went on his first operation in A Flight. Fighter aircraft attacked the flight and there were two bullet holes near his turret. The first bullet came in through the top of the fuselage, severed the trigger cable and then went into John's heart. This killed him and then he fell out of the turret against the starboard side of the fuselage. As he lay there a second bullet entered the side of the fuselage and also entered his heart. The poor lad didn't have a chance.[5]

The AOC, who had hardly set his feet on the ground when called to attend the funeral, was soon able to sum up the situation that awaited him; he later reported:

That evening I attended a conference with the Prime Minister and C-in-C to discuss the war situation generally. Every pressure was brought to bear on me to employ my force in the same manner as the Greek Air Force, in close support of the land forces. I appreciated, however, the best help I could give to the Greek armies was to concentrate my small bomber force on the enemy's disembarkation ports in Albania and the important centres in his lines of communication. I argued that such a plan would do far more to delay his advance than if I attacked his forward elements. If, however, the situation deteriorated considerably, and a break through occurred, I would of course devote the whole of my force to the immediate task of stemming the enemy's advance.

One of the main difficulties I experienced in establishing my force, and one which was a constant handicap throughout the whole campaign, was the extreme scarcity of aerodromes suitable for the employment of modern aircraft. There were no all-weather aerodromes, and on the mainland of Greece there are few areas in which aerodromes of any size can be made. In the Salonika area, the country is flat and a number of dry-weather aerodromes already exist. *For political reasons, however, I was not even allowed to reconnoitre these grounds, let alone use them.*

The main disadvantage of the aerodromes near Athens was that they were a long way from the front and it meant long hours of flying to and from the targets. They were, however, better drained and were only out of action for a few days after heavy rain. Furthermore, being near the sea, they were not so liable to get completely covered in by low clouds. During my first week in Greece, I made a tour of all possible sites and on my return pressed the Prime Minister to undertake immediately the construction of all-weather runways at Araxos and Agrinion.[6]

It is interesting to speculate whether the AOC undertook these site inspection flights in company with Wg Cdr Lord Forbes in the Q.6.

More Blenheims were on their way, five of 84 Squadron's A Flight, led by Sqn Ldr Dudley Lewis arriving at Eleusis at 14:40 on **8 November**. Each Blenheim carried three ground personnel in addition to the crew. Three Bombays carrying kit and equipment arrived later.

32 Mira carried out its first raid on this date since the arrival of the RAF. A section of Blenheims departed from Larissa/Ampelonas to raid targets at Kalpaki, north of Yannina. Returning to base after dark, they were prevented from landing by airfield defences that thought they were Italian aircraft, and thus they diverted to Tatoi/Menidi, where airfield gunners again gave them a hostile reception. By now low on fuel they circled the airfield until identification was established and they were given clearance to land, but unfortunately one crashed in which Capt. Lambros Kousigiannis broke his back, though he survived this accident.

On **10 November**, the RAF Blenheim detachment moved to Tatoï/Menidi. An RAF officer remembered:

This was the Greek Air Training School and we were installed in the cadets' house (unfinished). We were not much better off than the men, who for the first few days just lay on the floor in the big hangar. Eventually the men got bedsteads and bedding and were reasonably comfortable. We took over a restaurant and hotel about two miles away. The mess consisted of a large room with glass windows on three sides, from top to bottom: a glorious spot in the summer. In winter, however, when it got cold, we used to eat in our greatcoats.

84 Squadron flew its first operational mission from Greece that morning. Three aircraft led by Flt Lt Arthur Mudie (L1385) carried out a raid on Valona, where a number of CR.42s and Mc.200s were seen on the aerodrome, but the extent of any damage was unknown due to poor visibility. They were back at 13:45 and Sgt Les Nuttall's Blenheim (L1386) smashed its tail wheel on landing due to the bumpiness of the aerodrome.

Following a number of uneventful fighter patrols over Athens, 30 Squadron's A Flight got into the thick of the action and despatched a three-aircraft bombing raid of the naval docks at Valona, led by Flt Lt Bocking, who reported:

I took off at 11:30 with three Blenheims and set course for Corfu, climbing to 18,000 feet. Two enemy aircraft were observed over Corfu at 12:40 on a parallel course about 9,000 feet below us, and climbing. These aircraft crossed in front and underneath us, apparently headed for Italy. At 13:10 we passed Valona, 15 miles out to sea heading north and observed a very large convoy of nine ships (three may have been troop carriers) escorted by three fighters, entering Valona harbour. We turned east to the coast, and then approached our target from north to south. We dropped our bombs in a salvo from 18,000 feet. All the bombs dropped in the vicinity of the docks. As we commenced to dive away, the AA guns opened up with heavy and accurate fire but always slightly behind us.[7]

All three returned safely. That night, six Wellingtons of 70 Squadron carried out nocturnal attacks on Durazzo and Valona, as reported in a subsequent RAF communiqué:

A most successful operation was carried out. Durazzo, a port of the Albanian coast, was completely gutted and the fuel depot destroyed. Three fires that were started on the jetty later merged into one, and our pilots saw the fires still burning when they were 100 miles on their homeward flight. In a night raid on Valona all bombs were observed to fall in the target area and what was probably a munitions dump was seen to blow up.

On **11 November**, 32 Mira suffered its first fatalities of the war when the Blenheim crewed by Lts Photius Maravelias and Yannis Kapsampelis, with Sgt Sivropoulos in the turret, failed to return from a recce north of Kelcyre. Intercepted at 10:30 by two G.50s of 395ᵃ Squadriglia flown by Cap. Piergiuseppe Scarpetta and M.llo Bruno Ferracini, it was seen to fall in flames at Vuva Poligani, a mountain area in the vicinity of Kelcyre. There were no survivors. Cap. Scarpetta's aircraft was hit by the return fire that broke the gears of the constant speed propeller and some parts of the main engine gear, but he was able to safely land at base at 10:50. Later in the day, at 12:30, returning to base from an uneventful sortie, Serg. Italo Ritegni of the same unit crashed and was killed.

Next day (**12 November**), Flt Lt Mudie again led three of 84 Squadron, on this occasion to bomb Durazzo, landing at Larissa to refuel. They were off again at 13:55 and flew above cloud at 15,000–17,000 feet. Oil and petrol tanks at Durazzo were hit and large fires started. Shipping was seen in the harbour and a cruiser was noted. AA fire was intense and a CR.42 was sighted but did not engage. Severe and accurate friendly AA fire was experienced on the way home but none of the Blenheims was hit even though the crews could hear the bursts.

The designated targets for 30 and 84 Squadrons on **13 November**, were the aerodromes at Argyrokastron and Kukova, respectively. Owing to very bad weather, an alternative target was attacked by the 84 Squadron flight—Valona. Here, the jetty was damaged and a small ship claimed sunk. Four CR.42s of the resident 364ᵃ Squadriglia scrambled at 16:20 led by Cap. Nicola Magaldi. Only one of the fighters was able to reach the bombers but attacked without apparent effect. AA was intense however, and Flt Lt Mudie's aircraft was hit in the port wing and fuel tank by shrapnel, but all three Blenheims were able to reach base. Meanwhile, Sqn Ldr Shannon, who was leading the 30 Squadron trio, reported:

The target situated in the Dhruno River valley was obscured by clouds at 5,000 feet. The aircraft flew direct to the target, up the valley, bombed and turned and flew back down the valley. One large fire and two small fires were observed. All bombs fell close to fighter aircraft on the ground. Two fighters took off and one fighter was seen in the air, but no interception took place. Considerable AA fire, heavy-calibre pom-pom and machine-gunfire took place. No damage or casualties occurred to our aircraft.[8]

A Ro.37 reconnaissance aircraft of 72° Gruppo OA and a Ca.133 transport were both destroyed on the ground. Three CR.42s of 365ª Squadriglia had scrambled at 16:05—already under the bombs of 30 Squadron—piloted by Sottoten. Armando Badessi, Serg. Aldo Innocenti and Serg. Domenico Facchini. Low clouds and very bad visibility hampered the interception and, on landing back, Facchini's aircraft went over a patch of soft soil and overturned; the CR.42 was written off, while Facchini was slightly injured.

On **14 November**, the Greeks launched an offensive along the whole front, which quickly began to crumble the Italian defences. To support this, the Greek air force made a maximum effort, and during the two opening days of the new fighting there was much aerial activity. The Greeks were aware that if the Italian reinforcements could be prevented from getting over the line, the scales would be turned against them. Three 32 Mira Blenheims were made available, but one of these failed to take-off when it became stuck in the mud. The remaining two attacked the southern Koritza airfield, where Capt. Dimetrios Papageorgiou's aircraft (B254) was shot down by a direct AA hit and disintegrated in mid-air. The other Blenheim (B253), flown by Capt. Panayhiotis Orphanidis, was damaged by the same explosion and was then attacked by three CR.42s. The Blenheim was claimed probably shot down at 10:00 by Tenente Torquato Testerini of 393ª Squadriglia. However, despite being badly damaged with a shattered tail plane, it limped into Sedes airfield with a wounded gunner, Sgt Sotiriadis. B253's observer, Sgt Despotides, reported:

> One CR.42 followed us all the way back to the base. The speed of the two aircraft was almost the same, and the stubborn Italian pilot was waiting for the deadly mistake of our pilot to turn for our base to Ampelonas so that he could come closer to us. Nevertheless, our experienced pilot did not make the mistake, but kept on with full thrust to the airfield of Sedes. The Italian followed us until Thermaikos gulf and gave up the chase. It seemed that he wanted to witness the crash of our aircraft which never happened but, as I was informed later, he left his signs on it by opening 165 holes on the wings and the fuselage with his guns![9]

It was Serg. Magg. Walter Ratticchieri, Testerini's wingman, who had resumed the chase of the Blenheim after his leader had exhausted all his ammunition.

Ratticchieri recorded that the badly damaged Greek bomber—which he had followed all the way back—had been obliged to force land close to its base, crashing in doing so, and subsequently he brought back the information thus leading to the upgrade of Testerini's claim.

With Italian troops fighting hard and rushing in reinforcements in an effort to hold Koritza, the Greeks called in the RAF to assist, and during the afternoon three of 84 Squadron set off to bomb the Pogradec-Koritza road. The weather was extremely bad. Only one Blenheim returned, L1536 flown by Sgt Les Nuttall, who recalled:

> We were over Lake Ohrid at about 6,000 feet and above the clouds. We could see nothing below so the flight commander [Flt Lt Mudie] ordered us to dive. We were astern of him and 350 mph showed on the clock. The other sergeant pilot [Sgt Sidaway] peeled off and we never saw him again. We got down into the valley and spotted a lot of transport and troops on the road that wound through the valley. The flight commander dropped bombs on the lorries and troops, and we machine-gunned them at the same time, doing a lot of damage. The ground fire was pretty intense, but it didn't hit us anywhere vital.
>
> I lost sight of the flight commander, but saw a stone bridge—a three or four arch affair—over a ravine, with a convoy crossing it. We let go at it, got a direct hit, and bits of our own bombs came back and hit us. We still had some bombs left and went down the valley towards Koritza, but there were no troops beyond the bridge. It looked as if we had blocked the road at just about the right time. The fighters came after us, and we nipped into a cloud and came home.

Observer Sgt Neal added:

> I saw the bombs explode at one end of the bridge and the whole thing collapsed in a great cloud of stones and dust, and fall into the ravine below.

The air-gunner Sgt Stan Davis reported:

> When I saw the ravine, the bridge no longer existed. I could see where it had been. Nothing could get across the ravine. Earlier on I saw the hits on the convoy. You could see lorries all over the place and chaps running like mad.[10]

Of the two missing Blenheims, L1389 flown by flight leader, Flt Lt Arthur Mudie (with Flt Sgt Ted Hibband-Lord and LAC Bill Chick) was believed to have crashed into the hillside, while L1378 flown by Sgt Bill Sidaway (with Sgt Arthur Friend and Sgt Cliff Hoare) was possibly blown up by its own bombs. There were no survivors.

Next day (**15 November**), it was the turn of 30 Squadron again, three Blenheims setting off shortly after 14:00 to raid positions north-east of Koritza. Flt Lt Al Bocking recalled:

30 Squadron was briefed to carry out a special bombing assignment. The Greek army had cut off an impressive number of Italian units and had them surrounded and isolated on a mountain peak in Northern Greece near the town of Koritza. There was to be a set-piece charge by the Greek army. They were to attack from all sides at once and overwhelm the defenders. The signal for the advance was to be the exploding of 3,000lb of bombs dropped on the summit (and, it was hoped, on the Italians' heads) by three Blenheims. The importance attached to this operation was enhanced by the presence with the Greek army of King George and Prince Paul of Greece.

I was to lead the flight with Bob Davidson on my right and Sgt Childs [known as *Joey*] on my left. The necessity that the bombing should occur on time, the distance to the target (about 250 miles), and the reported intense activity of enemy fighters, all combined to make it imperative that we have some kind of fighter protection if we were going to live long enough to reach the target. Fighter escort was therefore provided—seven high-wing monoplanes flown by Greek pilots.

As we approached the target (or what we fondly hoped was the target) we came under heavy attack by CR.42s. All seven of the escorting Greek fighters were shot down [*sic*] before we released our bombs, and Sgt Childs' Blenheim burst into flames and exploded as we got the bombs away. Bob and I, in tight formation, headed for the deep valleys and set course for home.
We stopped only momentarily at the airfield in order to get rid of the aircraft before we continued our headlong flight towards *Zonar's Bar*, where we talked over this frightening business in a peaceful hush broken only by the subdued tinkle of ice-cubes.[11]

Sgt Eric Childs' aircraft (L1120/VT-N) was shot down in flames jointly by Serg. Walter Rattichieri and Serg. Domenico Tufano of 393ª Squadriglia, although they each claimed a victory. The 22-year-old pilot from Cornwall, and his crew Sgt John Stewart and LAC Don Stott were killed. The escorting PZL-24s, from the newly formed 22 Mira, apparently abandoned their charges and engaged a flight of G.50s. An RAF communiqué issued in Athens stated that:

Low-flying RAF planes successfully attacked three separate motor transport and mule columns on the Argyrokastron and Valona roads. The columns, which were rushing relief to the hard pressed enemy forces north of Korce [Koritza], were thrown into confusion. Vehicles were set on fire and lorries overturned. The mules stampeded.

Greek Blenheims were out again on **18 November**, tasked to bomb positions in the Argyrokastron area. The aircraft flown by 1/Lt Alexandros Malakis lost formation due to cloud and reached, by mistake, the town of Permet. The crew, believing they were over Agroykastron, released their bombs on military positions around the wrong target but, in the event, they were later informed that they had destroyed an important target. Sadly, however, at least one of their bombs hit a military hospital, killing some 50 mainly Italian military patients.

30 Squadron's K7095 was airborne from Eleusis at 03:45 on the morning of **18 November**, to carry out a recce of the port of Valona. Crewed by Plt Off. John Jarvis, Sgt Walker and air-gunner Sgt *Lofty* Lord, the Blenheim emerged from 10/10 cloud over the harbour, where some 30 small vessels were sighted, together with two others of about 5,000-tons; in the outer harbour a large vessel (approximately 10,000-tons) and another of 5,000-tons were observed with half-a-dozen smaller craft in attendance. In addition, a convoy of medium-sized was seen approaching from the north. On receipt of this news, 30 Squadron despatched a flight of Blenheims to attack the ships. Among the Blenheim crews involved was new arrival Plt Off. James Kirkman, an air-gunner, about whom Flt Lt Bocking wrote:

It was about this time that P/O Kirkman joined the squadron. Kirk was a character. Before the war he was an archaeologist and used to dig in Palestine. He was a scholarly gentleman, possessed of grave dignity that well suited his greying hair—and he stuttered! How he had ever become a Blenheim air-gunner is one of the minor mysteries of the war. The rear-gunner's compartment of a Blenheim was always cold and in Greece, without proper winter flying-clothing the air-gunners suffered. Somewhere Kirk had picked up a civilian winter overcoat. Wearing this over his uniform and parachute harness, and with his seven-foot-long old-school scarf (vivid as only old-school scarves can be) wrapped twice around his neck and tucked into his belt, he presented a sight calculated to strike terror into even the most intrepid Italian birdman.

The ground crew thought the world of Kirk. They would hurry him into the Blenheim, leaving his helmet and its radio earphones on the wing and (of course) out of his reach. Then they would back and wait in silent glee for Kirk to beam down from the back with an owlish stare and ask someone to "P-p-please p-p-pass up my e-e-electric h-h-hat, l-l-like a g-g-good f-f-fellow." It didn't take me long to notice that Kirk never deprived the ground crew of their little joke.

I took Kirk on his first operational raid. Being the only commissioned air-gunner in the squadron he felt badly about being the least experienced. I explained that experience only came by going out and (even more important) coming back often enough, and, if he was to be my air-gunner, I hoped that he would become very experienced indeed. This first raid of Kirk's was a typical one. The target was the harbour of Valona. The weather was terrible, and the only way to get by the now snow-covered 10,000-foot peaks was up the Argyrokastron Valley and directly over the fighter base at Tepelene. If you made it past these obstacles you came into clear blue sky right above the anti-aircraft defences and smack into the enemy fighters, who had long since learned that RAF HQ in Athens always directed that time over the target would be 13:00 hours. It was rumoured that the Italian pilots had a pool on the number of minutes early or late that the three Blenheims would be as they crossed the last mountain!

On this occasion the enemy pilots were some miles to the north when we arrived in the clear some five minutes' flying time from the harbour. I spotted them instantly. Ignoring the familiar hollow feeling and the palms that became slippery on the control wheel despite the intense cold, I tried to evaluate whether we could reach the target, drop the bombs, and get headed for home before they caught us. I decided that the distance which still separated us gave us a chance of even getting away completely. As we started in, the flak reached up and pockmarked the sky around us, and I saw the fighters on the horizon wheel in our direction.

So far there had been no sign from Kirk in the back that he was awake. I was about to lift him out of his seat with a bellow over the radio, when suddenly spluttering noises in my earphones indicated that he had sighted the enemy. I cut short his excited "G-g-gunner to p-p-pilot …" by saying that I'd had them sighted for several minutes. A chastened silence ensued, which lasted until we had dropped our bombs and headed for home at maximum speed.

The enemy fighters slowly gained on us. The usual chatter between aircraft died away. If we were overtaken, our destruction would be more or less a foregone conclusion. While we flew on, pardonably somewhat tense, suddenly the radio silence was broken by a plaintive request: "I s-s-say, old boy, s-s-slow up a b-b-bit! I c-c-can't reach the b-b-bastards!" Needless to say, Kirk's request went unheeded![12]

Reinforcements now arrived in the form of Gladiators of 80 Squadron, B Flight arriving initially, followed by A Flight. On **19 November**, B Flight flew up to Trikkala near Kalambaka in the morning, joining the resident PZL unit (21 Mira). The Gladiators were in action that afternoon, claiming no fewer than six CR.42s and two probable, and three G.50s (actual losses were three CR.42s plus one damaged with the pilot wounded, and one G.50). One RAF pilot was wounded. Over the coming weeks the Gladiator pilots would cover themselves in glory, accounting for many of their opponents, both fighters and bombers, but seldom were they available in sufficient numbers to provide escort for the Blenheims.

Next day (**20 November**), 30 Squadron suffered the loss of Blenheim L1166/ VT-K when Flg Off. *Bud* Richardson (actually Carlton de Wayne Richardson, a Canadian from Toronto) became lost during a three-aircraft raid by A Flight in bad weather. It was obviously an unwise decision to send off the aircraft when the cloud base was barely a few hundred feet. As they flew along the Gulf of Corinth the visibility decreased rapidly and so they flew on in open formation and climbed to try and get above the storm. Oxygen was not switched on until they passed the 10,000 feet as usual, for oxygen was in short supply and could not be wasted. At about 16,000 feet ice was encountered, the aircraft began to wallow, and there was a danger of losing control. As the aircraft had lost contact with each other for some time, the pilots each decided to turn back.

It seems they were flying just above 22,000 feet when Flg Off. Richardson's aircraft iced-up so badly that it became unstable and just fell out of the sky, out of control. As they plunged earthwards all the perspex windows in the cockpit blew in and Richardson told the crew to bale out. This they were unable to do due to the pressure of the slipstream. In fact Richardson had to pull the observer back down into his seat by his parachute harness as he lay half in and half out of the aircraft. As he fought with the controls to regain command of the aircraft, it performed two loops, three rolls and various other gyrations before it broke through the clouds at 7,000 feet above a small lake, with mountains rising sheer into the clouds all around them. Richardson ordered the bombs to be dropped 'safe' into the water, much to the consternation of a lone fisherman on the lake, and carried out a hurried wheels-up landing on a small beach at the lake's edge. The crew was out of the aircraft and running clear before the Blenheim slid to a halt on a beach at Zagora, east of Volos.

As Richardson and crew stood there a small crowd came into view brandishing pitchforks and the like and advanced on them in a most threatening manner. They were local Greek peasants who had mistaken the crew for Italian aviators. After a few tense moments and the quick removal of flying gear to reveal their uniforms underneath, they were recognised as RAF personnel and all was well. They were taken to a nearby village and hailed as heroes. They soon discovered that there was no telephone in the vicinity so could not inform the Squadron that they were safe and give their approximate position. The villagers fed them well from their own meagre supply of food and plied them well with plenty of local wine and generally made much fuss of them. At last they indicated that they were very tired and would like to sleep. They were found beds and were asleep in no time and so for them ended a very busy day.

The following morning Richardson discovered that the only means of transport was by mule. They set off with guides and mules up a track and continued until the end of the day when they reached a road and another village, but still no telephone. It took a further day by mule and then lorry to reach a village that did have a telephone before they could get news to the Squadron that they were safe. One more day by lorry brought them back to camp. L1166 was dismantled and salvaged by a team from No. 33 Air Stores Park a few days later.

By this time the Greeks had captured Koritza and Leskoviku, and in the south had re-crossed the Kalamas River. With a foothold secured on Albanian soil, and with the valuable lateral road south from Koritza in their hands, they now stopped to consolidate. Italian morale was now at low ebb, and only in the air could they hit back effectively. The loss of Koritza and the closeness of Greek forces to Argyrokastron had precipitated withdrawal of Italian units to the main Albanian airfields, which were now becoming very crowded as a result. The RAF intended a nocturnal raid for the night of **20/21 November**, as indicated by 30 Squadron orders:

> The Greek forces have continued their advance and the enemy is retiring in disorder. It is expected that during the night there will be considerable congestion in the Argyrokastron and Tepelene area. 84 Squadron are to carry out with three Blenheims operations similar to those detailed below, but against Argyrokastron.
>
> The intention is to attack the road junction and village of Tepelene with a view to destroying and disorganising military movement in this area.
>
> 30 Squadron are to provide three Blenheims which, if not bombed up at the time of receipt of this order, are to be loaded with the maximum number of 40 lb bombs. If the aircraft are already bombed up with those of other calibre these may be used. Aircraft are to take off and attack Tepelene by moonlight, and are to land at Eleusis by daylight. If weather is such that Tepelene cannot be recognised, the port area of Valona harbour is to be attacked as an alternative target.[13]

Flg Off. Derek Walker led off the three 30 Squadron machines at 03:45, but heavy cloud covering both target areas prevented an attack by either squadron and all aircraft returned safely to base.

The 84 Squadron detachment (A Flight) at Tatoi/Menidi now welcomed the arrival of its B and C Flights, bringing it up to full strength once again, while Blenheims of 211 Squadron also began arriving, the transfer being completed within two days. Air Chief Marshal Longmore flew to Athens on **22 November**, on board a Sunderland, for a meeting with Air Vice-Marshal D'Albiac, and to learn first-hand how the war was progressing:

> I found him [D'Albiac] established with his headquarters in the *Grande Bretagne* Hotel. King George, General Metaxas (the Prime Minister) and General Papagos, the C-in-C of the Greek Forces, also had their headquarters in the same building and I was granted an interview with them.

The King appreciated the prompt arrival of the Blenheim squadron [30 Squadron] to protect Athens, but having listened to the BBC broadcasts during the Battle of Britain giving details of the splendid performances of the Hurricanes and Spitfires, he asked why none of these fighters had been sent to Greece. Papagos seemed rather subdued and not as pleased as I should have expected with the successes of his Army. On the other hand, Metaxas impressed me considerably; he seemed alive and quick to grasp a point ... He was proud of the Greek successes.[14]

During his short visit to Greece, Air Chief Marshal Longmore made time to visit the various RAF units, some of the flights being made in Wg Cdr Lord Forbes' Q.6:

In company with D'Albiac I visited all our RAF units. At Eleusis, just to the west of Athens, 30 Squadron Blenheim fighters and a flight of 80 Squadron's Gladiators were installed for the fighter defence of Athens, on an aerodrome which was liable to go out of action for short periods after heavy rain. Arrangements were being made for a proper hard-core runway. At Tatoi, renamed Menidi, the other side of Athens, the aerodrome was more weather-proof and here I found 84 and 211 Squadrons. These Blenheims continued to operate whenever weather conditions permitted against military objectives in support of the Greek Army, against enemy aerodromes and the Italian base port of Valona.

Wing Commander Lord Forbes flew us up to Trikkala in his Q.6 to see 80 Squadron, but the landing ground was so water-logged we had to land at the adjacent aerodrome of Larissa, at the time occupied by some Greek air units. D'Albiac arranged for them [80 Squadron] to use Larissa during the bad weather period as the aerodrome there was reasonably weather-proof. Both Trikkala and Larissa were on the east side of the Pindus mountains which had to be crossed on every sortie in support of the Greek Army in Albania.[15]

211 Squadron took the task of getting ready for instant operations very seriously, flying its first sorties on **24 November**. Sqn Ldr Tommy Wisdom was at the airfield to welcome them back. However, one was missing, L8411 flown by the CO, Sqn Ldr James Gordon-Finlayson (known as *The Bishop* or simply *Bish* due to his portly countenance). Wisdom wrote:

211's first Grecian adventure was over the port of Durazzo. Five hours later George [Flt Lt George Doudney] told me about it. Despite filthy weather the three flights had navigated themselves across the mountains in ten-tenths cloud at 2,000 feet, ascending over the target in the Adriatic. Great success was achieved in this first raid. Barges in the harbour were shattered by the violence of the tremendous explosions and a ship had been hit. Fighters were up, and the AA barrage was heavy. All the aircraft had returned except *The Bish*, their leader. George, who had been shot up, said he saw *The Bish* had been hit, and thought he had gone down in the sea. We spent an unhappy evening.[16]

G.50 pilots from 24° Gruppo claimed three Blenheims, one by four pilots led by Tenente Domenico Pancera, another by Tenente Divo Bartaletti, and a third probably destroyed by Bartaletti and two others. In fact, Flg Off. Ken Dundas bellied in at Tatoi/Menidi with a damaged port engine and no hydraulics, while Sgt *Jock* Marshall's badly damaged L1481 was just able to reach Larissa, similarly with its port engine unserviceable. The crew was flown back to Tatoi/Menidi aboard a Greek Ju 52 next day. The subsequent RAF communiqué stated:

> The attack was directed against shipping in the harbour, the quay and jetties, and harbour buildings. One direct hit was registered on a 10,000-ton ship, and another on a smaller ship, which immediately burst into flames. Bombs fell on a quay close to another vessel. One heavy salvo fell 50 yards on the land side of the harbour jetty. One plane failed to return.

However, Sqn Ldr Gordon-Finlayson and his crew, Plt Off. Gerry Davies and air-gunner Plt Off. Arthur Geary were safe, as the CO later recalled:

> Just as we released our bombs we received direct hits from AA. One tore a large hole in the port engine cowling, but the motor continued to function, despite the fact that oil was pouring out. The other engine was hit and stopped almost immediately. The aircraft was holed in many places—there was an enormous rent right through one wing—but it was still flying, though the force of the explosion had put us on our back. Not one of us was touched, though the logbook in Geary's pocket was cut in half by a piece of shrapnel.
>
> We flew on, though slowly, and unable to gain height on our one engine. The cockpit was full of petrol fumes, and I was afraid we should either pass out or that the aircraft would catch fire. We flew dead over Valona at little more than a thousand feet, but the Itis either didn't see us or thought we were one of theirs. We were a sitting bird all right; but no one came near us. We flew on for nearly two hours, and then we spotted an island just off the coast—Corfu. We had a look at it, and decided there was only one place to attempt a landing—a strip of beach about 20 yards wide. I told Davies and Geary they had better jump, but they preferred to stay with the aircraft.
>
> Well, we put the aircraft down all right, although we could not get the wheels out and had to make a belly-landing. Some of our bombs were still on board, and they bounced along the beach behind us as we ploughed through the sand. We climbed out and congratulated ourselves. There were other difficulties,

though. Davies walked up the beach to some peasants, who at once ran away screaming. Then a man with a rifle appeared, and looked threatening. We put up our hands and yelled "Inglese, Inglese." A look of amazement spread over the man's face: he replied in American, "Are youse guys English?" Then the locals, doubtless collected by those who had seen us first, arrived to the number of about a thousand, and again things looked extremely dangerous. They were kept from throwing us into the sea—the most popular suggestion, we gathered—by our American friend. At long last we persuaded the villagers that were friends.[17]

They persuaded the owner of a fishing boat to take them to the mainland, where a friendly Greek provided a car and drove them over the mountains to the village, from where they travelled by mule to a railway station, and a week after their crash they arrived back at Tatoi/Menidi. L8411 was later located on the salt flats near Gastouri by a salvage party from No. 33 Air Stores Park, dismantled and taken back to base by boat.

84 Squadron despatched six aircraft to raid Valona on **26 November**, three G.50s intercepting one section. Flt Lt Bob Towgood, the Canadian flight leader, was attacked but his gunner claimed strikes on one G.50 and the Blenheim evaded without damage. Similarly, Flg Off. Johnny Evans was able to avoid the fighters and dropped his bombs on a line of Italian bombers on the airfield. Meanwhile, 211 Squadron sent three aircraft to attack Tepelene, but owing to weather conditions the flight had to return without bombing. The following day, **27 November**, Greek Blenheim B256 was shot down by AA fire near Pogradec, killing 1/Lt Alexandros Malakis and his crew, Sgts Asterios Liapis and Christodoulos Filippidis. Six of 211 Squadron took off to attack the port of Durazzo but also had to return without bombing as there was no cloud cover for the bombers after they made their run up. Orders issued by Air Headquarters made it clear that aircraft were only to approach and bomb when there was ample cloud cover. Sgt Jim Dunnet was on this operation as observer to Plt Off. *Herby* Herbert. They were to refuel *en route* at the newly constructed landing ground at Araxos:

Shortly we reached the end of the Gulf, and were circling in toward the landing ground on the left side of the coast. The Squadron broke up over the drome and the planes circled around waiting for their turn to come in. The drome wasn't too easy to spot, I thought, there weren't any buildings around, nothing except a bare grassy stretch; fortunately there were a few of the local inhabitants working around the petrol dumps, or we might have easily missed it; rather marshy looking from the air. One by one the planes touched down and taxied towards the refuelling dump. I climbed out as the engines gave a rasping grunt of protest, and wheezed to a stop.

A lorry had come up to the plane with a load of petrol and oil cans which were dumped noisily on the ground with all haste, and before much talking could be done, there was a clash of gears and off raced to the lorry to the next plane.

"Well, I suppose we've got to fill the bloody thing ourselves with petrol and oil," I said with a rather vacant look around, "there doesn't seem to be any ground wallahs about at all." "There wouldn't be, obviously in a place like this, Dunnet," *Herby* remarked, "it is only just being constructed and is only intended as an emergency landing ground." He turned to the gunner. "Will you go and get the axe out of the plane, Young. We'll need something to batter in the tops of the tins."

I looked around; holes were being hammered in tins everywhere; with a banging and shouting, crews were scrambling on tops of wings, fiddling with catch fasteners, opening up panels to get at the fuelling system, oil was being drained in, petrol was gurgling into thirsty tanks. "Give a hand here, Dunnet," my pilot shouted from the top of the wing. "Pass me up those cans will you?" *Jock* was busily battering holes in them to allow the petrol to pour out easily. I staggered under the wing with one of the cans and hoisted it up to the wispy haired youth kneeling on the wing; the cursed tanks never seemed to have enough, I thought, as I staggered to and fro with cans of fuel, but at last the slow process was over, and the more difficult task of putting the oil in arose.

We felt satisfied with our efforts and sat on the grass watching the others struggling away with loaded containers. Most of the Greek labourers had come up to have a look at the planes; one group approached our plane. Hesitatingly the men hung back, until invited forward to have a really good look; shyly they came, tough, bristly-chinned peasants. I showed them the bombs, they muttered to themselves, then broke out into an understanding laugh, as *Jock* said, "For Mussolini, boom, boom." Everybody felt the spirit of friendship amongst them. One of the strong sturdy chaps fished about in a bag he was carrying, and brought out a bottle of straw-coloured wine and a loaf of bread, urging with his gesticulations that we should have some.[18]

Once all the Blenheims had been refuelled, Sqn Ldr Gordon-Finlayson led the aircraft off to Durazzo, but the operation was eventually aborted due to lack of cloud cover in the target area.

Three aircraft of 211 Squadron bombed enemy shipping disembarking troops in Sarande harbour on **28 November**. The bombing was done from 12,000 feet and several near misses were observed. Nine aircraft of 84 Squadron set off to bomb Durazzo, refuelling at Araxos *en route*, but several of the aircraft, unable to find the target under cloud, bombed Elbassan instead. Plt Off. *Dickie* Bird's aircraft came under attack, apparently by G.50s, and L1385 was crash-landed in a dried-up river bed. Bird and his crew, Sgts Stan Davis and Eric Scott, were taken prisoner. Sgt Jim Hutcheson, flying L1892, commented: "After letting my two 500 lb bombs go, I was set on by a couple of CR.42s but fortunately I got clear."

Over Durazzo seven G.50s of 24° Gruppo were airborne, four from Tirana led by Tenente Domenico Pancera, and three of the local defence section led by Tenente Divo Bartaletti. The latter trio intercepted a Blenheim and it was claimed probably shot down at 13:35 near Devoli. This was obviously Plt Off. Bird's aircraft. At about the same time CR.42s of 160° Gruppo claimed another Blenheim probably shot down over the Koritza area, possibly Hutcheson's aircraft.

Tepelene was the target for nine of 84 Squadron on **29 November**, an escort of four Gladiators of 80 Squadron being provided. The weather turned very cold and cloudy and the mission was uneventful. The Gladiator pilots, meanwhile, took the opportunity to search for a missing pilot brought down the previous day, but then encountered a formation of Italian bombers though they could claim only two damaged.

There was no flying on the following two days. The conditions experienced in Greece were the opposite extreme from those in the desert and the operational crews were having and extremely difficult time in adjusting themselves to the cold wintry conditions. The ground personnel also felt the cold keenly. Nine of 211 Squadron stood by to take off on a raid on the last day of the month but were unable to carry it through owing to the extremely bad weather. All aircraft were grounded.

Of this early period, American war correspondent Leland Stowe, who was visiting Menidi, wrote:

> The squadron leader's face had impressed me with its joviality the first time I met him. It is not the same face now. You could see the strain of that flight written on it when he walked in and sank into a chair:
>
> "We had a 90-mile per hour gale against us all the way. We went up high, trying to shake off the cloud; it was the worst weather over these mountains we have ever struck. Finally we had to turn back, though some of the others may have got through."
>
> The others will be coming in any time now. We walked out to the field. Then the first plane swoops in. The pilot leaps down: "Could not get through. Everything was freezing up." The second plane roars over the field; then another. The pilot's face is sweating as he pulls his helmet off and jumps down. This time it is a different story.
>
> "Fighters all round us. I looked down and saw three blocks right under us. I let bombs go right between two of them. I pulled out of the next dive when the mountain was coming right up at us. Stickiest show I ever want to see."
>
> There are no easy days for men who bomb and fight across these diabolical mountains. Clouds are ever enveloping their peaks. These are the men who

joust with death every day, knowing fully what it means and how long are the odds which they face.[19]

With the Blenheim squadrons doing their utmost to support the Greek stand, local Greeks took the RAF personnel to heart. 30 Squadron's Sgt Johnny Vellacott recalled that whenever he and his cohorts, including his best friend *Lofty* Lord, ventured into the capital in search of some refreshments they were lauded wherever they went. On entering a bar the locals would stand and applaud the bemused airmen before plying them with free drinks and food. On one occasion several of the tipsy aircrew found themselves stuck without any transport back to Eleusis. Luckily they were able to commandeer a steamroller upon which they were able to make their merry way back to base before parking it outside the main gate! It was returned to the rightful owners the next day. Of this period, Flt Lt Al Bocking noted:

> Athens, with its lights and warmth, was close to hand. Athens, at that time, was a city drunk on victories, living in a fool's paradise, while the Germans, with whom Greece was not yet at war, sat in the restaurants and bars, fingering their swastika pins, keeping their eyes open, and watching the celebrations with cynical eyes.
>
> This German business was confusing us. Here we were, sitting in *Zonar's Bar* side by side with the *Herrenvolk*. Across the street, at the German Embassy, the Nazi flag was snapping defiantly in the breeze. But war makes strange bedfellows and, as long as we were here to help the Greeks fight the Italians. We had to put up with the Germans, who were still their friends. To add to our confusion, an American officer, Major [Demas] Craw, was attached to us as an observer for a still neutral United States. He, of course, had (ostensibly) to be friendly with everyone.[20]

Two officers of the United States Army Air Force, Colonel G. C. Bower and Major A. T. Craw, had been sent to Greece as military observers. Both would fly as passengers in Blenheims and Wellingtons on a number of raids during the coming months. Bocking continued:

> Major Craw was one of the finest officers and gentlemen it has ever been my privilege to meet. His one ambition was to get in the fight. He hated the Germans for the heartaches and bloodshed they had caused, he despised the Italians for the jackal they were, and he was firmly convinced that his country would eventually join us in our fight for freedom. We had great difficulty in keeping him out of our combat aircraft in raids over enemy territory, where, as

a neutral observer he was not supposed to be. On one or two occasions we did not keep him on the ground.[21/22]

Another story of the Athens night life came from the pen of RAF Press Officer Sqn Ldr Tommy Wisdom, who had arrived earlier in the month:

One night some of us were dining together at *Maxim's* [another night club/ restaurant] when the deputy assistant provost marshal whispered that the table next to us was occupied by a member of the Gestapo in Athens 'on vacation'— these Germans were always on holiday—with his girlfriend. With one accord we all took violent exception, not only to having Germans in the place at all, but also to having them listening to what we were saying, even if it was harmless.

One of our party, who spoke German, politely told the Huns to get out. The Gestapo man refused. It looked as if we were going to involve ourselves in the incident, which he doubtless wished to provoke. Englishmen from other tables joined us, and the word went round that the Hun should be kicked out if he wouldn't go quietly. Mac, who spoke German, moved over to the table and spoke for a few moments to the Gestapo man and his girlfriend quite nicely, saying that it would be far wiser if they left.[23]

CHAPTER 3

December–Winter Operations

Ice was in the clouds, and the clouds came below the mountain peaks. They hadn't a chance. But the raids went on.

Sqn Ldr Tommy Wisdom

The beginning of December saw 30 Squadron make a concerted effort to disrupt embarkation of troops and supplies from ships in Sarande harbour. The area was heavily defended by batteries of AA guns situated around the harbour, combined with firepower from destroyers. In addition to defending the supply ships the destroyers had been shelling the advanced positions of Greek troops. Three Blenheims were despatched to raid Valona on **1 December**, led by Flt Lt Al Bocking, who recalled:

> On one of the early raids, Bob Davidson, myself and Sgt George Ratlidge tried to get through the mountain passes. The weather was stickier than usual, and, since we were at 7,000 feet with mountains 9,000 feet high around us, we had to go up through cloud. We tried to get above it, but at 16,000 feet ice was forming on the wings and the controls began to get very heavy. The cockpit was full of snow, and it was difficult to see. Then ice-glaze—the most dangerous sort—began to form. Just as we were wondering if it would be necessary to jump, we found a hole in the clouds, through which Bob and I came down and steered a course for home
>
> The third aircraft was not so fortunate. Ratlidge had reached 20,000 feet and was flying in the clear, just on top of a level cloud-layer. But at that altitude the machine was wallowing; now and then it sank back into cloud, whereupon ice immediately formed. Suddenly, probably on account of carburettor icing, one engine failed. The Blenheim immediately went into a spin. Ratlidge ordered the crew to jump, and then it was discovered that the observer's pack had been thrown down the fuselage and out of reach.
>
> The pilot and air-gunner stayed with the observer. Still spinning, the aircraft came down through cloud into clear air at 7,000 feet, and they found themselves in a narrow valley with mountains rising sheer on either side of them. Ratlidge

brought the aircraft out of the spin, only to find that both engines had stopped. His luck held, however. A small field, the only one for miles around, appeared dead ahead; and, with a small prayer of thanks, Ratlidge slid the Blenheim on its belly.[1]

The Blenheim (K7103) had force-landed in Khalkis, and a party from the RAF's No. 33 Air Stores Park—a Repair & Salvage unit—was sent out from Daphnie to salvage it three days later.

Next day (**2 December**) saw nine aircraft of 211 Squadron set out again to raid Valona. They bombed the power house, ammunition dumps and the harbour at Valona. It was a successful raid, bombs being observed to burst on the jetty and among buildings. Fires were started and one building was demolished. The leading flight was attacked by ten CR.42s (six of 365[a] and four from 364[a] Squadriglie), as reported by Sqn Ldr Gordon-Finlayson (L8513):

> We had to go in rather low because of cloud, and the fighters were waiting for us. They were completely out of luck, however—while they were chasing one flight another went in and dropped its bombs. We saw a big blaze with a tall column of black smoke above it, and it looked as if we had hit something quite important. One of the fighters caught the concentrated fire from one flight and it came down in a vertical dive with smoke pouring from the fuselage. My aerial was shot away and George Doudney got a bullet through his helmet, but that was all the damage they did to us.[2]

Flt Lt Allan Farrington (L6670) reported that one CR.42 shot down by cross-fire with the leader's machine, the two gunners being Sgts *Ace* Martin and *Taff* Jones (with the CO), but no CR.42s were reported lost. The Italian formation, led by Ten. Col. Rolando Pratelli, had taken off from Valona at 13:40 to carry out a sweep of the Konispol-Corfu area, and were on their way home, low on fuel, when the Blenheims were spotted at about 8,000 feet heading for the harbour and airfield. The Italian pilots engaged five of the Blenheims before they escaped in clouds. Although two Blenheims suffered slight damage, no claims were submitted. Flg Off. Paul Pickersgill was was forced to land L8466 at Araxos on the return journey; neither he nor Sgts Harry Taylor and *Paddy* Duffy were injured; the aircraft was later salvaged.

30 Squadron was tasked with attacking the ships at Sarande on **4 December**, three Blenheims flown by Flt Lt Al Bocking, L6672 piloted by Plt Off. *Butch* Paget and L8462 flown by Flg Off. Derek Walker, (with Sgt *Lofty* Lord as his Wop/AG), took off from Eleusis at 11:45 with a mixed payload of GP and incendiary bombs. The aircraft, flying at low level, scored a direct hit on the forward starboard quarter of a destroyer with their first salvo but their second salvo fell just 15 yards astern of the ship. *Lofty* Lord, in his logbook, claimed the destroyer to have

been badly damaged, while Paget's Wop/AG, Plt Off. James Kirkman, claimed that the destroyer had been sunk, but this could not be confirmed as the aircraft disengaged due to heavy AA fire. Of this sortie, Flt Lt Bocking wrote:

> I went over, flying high, and dropped to 14,000 feet. I could see Italian fighters at a distance, but they did not see me. As we were about to go into a dive, I called up the rest of the crew by telephone [intercom] and said: "This is the moment I dislike most." The observer answered, chuckling: "Well, I think this is the best part of the trip." We dived to 500 feet and dropped the bombs; they fell on the stern and disabled the destroyer. We made a second run through pom-pom and other anti-aircraft fire, and turned around the masts, machine-gunning the crew.[3]

Later reports claimed that the destroyer, which had been attempting to leave the harbour, was damaged to such an extent that the Italians abandoned it, half submerged and listing to starboard. However, the Greeks reportedly later salvaged the destroyer and put it into service.

Meanwhile, on this date, 211 Squadron sent three flights (nine aircraft) armed with 250 lb bombs to attack retreating Italian columns at Tepelene. Bombs were observed to burst amongst M/T concentrations. All returned safely. Next day (**6 December**) three of 30 Squadron's fighter Blenheims returned to the same area to strafe the Sarande-Valona coast road. One Blenheim was forced to return early with engine trouble and the other two were both obliged to force-land during their return flight; both had been damaged by AA fire and were out of fuel. New Zealander Flg Off. Bert Blackmore, flying with the Squadron's armament officer Plt Off. Richard Crowther as gunner, came down on the island of Corfu in K7100. The aircraft was located by a party from No.33 Air Stores Park a week later, in a bog 20 miles north of Kerkyra. The port undercarriage and wing were broken and the aircraft had to be dismantled and sent back by ship. Meanwhile, Plt Off. John Attwell with Sgt Max Walsh landed L1097 some 20 miles north of Agrinion; the salvage party found the aircraft had carried out a near perfect landing, and it was later flown back to base; both crews were unhurt.

Eleusis saw the arrival of a Hudson of 2PRU to assist with photo-recce duties not only over the front lines but to also keep an eye on developments in Yugoslavia and Rumania. It would return to Cairo at the end of the month, the Blenheim units sorry to see to it go. During the month it had taken some pressure off the crews, who were not trained reconnaissance personnel.

Bad weather—low cloud and heavy rain—curtailed all flying for the next two days. On **7 December**, 211 Squadron at last succeeded in sending eight aircraft to Valona, taking off at 07:10. One fairly large vessel repotedly received a direct hit while bombs were seen to fall near others. The operation was repeated in the afternoon, nine aircraft of 211 Squadron taking off at 13:00, and were joined by six more from 84 Squadron. Extremely severe weather was encountered, as noted by Sqn Ldr Gordon-Finlayson:

> As soon as aircraft entered cloud, frost accumulated on the leading edges, wireless mast and airscrew. Large chunks were thrown against the cabin by the propellers. The temperature was minus 20 degrees Centigrade. The aircraft shuddered heavily.[4]

Two (L1388 and L8374) of 84 Squadron's leading trio were forced to return early due to heavy icing, landing safely at 16:05, while two of 211 Squadron crashed into hills. Flg Off. Paul Pickersgill and his crew of L4926 (Sgts Harry Taylor and Norman Hallett) were killed; their bodies were recovered and buried at Agrinion. Plt Off. Guy Jerdein, Sgts James Barber and John Munro, the crew of L1535, were buried at Rama. The remainder of 211 Squadron's aircraft were also obliged to turn back due to the weather.

Meanwhile, the second 84 Squadron trio was intercepted over the target by three CR.42s of 365ª Squadriglia, led by Sottoten. Lorenzo Clerici, that were patrolling over the city. Flt Lt Les Cattell's L8455 (with Sgts Horace Taylor and Frank Carter) and Sgt Michael Cazalet's L8457 with Sgts Ken Ridgewell and Cliff Forster being shot down at once, while Flg Off. Ken Linton force-landed L1381 near a lake south of Sarande after his aircraft had been badly damaged by a single long burst of fire from one fighter. From the two former aircraft only Cazalet's gunner, Sgt Forster, survived to be taken prisoner. L1381 was later salvaged by a party from No. 33 Air Stores Park, dismantled, and sent back by boat.

The Italian pilots—Sottotente Clerici, Serg. Pasquale Rivolta and Serg. Mario Angeloni—jointly claimed one Blenheim, which was seen to go down in flames, and a second that was seen to enter the clouds inverted. Clerici then saw another bomber that was trying to reach Valona's harbour. He attacked and forced it to change course and then hit it in the left engine, finally seeing it disappear into clouds. This was obviously Linton's aircraft. Italian records reveal that the wreck of the first bomber was found south-east of Draschiovice. The second bomber initially considered only damaged, was found a day later, totally destroyed. The third bomber, attacked by Clerici alone, although followed out to the sea, was not seen to fall and only credited as probably shot down.

The remaining two 84 Squadron Blenheims (the other, Flg Off. Bobby Campbell in L1847, having aborted due to oxygen problems), led by Flt Lt Graham Jones, continued to Valona, meeting severe opposition from the defending CR.42s over the target. Nonetheless, they released their bombs and safely returned, believing that they had shot down one of the attacking fighters.

150° Gruppo's 'Alarm Section' comprised of Tenente Franco Gatti and Serg. Pietro Secchi of 365ª Squadriglia, had scrambled at 14:50. Unable to see anything, they were returning to base when they saw two Blenheims under attack by other CR.42s. They cut across the path of one of the Blenheims and machine-gunned it until it dived for safety into the clouds. The pilots reported that it was last seen "flying in a strange way as if it had been badly damaged." It had certainly been a black day for the Blenheim units—five aircraft lost, four totally, with 11 crew members killed and one taken prisoner. Of 211 Squadron's losses, Sqn Ldr Wisdom, the Press Officer, wrote:

'*The Airedale*', P/O Jerdein, who got his nickname because his hair was thick and curly like an Airedale … was killed. He was a good fellow, keen as mustard on his job. With *Pickers*, a great songster, they both crashed while returning from a raid in filthy weather. Ice was in the clouds, and the clouds came below the mountain peaks. They hadn't a chance. But the raids went on.[5]

Three aircraft of 211 Squadron took off at 08:00 on **9 December**, to again bomb Valona. They were again forced to return due to adverse weather conditions. A second attempt was made by the same aircraft at 11:30 and this time their objective was reached. Bombs were seen to fall on a jetty and in the town. On the return flight Sgt *Jock* Marshall (L1481) came upon a Z.506B, as noted by Sgt *Nobby* Clark:

Get out under cloud through a valley to the sea and encounter a single Cant floatplane –*Jock* gave chase, firing away, and took us right under it so *Haggis* [Sgt Bill Baird] was also able to have a go.[6]

However, no hits were claimed nor sustained and both crews went on their respective ways.

During the next two days 211 received four replacement aircraft (L1482, L1528, L8514, and L8631), and two complete crews from Egypt, while 84 received three aircraft, with two more to imminently follow; and also two replacement crews, one commanded by Flt Lt Tony Plinston, a New Zealander, and Flt Lt Bill Russell, the latter recalling:

We [Sgts Ken Dicks and Alan Blackburn] had been serving in 107 Squadron in the UK we stupidly volunteered to fly a brand-new Blenheim IV out to the Middle East. We thought we would be posted to a squadron with this beautiful aircraft which had all the latest gear, two guns in the turret and a blister gun under the nose. Barely had we got our kit out of the aircraft at Abu Sueir than it was whisked away never to be seen again. After a week we were posted to 84 Squadron, flying to Menidi in a rather clapped-out old Blenheim I.[7]

84 and 211 Squadrons also received a visit at this time from Wg Cdr Lord Forbes in his capacity as Senior Staff Intelligence Officer BAFG, who arrived in

his Q.6 to discuss latest intelligence reports with Sqn Ldrs Gordon-Finlayson and Lewis.

Five Blenheims of 84 Squadron raided Valona on **10 December**, led by Sqn Ldr Lewis. An ammunition dump, an M/T park and buildings were hit in addition to a ship in the harbour, which allegedly received damage to its stern. Ten CR.42s were reported, but only two were in fact airborne on patrol when the Blenheims arrived. Tenente Aldo Marchetti and his wingman were able to engage but no claims were submitted owing to cloud cover, which enabled the Blenheims to escape.

With no Wellingtons operating from Greece since the departure of the 70 Squadron detachment, night raids had been much reduced. However, late on **13 December**, four such aircraft from 148 Squadron on Malta made the long flight to attack Valona. Bad weather conditions forced the leader to turn back, but two of the remaining trio reached their target, the third bombing the secondary objective, Crotone. All returned safely to Malta before midnight. Next day however, a new detachment of four Wellingtons from 70 Squadron reached Menidi, and these raided Durazzo. Again weather was bad and the leader was forced to turn back, flying direct to the unit's home base at Kabrit. The other three attacked the target and returned to Menidi, reporting seeing a large fire in the harbour area as a result of their bombing.

Following another spell of bad weather, 211 Squadron was able to despatch a raid of nine aircraft at 07:25 on **14 December**, the target once again Valona. Although visibility was poor all bar one reached the target, noted by the CO:

> A passage was found between low rain clouds in the Gulf of Corinth and the Messologni area. The temperature was minus 32 degrees and gun turrets froze up. One pilot had to leave formation and lose height as he was unable to use his hands.[8]

L1481 was the aircraft forced to turn back when some 40 miles from Valona owing to icing of controls. The pilot was Flg Off. Alonzo *Buckshot* Barnes, an Australian in the RAF, who was in fact currently 211 Squadron's M/T officer! A former Gladiator pilot with 112 Squadron, he had been demoted and grounded following a misdemeanour[10] and eventually found himself posted to 211 Squadron. Still very keen to fly and to be involved actively in the war, he had persuaded Sqn Ldr Gordon-Finlayson to allow him to fly from time to time to keep his hand in. On this occasion, however, he was to be disappointed. And it turned out to be his ninth and last opportunity. On the return flight Flt Lt *Buck* Buchanan ran low on fuel and landed L8514 at Araxos, where it tipped up on to its nose; the aircraft was abandoned.

Four 84 Squadron machines led by Flt Lt Towgood also took-off, at 10:25, to bomb targets at the mouth of the River Voiussa, but as nothing worthy of their bombs was seen, they bombed instead Valona aerodrome. Two of the Blenheims released their bombs prematurely although the other two crews believed they were on target and reported severely damaging a CR.42 about to take-off.

A further two aircraft took off for Yannina next day (**15 December**), from which another attempt was to be made at a photographic recce. One aircraft, flown by Plt Off. Tommy Thompson, damaged its tail wheel on landing at Yannina and was unable to continue the operation, while the other aircraft, L6670 flown by Plt Off. *Herby* Herbert, returned to base having completed a successful visual reconnaissance, but no photographs were obtained owing to camera failure. The aircraft landed with its undercarriage retracted due to port engine seizure. Air temperature was minus 50 degrees Centigrade at 23,000 feet and the gunner, Sgt Duffy, suffered severe frostbite to his fingers and toes, which necessitated admission to hospital. He was joined in hospital a couple of days later by observer Sgt Andy Bryce, who had been injured in an M/T accident while travelling in an army vehicle. L6670 was dismantled by No.33 Air Stores Park personnel and sent to the RHAF's aircraft factory to be rebuilt.

Three days later (**18 December**), three Blenheim IFs of 30 Squadron flew a morning offensive reconnaissance up to Valona harbour. Here they bombed seaplane hangars, but were then intercepted by six CR.42s and three G.50s. Plt Off. *Butch* Paget's aircraft (L8462) was hit in the port engine and caught fire, crashing into the sea eight miles west of Sarande. Lost with Plt Off. Paget were Yorkshireman Sgts George Sigsworth and Lancastrian Bill Tubberdy. Meanwhile, Flt Lt Bob Davidson fought a CR.42 briefly (believing that he had probably destroyed it) but then had to turn his attention to his colleague, flying over the spot where the Blenheim had ditched and dropping his dinghy; however, Paget's aircraft had sunk like a stone with the loss of all the crew.

The official Italian version of events was very similar. A section of three CR.42s from 363ª Squadriglia that had taken off at 12:05, led by Sottotente Ugo Drago (with Serg. Mario Scagliarini and Serg. Enrico Micheli), were over Valona when three Blenheims were seen approaching coming from the Shushice valley at 12,000 feet. The Blenheims were obliged to enter clouds over the Karaburunit peninsula. Three more CR.42s, from 365ª Squadriglia led by Tenente Franco Gatti (with M.llo. Virginio Bodini and Serg. Mario Angeloni) joined Drago's Fiats in the pursuit. The bombers were followed as far as Butrint and believed hit many times—and all three claimed probably shot down, credited to all six pilots.

However, three G.50s of 395ª Squadriglia led by Tenente Livio Bassi were also airborne over Valona when the Blenheims arrived, and were soon joined by that flown by the CO, Cap. Piergiuseppe Scarpetta. They also reported attacking the Blenheims but broke away when they entered cloud, all apart from Bassi, who continued the pursuit for 25 minutes until the Blenheim was seen to hit the sea close to Corfu. It seems that Bassi delivered the *coup de grâce* to Plt Off. Paget's aircraft.

On landing back to base, one of the CR.42s, damaged in the engine by return fire (presumably Davidson's victim), hit the wing of a parked Fiat G.18 transport and overturned. The pilot was however unhurt and his aircraft deemed repairable.

That night, British battleships HMS *Warspite* and *Valiant* shelled Valona, damaging thirteen of 150° Gruppo's CR.42s on the airfield. The Royal Navy was not to escape its current round of operations without loss on this occasion, however, for the submarine HMS *Triton*, which had recently sunk a 6,000-ton freighter off Durazzo, was itself intercepted in the Strait of Otranto, and sunk by the Italian torpedo-boat *Confienza*. While Valona was being bombarded, three Wellingtons from Menidi were raiding Brindisi railway station—on the mainland—and oil storage tanks, large fires being started. On this occasion AA was heavy and one was hit in the port engine, the airscrew breaking loose and flying off. By skilful handling while the crew jettisoned all moveable equipment, the pilot was able to fly back to Greece at 1,000 feet and land safely at base.

At last, with dawn on **19 December**, the weather cleared over the Larissa Plain, and in fine conditions nine Blenheims from 84 Squadron were off early to bomb Valona and Krionero. Only Serg. Arrigo Zoli of 395ª Squadriglia was up and he engaged the bombers, but after a couple of attacks his guns jammed. Back at base he was credited with a probable. Three Blenheims sustained damage; the gunners claimed damage to one Fiat in return. Flt Lt Plinston was on his first op since arriving in Greece:

> It was a beautiful day, no cloud over the Gulf of Corinth, cloud over the mountains and then clear skies again over Valona. A ship was moored alongside the quay but regrettably there were no direct hits. On the way back three Italian fighters came up to have a look but did not press home their attack. It served to remind me how an enemy fighter helps to improve your formation flying.[10]

Further success was claimed by 154° Gruppo on **22 December** when five G.50s—four from 361ª Squadriglia and one from 395ª Squadriglia—scrambled from Berat at 11:00 and intercepted nine 84 Squadron Blenheims led by Sqn Ldr Lewis raiding the Kucera oilfields; a sixth G.50 flown by Serg. Manfredo Bianchi of 395ª Squadriglia was also up on a lone patrol over Kucera. Bianchi engaged and claimed three of the Blenheims shot down in flames, and was soon joined by Serg. Arrigo Zoli of the same unit claimed a fourth; a fifth was believed to have been probably shot down. Two of the G.50s were slightly damaged by return fire, including that flown by Bianchi.

Two of the Blenheims were actually shot down, L8471 going down with the loss of Flg Off. Peter Miles and his crew (Sgts Frank Moir and Bert Brooker), while Flg Off. John Evans managed to bale out of L8374 near Koritza. Both were probably shot down by Serg. Bianchi, since Sqn Ldr Lewis reported that both fell victim to a single fighter. Three other Blenheims were damaged, some by

AA fire; L4818 flown by Flt Sgt Alex Gordon DFM, a Scot, was badly shot up during attacks by several fighters, his Irish air-gunner—Sgt George Furney DFM from County Antrim—receiving a severe head wound. Despite this, Gordon was able to fly the aircraft 200 miles back, landing at base with the starboard engine dead—a remarkable accomplishment. Both had been decorated for their performance in desert operations before transferring to Greece.

Flg Off. Evans later returned, reporting that the cockpit of his aircraft had suddenly become a mass of flames. The observer, Sgt Harry Offord, had made an immediate and successful evacuation of the aircraft, but Sgt Alf Sargeant, the Welsh air-gunner, was killed. Meanwhile, Evans, who had been hit in one arm, got caught up in the shroud-lines of his parachute so that the jerk as this opened broke one of his thigh bones:

> As a result, I arrived on earth a good deal faster than I should have done. Fortunately we had fallen in Greek lines, and my sergeant [Offord] brought some soldiers from a village, and they carried me into a hut. The Greeks were grand; they bandaged me up best they could, and their commander told four men to carry me back to safety. For three days they carried me on a stretcher over mountain tracks. Sometimes I lay on the stretcher and looked over the edge to see the ground a thousand feet below; but those chaps—despite the snow and mud—never slipped once. Finally we reached a town, and they patched me up and put me on the train for Athens.[11]

From the carnage inflicted on the Blenheims by the G.50s it was obvious that a change in tactics and defence needed to be considered. Flt Lt Bill Russell recalled:

> As a result of the hammering we had received, Flt Lt Towgood and myself decided to start experimenting with extra guns. He fixed up a Lewis gun firing backwards from an engine nacelle, while I got one attached rear of the bomb-bay, the idea being to load a full drum of tracer to hose rearward at any fighters repeating their tactics of the 22nd, which were to cruise along astern and below and pick us off at their leisure. Before we could try the system out, Sqn Ldr Lewis got to hear of it and we were both bawled out for making 'unauthorised modifications to aircraft' and that was the end of that.[12]

Christmas Eve saw an attack by seven Blenheims of 211 Squadron, led by Sqn Ldr Gordon-Finlayson, against buildings and dispersed aircraft at Valona. Low cloud necessitated the attack being carried out from 1,500 feet. The CO related:

> One after another the Squadron flashed through the gap, and heading straight for Valona aerodrome we released the thunder and lightning of our bombing attack, machine-gunning the surprised and panic-stricken enemy.[13]

Plt Off. Eric Bevington-Smith in L1482 recalled:

> We assembled five crews [*sic*] and set off for Valona. The weather was appalling, with a cloud base below 2,000 feet and we flew along the Gulf of Corinth and up to Valona, where the cloud base was 1,700 feet … we just managed to slip through in line-astern, went up into cloud again, and by good luck came out of cloud over Valona and dropped our bombs. The AA had not yet woken up, so we put our noses down and went flat out for the harbour entrance. When we were at about 500 feet we met an Italian cruiser and destroyer coming in for Christmas. We turned our front machine guns on and dived on the ships, and as we passed our rear-gunners sprayed the decks. It worked; we were at least two miles away before shellfire started bursting round us and a quick change of course to the south got us away. If only those Italian gunners had not assumed that at the entrance to the harbour of their home port, they were safe![14]

On Valona airfield one CR.42 was destroyed by the bombs and two more were damaged. The AA defenders claimed one Blenheim probably shot down. A cruiser was encountered and strafed, all aircraft surviving her barrage. Three 363ª Squadriglia CR.42s flown by Sottoten. Romeo Della Costanza, Serg. Enrico Micheli and Serg. Mario Scagliarini were scrambled and the leader was able to engage and open fire; he believed that he had probably shot down a Blenheim, but this was not the case.

On **Christmas Day** five Blenheims from 84 Squadron were despatched to Corfu in foul weather to drop sacks of gifts on the esplanade for the children of this island, and also a dozen bundles of leather jerkins. During the afternoon more aircraft appeared overhead—but this time they were three Italian bombers which dropped a number of bombs on buildings near Corfu harbour, several of which were hit. One bomb went through a window of the National Bank of Greece building, piercing the concrete floor and exploding in the basement which was in use as an air raid shelter, and where on this festive day a dance was in progress. Eighteen people were killed and 25 others injured. Elsewhere in the town three others were killed and five hurt.

The rest of the holiday passed quietly enough as far as the RAF was concerned, although Boxing Day (**26 December**) brought with it renewed fighting. Eight aircraft of 211 Squadron carried out an offensive reconnaissance of the Himare-Valona road and bombed Krionero on completion of the recce. The formation was intercepted by a reported nine fighters [in fact only six CR.42s of 364ª Squadriglia led by Cap. Luigi Corsini]. One Blenheim (L1482 flown by Plt Off. *Herby* Herbert) landed with its undercarriage retracted due to damage to its hydraulic system inflicted by fighters, as observer Sgt Jim Dunnet graphically recalled in his account of the flight and the fight:

I gave myself a moment's musing of the greatness of the past, something of whose splendour still survived in the landscape of this noble country. Patras, away on my left, shone whitely at the base of the brown hills—Patras where the sweet plump little olives came from. I glanced across at the plane on my left, and felt a little more comfortable and secure; that was *Pongo* [Sgt Waring] over there in the turret, just a little black-helmeted head turning now and then in our direction with rude gestures. With *Jock* [Sgt Bill Young] behind us and *Pongo* over there on the left to assist in cross-fire, not to mention Geary, the pilot officer gunner who was flying in the CO's machine, I felt nothing could happen to us. It was good to have your pals right alongside you, fighting and protecting each other to the utmost. *Jimmy* James was tucking himself well in to the leader—that's the stuff, he was a damn good formation pilot, old *Jimmy*.

I turned my attention to the landscape, or rather seascape, again. We had turned north heading for our target. I looked down through the thin drift wires of the bombsight at the foam-capped waves. Drift 5 degrees port, I checked up on my navigation instruments; the wind had changed; a few moments' calculation, rapid alterations of settings on the bombsight and everything was set. I felt the usual tense feeling set in, as Valona appeared in the distance, came swiftly towards us. I bent my head over the bombsight, hell! Nearly forgot to select the bombs. I scrambled back hastily and flicked the bomb switches over. *Herby* was intent on scraping the leader's fuselage with his wingtip, close in. That was the stuff.

Here we are, the town of Valona came in my sights. Out of the corner of my eye I could see the feathery trails of tracer curl up from the ships in the harbour. There, it had started: the bursting black puffs which seemed to float lazily past us so harmlessly. I pressed the firing switch viciously. Hope that blasts to hell some of you down there. I looked round to grin at my pilot only to see a tense, straining face, felt the plane lurch heavily in a screaming turn, and looked round. The leader was wheeling round and away, going like hell. I heard our own engines roar as we banked around after the CO. What the hell was wrong? There wasn't much AA being thrown up. The intercom rasped in my ears. "Fighters!" It was *Jock's* voice, hoarse with excitement, his Vickers rattled into life. Where the hell? I twisted in my seat, my eyes roved the sky, can't see; there they are, there must be a dozen of them, CR.42s! I crouched back involuntarily as I watched a tiny vicious-looking biplane turn in towards us, saw the red tracer leap from *Jock's* gun and curl towards it. "Go on, *Jock*, get the bastard!" The whole Squadron were now bunched in close together, noses slightly down, engines screaming with full boost as we raced madly for home, turning and twisting to evade the fighters swarming round us like bees. It was useless to say I was cool, I was rather more excited than afraid, fear had no time to enter into such rapid action. I didn't like to look around again, knowing I would see some blunt-nose biplane turning in to spit a hopeful burst at us.

I saw *Pongo* clamp a fresh pan on his gun and fire a long burst at something behind, then I crouched against the side as I saw fiery darts whip and crackle between the CO's and our wingtips—tracer bullets! Then we were hit. I cast a swift glance in the well, but couldn't see for smoke in which there seemed to be red darting streaks, then only smoke. I choked as the fumes got in my throat; I clutched the pilot's arm, who shook me off, his white face was straining on keeping formation. I looked again in the well behind, the smoke had cleared and I couldn't see anything very wrong; no fire; the engines were still roaring along. I heard the dull chatter of *Jock's* gun, so he was OK. A fighter zoomed up and away to our right, two more were wheeling down at us from above and behind; angry red streaks darted at them. "Good old *Jock*, go on, give 'em hell!" I wished I had a gun; to just sit there and watch them shoot at you! Turrets were swung feverishly from side to side; guns were elevated, depressed, dancing and chattering leaden streams out at the never-ending attacks.

Why the hell isn't there sufficient cloud? Bloody stupid to go in there and think we wouldn't be attacked. "Go on, *Jock*, get that bastard, fire, man, fire!" A thin-winged biplane came screaming straight at us from above; no answering red tracer leapt from the back as *Jock* was too busy engaging a fighter from the other side. I felt the plane shudder under me as the pounding impact of tracer sliced into the wing—the engine? I could see the structure of the interplane strutting of the CR.42, the Italian markings on the undersurface of the wings, the flash of its wheels as it zoomed up and away showing a green and brown belly. I cheered in delight as from somewhere red streams of tracer whipped through the air, and into the fighter, into his belly, bloody fine. I watched the Italian plane suddenly belch black smoke; slowly it turned over on its back. There was an orange spurt of flame, dense outpourings of black smoke, then it started a long plunge to its fiery end; the long black trail hung in the sky like an agonising finger reaching towards heaven, and going so rapidly to hell.

As if that had been a signal, the fight broke off abruptly, the guns stopped their hammering tattoo behind us, and throttles were eased back to normal cruising position; I couldn't see any more fighters behind us; Corfu was below us, thank God! It was over—we had been hit, though how much I didn't know. I thought it a miracle we were still in one piece. Thank God the engines hadn't stopped or caught fire; I had heard the bullets smacking into the metal of the wing. Well, let's hope we get back OK. I turned to give a reassuring thumbs-up to the pilot. Herbert had relaxed a bit, his pale complexion had gone grey with sweat, his tense grip on the stick relaxed a little, and he grinned back at me. I looked at my watch—we had been chased for a quarter of an hour. I took a look around the sky. The Squadron seemed to be quite intact, good show, and they had got one fighter at least. I picked up the mike. "Did you shoot that fighter down, *Jock*? Are you OK back there?" "Aye, aye, everything's OK here, they shot our aerial away though and ah think got us in the side. It's OK though.

Pongo and I got that bastard between us," *Jock* chuckled. "Made a wizard fire, didn't it?"

The countryside below us shone with a new and purer light as we purred home contentedly; the air was light, fresh and clean; it was as if a new life had opened out to us; everything was radiant and alive, even the dark masses of towering mountains which had appeared so ominous and foreboding earlier, now looked cheerful and friendly. It was not until we had reached Tatoi and were circling the aerodrome before landing that we discovered the undercarriage would not come down. So that's where the bullets went, I thought. "We can't get the wheels down, *Jock*," I spoke through the mike. "We'll have to do a belly-flop."

We fired a red Very light, circled once more, then straightened out and came in; I tensed my body as I saw the landing ground sweep up to meet us, then relaxed again. I had read in books about how to relax every muscle when coming in for a hard knock, but still I found myself just as tense again. I prepared myself for the shock. We were levelling off now skimming just a few feet off the ground, getting lower, lower. I looked out, the props were only inches off the grass; I looked to the front again, not wanting to see them bite into the ground. Crunch! We were rocked and flung about from side to side as the plane dug savagely in and ploughed through the turf viciously, like a bucking bronco. Smashing and wrenching noises assailed our ears, a final torturing 'scrunch' and everything was very still and quiet. For a split second we sat there, feeling rather dazed, unable to collect ourselves quickly enough, then with a sudden burst of unleashed energy, I sprang to my feet, yanked the escape hatch open and dragged myself out, quickly followed by the pilot. A hasty glance around—no fire, everything was OK. *Jock* was out, standing on the grass, rather dazed but still grinning. With a rush and screech of brakes the ambulance and fire tender pulled up alongside, anxious enquiring faces looked down at us. Yes, all OK, nobody hurt, everything all right.

"Hells bells, look at this." I turned around at *Jock's* exclamation and walked over to where he was pointing with an amazed finger at the fuselage. Hell! We were damn lucky! We examined a neat line of holes drilled straight along the upper side of the belly running from just under the gunner's cockpit to about a foot from the cockpit. Another split-second's firing and that fighter would have riddled us. I wriggled my shoulders in distaste; so that was the red fire and smoke I had seen when I had looked back in the well—tracer bullets! God, they had been bloody close too! [15]

Although five other aircraft were hit by machine-gunfire all returned to base without injury to any of the crew members: L1481 Sqn Ldr Gordon-Finlayson; L6657 Sgt Sid Bennett; L8449 Flg Off. Alan Godfrey; L1487 Plt Off. Tommy Thompson; L8533 Sgt *Jimmy* James. Cap. Luigi Corsini reported intercepting eight Blenheims over Durazzo at 11:45, his pilots claiming two shot down and two probables. Credit for the victories went jointly to Cap. Corsini, Tenente Alberto Spigaglia, Sottoten. Giuseppe Gianelli, Sottoten. Pasquale Faltoni, M.llo Ugo Guidi and M.llo Guglielmo Bacci. One of the Fiats came back damaged by return fire.

Information received revealed that important Italian reinforcements were being unloaded at Valona. On **28 December**, Flg Off. *Duke* Delaney lead a formation of three 211 Squadron aircraft to attack the shipping and foreshore at that harbour. The operation was repeated the following day (**29 December**) when a further encounter between British and Italian machines was next recorded. On that day three of 30 Squadron's Blenheims were off on a morning offensive reconnaissance over Valona, where Italian reinforcements were known to be disembarking. The bomb-aimers had just released their bombs on the port when three G.50s of 361ª Squadriglia, that were patrolling over Valona, engaged. Serg. Arrigo Zoli dived to attack, hitting K7104 in the port engine, which burst into flames. The bomber, in the hands of Flt Lt Harry Card crashed into the sea; while two parachutes were seen, there were no survivors. Meanwhile, Zoli also attacked both the other Blenheims, claiming one more shot down and the third probably so; Plt Off. Alex Crockett's L6672 was seriously hit but made it back to Eleusis, where it belly-landed; although hit in fuel tanks, wings and fuselage, Sgt Tony Ovens' aircraft (K7105) also returned damaged.

Early on the morning of **30 December**, five fighter Blenheims of 30 Squadron set off to patrol over the Preveza-Levkas area. On arrival the formation split into two patrols of three and two, and after about an hour Sgt Fred Goulding, gunner in Sqn Ldr Shannon's aircraft in the latter pair, spotted a Z.506B floatplane of the 190ª Squadriglia, 86° Gruppo, below, as this was carrying out an offensive reconnaissance along the Greek coast in the hands of Tenente Domenico Bazzi. Shannon dived to attack, firing with his front guns and making several passes, closing to 25 yards, until all his ammunition was exhausted. He also closed to allow Sgt Goulding a shot, but the latter was hit in the knee by an explosive bullet fired from the floatplane's dorsal gun position. The CO broke off and headed for home, but quickly realising how badly hit his gunner was, he put down at Agrinion for help. Although a doctor arrived within minutes, Goulding was already unconscious and died shortly afterwards from loss of blood. *Bud* Richardson later reported:

> I then did a series of quarter attacks, closing to 50 yards, pumping lead into the aircraft until I wondered whatever was holding it up. By this time my ammo was running short so I decided to let my air-gunner have some fun, and in pulling ahead and in front of the front end of the enemy aircraft three or four times, the air-gunner was able to get home some bursts into him. By this time the aircraft had slowed down considerably, and I decided to make a final attempt to get the pilot, so I pulled away in front, turned, and did a front

quarter attack, opening fire from 50 yards and holding until I had to pull away in case of colliding. The aircraft dropped a wing and crashed into the sea—two seen waving a handkerchief and three or four lying on a wing. I dropped dinghy and returned.[16]

On returning to base, Richardson was later informed that the Greek Navy had picked up the Italians. However, records show that Tenente Bazzi, along with second pilot Serg. Elisio Acuti, Av.Sc.Mot. Libero Mera, Av.Sc.Arm. Salvatore Di Salvo, and 1°Av.Mot. Cosimo Buorngiorno, were all reported killed in action.

The death of Sgt Goulding caused a deal of animosity amongst the gunners of 30 Squadron, as they felt that had there been an observer aboard the aircraft to treat him, he may well have survived. Having to fly without an observer meant there was nobody to administer immediate treatment should a gunner require such attention. It is not known if the air-gunners union approached Sqn Ldr Shannon with their troubles, but it was soon out of his hands since his posting was announced two days later and Sqn Ldr Robert Milward, known as *Percy*, who had previously commanded a flight of Blenheims of 39 Squadron based in Aden, for which he was awarded the DFC, arrived to take command.

At Kazaklar airfield, three Blenheims of 32 Mira were being readied for an operation when the leader, Major Charalambros Potamianos, was called by HQ to proceed to Paramythia with haste, where he was to assess the suitability of the airfield for use by Blenheims. An RHAF Anson had already arrived to convey him to the mountain airfield. Capt. Panayhiotis Orphanidis (a native of Rhodes) was instructed to take over his aircraft (B252) and crew, and to lead the mission. Major Potamianos recalled:

The pilot of the Avro Anson had the order to take-off immediately. However, I wanted to watch the departure of my group and told him to switch off the engines and disembark for a while. First to be airborne was the aircraft of Lt Kleanthes Chatziioannou, second was [Lt Michalis] Stratis and last in the row was Orphanidis. Suddenly, a terrible, massive clash was heard. Orphanidis' Blenheim was no more than 500 feet over the ground when we turned our eyes on it just to witness a big explosion in the downside of the aircraft and watch its horrible crash moments later. The aircraft came into the ground and caught fire immediately. Everyone left their tasks in panic and many of them were running to the crash site. That moment I yielded to them "What are you doing? Haven't you ever seen an aircraft crashing? Go back to your jobs now!" in an effort to calm down my Squadron's men. Then, I got into my mess and I just couldn't keep from crying…[17]

The three crewmen were instantly killed. A fault with the bomb arming process was assumed to have been the cause.

Meanwhile, Lt Chatziioannou, who was circling over the airfield, waiting for the other two aircraft to join the formation, witnessed the tragic event which shocked him and immediately landed back to the airfield. When he disembarked the aircraft, he complained to the doctor of the Squadron about stomach disorders. The doctor advised him not to fly and asked Major Potamianos to change the crew, as it seemed that Chatziioannou was unable to fly after the shock. Unfortunately, there was no other stand-by crew that could take his position. Finally, the two Blenheims took off to bomb positions at the area between Kelcyre and Berat. After the bombardment, they were chased by two CR.42s of 363ª Squadriglia. Sottoten. Maurizio di Robilant attacked the aircraft of Chatziioannou (B260), which crashed in flames near Valona. None of the three crewmen were seen to bale out. With Chatziioannou died Sgts Arabatzis and Sotiriadis.

Meanwhile, nine 211 Blenheims bombed stores and store buildings south of Valona. Two CR.42s and one G.50 of 395ª Squadriglia were encountered. The latter, flown by Sottoten. Giuliano Fissore, attacked Sgt Sid Bennett's aircraft at 7,000 feet, when some 20 miles south of Valona. With its port engine on fire, L1540 left the formation and nothing further was heard of it, but Fissore observed the Blenheim crash in flames and no one leaving it before it hit the ground. In addition to Sgt Bennett, Sgts Bill Tunstall and Les France were also lost. Their aircraft came down about ten miles from Valona and the bodies of the three NCOs were recovered and buried in the Albanian village of Mavrove, just east of the main road to the mountainous south.

Air Vice-Marshal D'Albiac, in the course of a talk to the war correspondents about the war in Greece, said:

> Flying conditions in Greece are more difficult than anywhere in Europe. The weather changes with great rapidity, making accurate forecasts impossible, and the natures of the country does not always allow landings when pilots are unable to regain their bases. Ice formations are another difficulty. Instruments freeze, and the airscrews get a covering of ice which makes it difficult to maintain sufficient altitude to clear the mountains. The temperature is never more than 28 degrees, and sometimes goes to minus 50 degrees. Those conditions, as well as the restricted number of air bases available to the RAF, make the operation of a large air force in Greece during the winter impracticable, but I believe that the RAF will be greatly reinforced when the weather improves.[18]

CHAPTER 4

January–February 1941

The Greek advance had lost its impetus by the beginning of the year as the result of increased enemy resistance, lengthened lines of communication and severe winter conditions.

Air Chief Marshal Sir Arthur Longmore AOCME

The New Year of 1941 found a situation of stalemate fast developing along the front line. The weather had clamped down hard, making movement on the ground difficult, and in the air on many days, well-nigh impossible. The Greeks were practically exhausted by the tremendous exertions of their autumn counter-attacks, and were still desperately short of transport, clothing and anti-tank and anti-aircraft artillery. The major part of their armed forces and most of their air power were involved at the front, leaving only four weak divisions on the frontier with Bulgaria. Should any threat from this area develop it was considered that nine more divisions and associated air support would be required to defend Eastern Macedonia and Salonika. Nothing however was to be allowed to alarm the Germans, and still no British land forces were to be accepted for service in Greece unless the Germans crossed the Danube and entered Bulgaria. RAF units should also operate only in the west and south, no squadrons being based in the Salonika area. Further reinforcements of air units within these parameters would however be accepted gratefully, allowing the RHAF to withdraw to Salonika to reform.

During January, therefore, the British High Command resolved to send two more squadrons to Greece, one of fighters and one of bombers, while planning at the same time to capture the Italian Dodecanese Islands—particularly Rhodes— to secure the Aegean and Eastern Mediterranean. In his Despatch for this period, Air Chief Marshal Longmore wrote:

The Greek advance had lost its impetus by the beginning of the year as the result of increased enemy resistance, lengthened lines of communication and severe winter conditions. The Greeks still retained the initiative, however, and after operations had apparently become static, they made a further advance, capturing Kelcyre on the 8th January, 1941, and thereafter making slow progress along the Northern side of the Kelcyre-Tepelene gorge. There was little activity in other sectors.

Although the Greek Air Force operated with success in the early days of the war its activities were much reduced latterly by the inability of the Greeks to make good their aircraft casualties. Thus, practically the whole of the air effort in this theatre devolved upon the RAF which was consequently called upon to attack strategical objectives, to operate in direct support of the Greek Army, necessary in order to maintain their high morale, and to provide the fighter defence of the Athens area. To meet these requirements Squadrons were employed in the following roles—Wellingtons operating by night attacked ports in Albania and to a less extent in S. Italy to interrupt the flow of enemy supplies and reinforcements to Albania. The primary role of the Blenheims was to provide direct support for the Greek Army by attacking: (a) enemy lines of communication and important centres behind the forward area to prevent the distribution of supplies and reinforcements, and (b) enemy positions in the forward area.

Blenheims also attacked ports in Albania by night and day and provided strategical reconnaissance of ports in Southern Italy and Albania. Hurricanes and Gladiators were employed in escorting Blenheims during many of their daylight bombing attacks, in maintaining offensive patrols and in protecting the Greek troops against enemy air action. Blenheim fighters continued to provide the air defence of the port and air bases in the Athens area. In addition to the commitments already referred to, Wellingtons and Blenheims operating from Greece were called upon to attack enemy aerodromes in the Dodecanese from which enemy aircraft were carrying out mine-laying operations in the Suez Canal, as well as air attacks on our convoys proceeding to Greece.[1]

The threat of German intervention was a real one, for early in the month of January Hitler would decide to send a strong contingent to Albania to bolster the Italians, planning for this move beginning under the codename Operation *Alpenweilchen*. The end of the Greek counter-offensive and reinforcement of the Italian forces brought a halt to these preparations in mid- February however, when it became clear that, with 21 divisions in Albania, the Italians should be able to secure their hold on Valona.

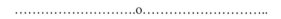

For 211 Squadron the New Year was marked by a tragic accident. Advice had just been received that Sqn Ldr Gordon-Finlayson had been awarded a DFC, while New Year's Eve was also Flt Lt Graham *Potato* Jones' birthday. With a triple reason to celebrate the squadron wined and dined at *Maxim's* in Athens,

but while returning to the Mess, one car containing several officers crashed into a tree, the Equipment Officer, Flg Off. Dennis Barrett, dying of the injuries he received, whilst Gordon-Finlayson, Jones and Plt Off. Ron *Twink* Pearson were also hurt though fortunately none of them seriously.

The early part of January was marked by continuous rain, airfields becoming seriously water-logged and operations rare. 211 Squadron was one of the few active at this time, eight Blenheims led by Flt Lt George Doudney in L8541 raiding Elbasan on **4 January**; on the return flight Plt Off. Hugh Clutterbuck force-landed L6657 at Araxos owing to error in navigation.

But the first real action of 1941 occurred on **6 January**, as weather permitted some more sustained operational flying. Nine Blenheims from 211 Squadron, again led by Flt Lt Doudney, reached Valona at 09:40, bombing the foreshore from 4,000 feet. Two CR.42s of 364ª Squadriglia 'alarm section' and three G.50s from 395ª Squadriglia were scrambled, intercepting as the bombers left the target. Tenente Livio Bassi and the two other G.50 pilots—M.llo Bruno Ferracini and Serg. Emilio Piva—each engaged a vic of Blenheims, Piva later recalling:

I shot at the engines and it caught fire, I always aimed at the engines, trying not to kill the enemy aviators, sadly many others aimed right at the cockpit. From the flaming bomber I saw two men jumping with parachute. I was happy they were alive and I started to turn around them to greet them. In doing so I noticed that they raised their hands, scared and I didn't understand why. Once back at base the Commander explained me why this had happened. British propaganda told RAF pilots that the Italians used to machine-gun pilots after they had been obliged to jump. Obviously it was not true. Nevertheless, sadly, the two Englishmen shot down by me died. They came down in open water and were found drowned. They were boys like myself and also today I often think to them.[2]

Although Piva's account has some anomalies, his victim was undoubtedly L8536 flown by Flg Off. *Duke* Delaney, which was seen to be badly hit, although it was believed that Sgt *Jock* McCord in the turret had shot down a 'Macchi' in flames. As the bomber headed away, the port engine stopped, but it headed on, accompanied by the formation leader, Flt Lt Doudney, whose own Blenheim (L8541) had also been heavily damaged. Near the frontier at Argyrokastron, Delaney indicated that he was going down to land. As he attempted to bring the aircraft down on its belly, it struck some boulders and cart-wheeled; Delaney and the crew (Sgts Vynor Pollard and *Jock* McCord) were killed outright. Doudney meanwhile almost reached Menidi, but he too was obliged to crash-land short of this base.

On the ground, part of the 34th Greek Regiment had encamped in the village of Topova, well inside the Albanian border. These soldiers had witnessed the final moments of Delaney's aircraft, as recalled by 2/Lt Panayotis Kaneuopoulos:

It was 10am when far on the horizon we saw an allied aircraft, which was coming into land. Moments later it touched down in a narrow field right across from us, overturned and exploded. The Regiment commander immediately ordered me to take a few soldiers and rush to the place of the accident. We went down the slope of the mountain, crossed the River Drinos and, after climbing up the opposite slope, we reached the scene of the tragedy.

All three airmen were dead. They wore uniforms and we scattered around the wreckage. I noted down the aircraft's distinctive markings and the names of the three airmen. We then carried, with great difficulty, the bodies to the village and in the afternoon buried them, with due military honours, in the modest cemetery of Topova. The personal affects we had been able to find were forwarded to the Division for their action.[3]

Meanwhile, Tenente Bassi was attacking and shooting down Flg Off. Bobby Campbell's L1487; the New Zealander later wrote from his hospital bed in Albania:

I was shot down into the sea not far from our target. The 'Old Maestro' [their Blenheim] was riddled and Appleyard [Sgt Ray Appleyard, the air-gunner] was shot twice in the head, not fatally, thank God. Beharrell [observer Sgt John Beharrell] is OK. I have a busted leg. We managed to get out before we sank and swam to the shore. Beharrell had the only life jacket as he could not swim. We left him to it as he was getting on OK and we had a hell of a job ourselves, being in the water for an hour or more. Beharrell was picked up by an Iti destroyer. It was rough, and the cliff almost perpendicular so we had a job getting out. We were captured about midnight. We were all in and had no clothes. I won't tell you any more about it …

Try to keep my gear together, *Buck*, and be a good chap and send that portrait of me home to mother. If my uniform etc could be sent via the Red Cross I should appreciate it as I have only a singlet and underpants of my own—no razor, toothbrush, and, of course, no money. I owe Allan 1,000 Dracs and I hope he gets it OK. I am very sorry at having to leave everybody—the chaps were all like brothers to me … Tell the *Bish* to hurry up and win the war. Your pal, Bob.[4]

Tenente Bassi, rather than pursue the remaining Blenheims, to his credit guided a destroyer to the area where the observer, Sgt Beharrell, was rescued; his capture was announced on Italian radio. Shortly before his own death, Bassi visited Campbell in hospital.

Two more Blenheims had also received damage, Flg Off. *Buck* Buchanan (L1490) reaching Menidi, while Plt Off. *Pip* Cox put down at Eleusis for temporary repairs to L1528. Losses were thus two Blenheims and one crash-landed, plus three more damaged. Meanwhile, CR.42 pilot Serg. Osvaldo Bartolaccini pursued Sgt *Jock* Marshall's L1542, which had been damaged in the tail by AA, but the gunner, Sgt Bill Baird, drove this off, reporting that smoke poured from its engine as it broke away; in his logbook he wrote:

> About 20 minutes after 'bombs gone' there appeared a large hole in the starboard tailplane, caused by a delayed action AA shell. I was exceptionally placed to observe this as the turret is fairly close to the tail on a Blenheim! The immediate result was the plane's desire to climb drastically, and *Jock* and the observer [Sgt Jack Richmond] both had to wrestle with the control column to regain straight and level. We still had to get back to Menidi down the Gulf of Corinth, but *Jock* decided to do just that. On arrival at base *Jock* was astonished to see the extent of the damage—one could put head and shoulders through the hole. It took till the 16th to repair it! This ranks high in many near things that came my way.[5]

Sgts Marshall and Richmond were later each awarded the DFM for their performance. When Sqn Ldr Wisdom received news of the missing Blenheims, he wrote:

> Three of our aircraft failed to return, the saddest words I have had to write. And I wondered, as always, whether any of my friends were aboard those three aircraft. Then I heard—the *Duke* was dead. That night a message came through to say that the crew of the aircraft had been discovered—all dead. The *Duke* had attempted a wheels-up landing in a tiny valley in which he was trapped. The only possible landing place was strewn with boulders, and the aircraft had struck these and cart-wheeled over.
>
>   Peasants from the village on the mountainside, not far from Kelcyre, buried the three men in the tiny graveyard. We were to salute the *Duke* and his crew when we flew together that way a month later. My friend, the *Duke*, wise-cracking, brave as a lion, and so young—he was only 21—was dead. It was many days before I could make myself believe it. The old gang were going one by one.[6]

A raid by seven Blenheims of 211 Squadron on **10 January**, to bomb retreating Italian troops on the Kelcyre–Berat road, was aborted owing to bad weather with low cloud covering the hilltops. At 10:30, eight aircraft from 84 Squadron attacked the same target, Plt Off. Ivor Goudge running low on fuel during the return flight. He crash-landed L8501 at Araxos, where the Blenheim was abandoned.

On **12 January**, Wg Cdr Lord Forbes arrived at Menidi in his Q.6, with the AOC Air Vice-Marshal D'Albiac and Grp Capt. A.H. Willetts on board. Apart from a morale-boosting speech on the progress of the British offensive in Libya, an important outcome of the visit was the establishment of a camp cinema at Menidi, courtesy of the Greek air force, which placed a hangar at the RAF's disposal for use as a cinema, while the necessary equipment was hired from a cinema in Athens. Two days later, 211 Squadron's diarist at Menidi noted the departure of Wg Cdr Lord Forbes in his Q.6, destination Turkey. It transpired that he was to attend a meeting between a British Military Mission headed jointly by Lt-Gen James Marshall-Cornwall, former Chief of the British Military to Egypt, and Air Vice-Marshal Sir Thomas Elmhirst, and the Turkish General Staff. The meeting was necessary to clarify the position of the Turkish Government following the movement of German troops to the Bulgarian border, thus posing a threat to both Turkey and Greece. Wg Cdr Lord Forbes would return to Menidi at the end of the month.

Plt Off. *Herby* Herbert of 211 Squadron was detailed to take vertical overlap photographs of Kasos Island, taking off in L1481 at 09:10 on **15 January**. He returned two hours later, mission unfulfilled. Low cloud down to sea level and icing conditions at 3,000 feet made the task impossible, as his report revealed:

> I took off and climbed southward through a layer of cloud at about 3,000 feet and proceeded along track. After about a quarter of an hour this layer closed up. I tried to climb through the cloud but after about half an hour and reaching 15,000 feet I was unable to climb higher owing to ice accretion. I decided to turn back and attempted to reach sea level. I came out of cloud after about 20 minutes flying on the return journey and proceeded to sea level through a gap. As the clouds were down to sea level in places, I decided that no attempt to reach the area should be made at low level. I landed back at Menidi at 11:30.[7]

Winter conditions made photo-reconnaissance sorties extremely difficult, with poor visibility, poor flying conditions, severe icing and temperatures sufficiently low to freeze aerial cameras and to give gunners frostbite. 211 Squadron attempted to carry out raids on **17 January** (three aircraft to Valona led by Sqn Ldr Gordon-Finlayson) and again two days later (nine aircraft to Elbasan) but both were aborted owing to low cloud. Sgt *Nobby* Clark, observer aboard Sgt *Jimmy* James' aircraft (L8533) noted:

> Wing icing causing aircraft to fall out of the sky—opt to stay with the aircraft and take a chance (we're beyond target and in enemy territory); jettison bombs, pans of ammo—it melts at 2,500 feet![8]

Three Blenheim bombers of A Flight of 30 Squadron took-off from Eleusis at 11:00 on **19 January**, for anti-submarine patrols over area of incoming convoy, while six of 84 Squadron carried out a raid on Berat. One pilot reported:

No fighters, but ack-ack was waiting for us. Sticky, but no one was hurt. Flight led in line- astern through the valley.

Two hours later, what was believed to have been a reconnaissance He111 appeared over Eleusis at 16,000 feet. No air raid warning was given and AA did not open fire; however, two Blenheim fighters were scrambled. One aircraft got up to 24,000 feet but could not contact enemy aircraft, which had now climbed to 30,000 feet. The aircraft had apparently made a complete recce of Eleusis and Menidi.

On **20 January**, 211 Squadron again despatched five Blenheims led by Australian Flt Lt Allan Farrington (L8513) to bomb Valona during the morning, at 10:30. Four 150° Gruppo CR.42s attacked just as they had finished their bombing, and two were slightly damaged, Sottoten. Ernani Loddo claiming one shot down into the sea. Escaping the fighters, all five were heading back to base when ten miles south of Corfu a Z.506B from 35° Stormo BM was sighted, and was attacked, as noted by Sqn Ldr Wisdom:

> Though the Blenheims had only a single front-gun they took turns in riddling the Cant, and when front-gun ammunition was exhausted they manoeuvred their aircraft so that the rear-gunner could have a crack, too. The Cant went down.[9]

It seems that Flg Off. *Buck* Buchanan in L1490 was given credit for its probable destruction. Closing to 75 yards, Buchanan inflicted severe damage and believed that he silenced the turret gunner, but return fire struck the Blenheim in one engine nacelle. However, the floatplane survived the attacks and on returning to base, the Italian gunner claimed to have shot down one Blenheim and possibly a second.

80 Squadron was still maintaining a detachment at Eleusis for the defence of Athens and at 12:20 on this date three Gladiators were ordered off to patrol over Piraeus, as Italian bombers were reported approaching from the west. Two minutes later two more Gladiators were ordered off to patrol 15 miles to the south-west, and two of 30 Squadron's Blenheim fighters were also scrambled, flown by Flg Off. Derek Walker (L4917) and Flt Sgt Don Innes-Smith. At 13:30 four Z.1007bis from 47° Stormo BT appeared over Athens and bombed from 13,000 feet, escaping interception, as the trio of Gladiators were patrolling at 10,000 feet and had no chance of reaching the bombers, although they did chase them out to sea. When a second formation of bombers approached however, the Gladiators had climbed to 15,000 feet and were well-placed to intercept, making a head-on attack as the bombers turned east for their target, but one was hit by return fire and crashed, killing the pilot.

Meanwhile, another Gladiator pilot attacked the same bomber at which the other had been firing, and was joined by the Blenheim of Flt Sgt Innes-Smith:

The height when first sighting the enemy was 10,000 feet, the position of e/a being practically underneath [by] about 2,000 feet. Our approach was presumably unobserved by the 5 enemy aircraft, which were flying in vic formation. Two stern attacks following a dive were made on the e/a, and my rear-gunner reports that e/a returned the fire from their rear guns, which were unobserved by me as I was concentrating on the front sight. My first attack was directed at No.4 aircraft and at 800 yards I opened fire, with no apparent effect on the enemy. The second attack I directed at No. 5 aircraft from 300–400 yards, also with no apparent effect.

The first attack was made over Megara, but the enemy was too fast to get in a second attack before AA opened, so I circled and attacked the e/a a second time. As the e/a turned south from Athens, they were attacked by Gladiators. I then concentrated on No.4 aircraft who had his undercarriage down. This aircraft caught fire and crashed into the sea as a result of attacks by Gladiators. The crew of four baled out.[10]

The Cant crashed into the sea ten miles south of Athens, exploding on impact. It seems that the pilot of the 263ª Squadriglia machine survived but second pilot Serg.Magg. William Bivati was lost together with 1° Av.Arm. Elio Cavadini, 1° Av.Marc. Carlo Forti, and 1° Av.Foto. Emilio Arcangelo Scaliati.[11] The other four bombers in the formation all suffered damage from the fighters' attacks. Flg Off. Derek Walker (with Sgt Crooks) noted:

Interception raid on Athens. Chased four Cant Z.1007s but could only get one attack in owing to speed. Innes-Smith shot one Cant down.[12]

211 Squadron was active again on **22 January**, Sqn Ldr Gordon-Finlayson (L8478) leading six Blenheims on an offensive reconnaissance over the Kelcyre-Berat road, and were joined by six of 84 Squadron. The latter crews were intercepted by two G.50s but made their escape. At Berat buildings were bombed from 6,500 feet, but at 09:30 a G.50 from 395ª Squadriglia flown by Serg. Magg. Manfredo Bianchi then intercepted with height advantage. He chased the Blenheims for ten minutes, claiming one shot down (his fourth individual victory claim). His fire had indeed struck four of the bombers (including the CO's), and in Flg Off. Alan Godfrey's aircraft (L8533) one bullet set a Very cartridge on fire, starting a blaze which must have looked as though it spelled the end for the machine; although preparing to bale out, Sgt *Peggy* O'Neill, the observer, managed to extinguish the fire with his boot, and the aircraft was able to return to base. Although badly hit by AA fire and damaged by fighter attack, Plt Off. Pearson managed to fly L8449 back to base, as observer Sgt *Jimmy* Riddle recorded:

Chig [Sgt Gordon Chignall, Wop/AG] phoned through to say there was nothing between him and the ground, astern of his gun turret—cables, wires and lumps of skin were flapping in the slipstream, and that he had lost one of his legs. We were flopping about all over the sky trying to reach cloud out of way of the fighters and I said I would crawl through to help him as soon as I was able to set course from a safe position. However, he phoned again to say that he had found his leg, completely numb and forced up under his seat by the blast. Upon landing he found a piece of shrapnel buried in the leg of his flying boot. Why none of us was punctured is a mystery, as both main planes, the fuselage and tail empennage was well peppered and most of the control cables to the tail were severed. One of the landing legs was severely damaged, but the engines were unscathed.[13]

Sgt *Jimmy* James' L6647 was also targeted, as Sgt *Nobby* Clark noted:

We catch it hot, lots of holes—we are No.3 in C Flight. No.2 [Godfrey] has a fire in the cockpit—we stay alongside with them, just in case. When the smoke clears, they wave OK.[14]

Aboard Plt Off. *Pip* Cox's L1528, Plt Off. Eric Bevington-Smith, the observer, recalled:

We were attacked over the target and escaped into cloud, becoming separated in the process. Flying alone, down the Ionian Sea and once we were south of Corfu, Cox let me fly, and I was stooging along with Cox dozing in the observer's seat. Casting my eye over the instruments, I thought something might be wrong and I shook him awake (the oil pressure was nil and the oil temperature very high). I had never seen Cox move so quickly in his life! As he took control, our starboard engine started emitting copious volumes of smoke, and had to be shut down. Cox decided to force-land at Araxos, on the north-west corner of the Peloponnese. We fired off red Very lights and the people on the ground fired them back, warning us not to land, but we had no option. We touched down alright on the partly constructed runway; as we did so the starboard engine burst into flames and Cox yelled to open the exit hatches and be prepared to get out. To do this I undid my seat belt, and as the aircraft slowed down the main wheels sunk into the ground, pitching the aircraft up on its nose. I was precipitated into the nose, hitting my mouth on the bomb sight, and losing four of my front teeth.[15]

The three airmen obtained a lift in a farm cart to Patras where they contacted the US Consul. He advised them that there was no train to Athens for four or five days, so they walked to the harbour, and there hitched a lift on a boat to Piraeus that night. 211 Squadron received three replacement crews (plus a spare pilot) two days later, including Rhodesian brothers Plt Offs Jack and John Hooper. Sgt George Kearns was the latter's gunner:

> I was a part of the crew that flew Blenheim N3559 [a Mark IV] to Greece on 26 February to be delivered to 11 Squadron. I was supposed to have been returned to Egypt by the Navy but it never happened and I was posted to Paramythia on 211 Squadron on 4 March 1941 and was crewed up with Plt Off. John Hooper and Sgt Len Page. As that crew, we flew 11 operations mostly in Blenheim L1496 until the evacuation from Greece began.[16]

During the afternoon of **25 January**, three of 30 Squadron's Blenheim bombers set off to raid Boultsov in Albania, but over the target area, at 15:05, six G.50s and a number of CR.42s were reported—in fact, there were just two G.50s flown by Tenente Enrico Giordananino and Serg.Magg. Ermes Lucchetta of 24° Gruppo engaged the Blenheims and jointly claimed one probably shot down. Aboard Flt Lt Tom Horgan's aircraft, as air-gunner, was Sgt Geoff Chapman:

> The flight from Eleusis to the Abanian border went according to plan and we were greeted with desultory AA fire as we crossed over the line. Air-gunners were expected to test their guns from time to time—this had been done—but I was horrified to find that this time my guns were frozen solid and just could not be budged! Whilst trying to cope with this embarrassment, enemy fighters were spotted in the distance. It seems that in our search for the supply base we had flown over an Italian fighter airfield. Our formation went into a swift shallow dive down to ground level to ensure that the fighter attack would be from above and forcing the fighters to break away above us also.
>
> We counted six G.50s and 12 CR.42s apparently in hot pursuit. By now the Vickers gun in my turret had unfrozen so we were all ready for action. The G.50s came in very swiftly in line-astern and broke away sharply above us. We could clearly see the underside of each aircraft and fired away madly … the G.50s hit No. 3 aircraft [L8443 flown by Sgt Les Stammers] and both his air-gunner [Sgt Akeroyd] and observer [Plt Off. Carter] were wounded, the former quite seriously but the aircraft was kept in formation. In a short while, the G.50s discontinued the close attacks and contented themselves with taking pot shots at us from about 400 yards or so. The CR.42s never joined in the fray, merely performing aerobatics at some distance behind the G.50s.
>
> We eventually found the target, there to discover that No.3 could not dispose of its load as the bomb rack had been damaged during the action. We duly returned to base. No. 3 made a safe emergency landing and the air-gunner and observer were whisked away to the Military Hospital in Athens.[17]

Sgt Stammers' air-gunner, Sgt Wilf Akeroyd, was wounded in the hand, arm and stomach. He was awarded a DFM, the citation stating:

In January 1941, this airman was the rear-gunner in one of a formation, of aircraft detailed to attack an enemy camp. Approaching the target, the formation was attacked by six enemy fighters and Sergeant Akeroyd was wounded in the finger. Later, he was hit in the right arm and finally in the stomach. In spite of his injuries he returned fire at every opportunity. His wireless set was smashed and when the attackers had been driven off, he crawled forward and informed the pilot of his injuries and the extent of the damage to the aircraft. He displayed great courage and fortitude throughout.[18]

Sqn Ldr Gordon-Finlayson (L1481) led a flight of six 211 Squadron Blenheims to carry out a bombing raid on a military camp at Elbasan on **27 January**. The weather was good but cloud cover scanty over the target. Bombs were dropped from 6,000 feet and direct hits were scored on buildings, which were enveloped in smoke as the formation turned away. A G.50 was sighted on the run-up to the target but made no attempt to engage the Blenheims, which had employed a new type of formation of five in a vic, with the sixth closely stepped down in the box.

Further reinforcements now began to arrive in Greece, nine Wellingtons from 70 Squadron having arrived on detachment at Menidi and Eleusis earlier in the month, while the air party of 11 Squadron had arrived at Eleusis on 23 January. This comprised six Blenheim Is and six Mark IVs, led by Sqn Ldr Peter *Long John* Stevens; the ground party would follow five days later, the unit moving forward to Larissa on the same day. RAF airman Marcel Comeau, a fourth generation Englishman of Nova Scotian ancestry, recalled his first meeting with Sqn Ldr Stevens:

He immediately showed concern over the state of my shoes—large sizes in footwear being unobtainable in Greece—but solved the problem by giving me a pair of his own. This incidentally enabled me to prefix any discussion on squadron affairs: "Well, if I was in the CO's shoes—as of course I am ..." He also gave me *carte blanche* to travel to Volos whenever I liked to search for shoes of our mutual measurements.[19]

By the beginning of January, 32 Mira had lost six aircraft with eighteen crewmen. The squadron was left with half of its original strength, and even some of these were out of use due to technical problems. Mainly for this reason, the Greek Blenheims flew no operations during the month. Five replacement crews arrived to fill the gaps left by those lost while Lt-Col Nikolaos Averof replaced Potamianos as CO. Wt Off Georgios Sakkis commented:

While our former leader would fill us with enthusiasm, his replacement gave us a number of lessons on bombing tactics which had great effect on the complement of our training, which made me feel ready to carry out any mission. Thus, even in January we had no war action due to the very few flyable aircraft, it was not a lost period, but useful for the crews and the squadron. This was shown by the fact that in the missions of 1941 the losses of our Squadron were extremely limited.[20]

By the end of January, the few remaining Blenheims were finally repaired and ready to go back in to action. However, the number of the aircraft was so small that the unit would receive a reinforcement of six ex-RAF Blenheim Is, including L6658 and L6670 from 211 Squadron, and L8384 and L8385, both ex-39 Squadron, amongst them; these were re-numbered B263 to B268. The Mark I was not favoured by the Greek crews as there were no floor hatches for emergency bale-outs, the aircraft requiring to be inverted, fighter-fashion, to allow personnel to drop free.

February 1941

February's bad weather led to an inauspicious start to the month. 11 Squadron's diarist at Larissa wrote:

> Work on settling into our quarters continued. The weather was, however, unfavourable, intermittent rain falling throughout the day. The aerodrome became unserviceable and very soft. Aircraft had to be continually moved as they were found to be sinking in the mud up to their axles. Large stocks of bombs and components arrived at the railway station and were unloaded and stored in the Greek air force's excellent underground bomb stores.[21]

Nonetheless, on the first day of the month, Sqn Ldr Gordon-Finlayson (L1481) led six 211 Squadron aircraft to bomb warehouses, a timber depot, and munitions dumps at Valona. Low cloud lay over the target area and at first it was thought that the attack would have to be delivered from 800 feet, but an opening was found permitting bombing from 3,500 feet. One small building was seen to receive a direct hit. L6657 flown by Plt Off. Hugh Clutterbuck had returned early owing to an electrical failure, and all the others returned safely. Further attempted raids by 211 over the following two days were aborted owing to adverse weather conditions.

On **2 February** one of 11 Squadron's Blenheims, N3580, force-landed near Salonika whilst attempting to reach Menidi, while a second, T2235, was lost on a flight from Eleusis to Abu Sueir, Kenya-born Sgt Doug Strachan and his crew—Sgts Gerald Date and Ron Clift together with passenger AC1 Ted Bradbury—being posted missing. Some of the new crews undertook formation training flights over the sea during this period. On **5 February,** 84 Squadron despatched three Blenheims at 07:15 to bomb supply depots on the Valona-Tepelene road. They became separated in low cloud on the way to the target, attacking individually. As they returned the port engine of Flt Lt Bob Towgood's L4833/VA-U failed and the Blenheim crashed near the boundary fence of Menidi airfield, the pilot being killed instantly when a propeller blade smashed into the cockpit, although the other members of the crew survived. Observer Sgt *Jimmy* Riddle witnessed the crash:

> We [with Sgt Gordon Chignall] were walking across the top of the airfield when she came in and the port motor cut at less than 50 feet. Down went the port wing into the deck. We waited a second or two in case anything blew and ran across to her just as the crash wagon got near. We found the Wop/AG [Sgt Peter Atherton] outside the kite, the pilot dead, apparently with a broken neck, and the observer [Sgt Bob Somerville] underneath a prop blade which had gone into the cockpit without in fact injuring him.[22]

Next day (**6 February**), Flg Off. Angus Nicholson of this unit was off in L1393 on a solo midday sortie to the Tepelene area. The weather again deteriorated, and in very poor visibility he was obliged to ditch in the sea near a small island in the eastern end of the Gulf of Corinth. Sgt Tony Hollist, the 19-year-old gunner from the Isle of Wight, was killed in the crash, whilst the observer, Plt Off. Dicky Day, was drowned. Nicholson alone managed to inflate the dinghy and reached the island from where he was evacuated to hospital.

Z.1007bis from the 47° Stormo and 50° Gruppo Aut. were also in action during the day, raiding Salonika once again. Here they reported being attacked by 'Blenheim fighters and Hurricanes', one bomber being damaged by one of the latter. No RAF Blenheims were involved, but it is possible that 32 Mira bombers became engaged whilst on a sortie to the front. However the 'Hurricanes' were undoubtedly the Bloch MB151 fighters of 24 Mira from Sedes airfield, one of which claimed a Z.1007 shot down.

211 Squadron again attempted to carry out raids although weather again interfered. Four of the six aircraft led by Flg Off. Buchanan were forced to return early, while the other two flown by Plt Offs. Herbert and Cox bombed through breaks in the cloud with unobserved results. The day also saw the move of six of 211 Squadron's Blenheims to join the Greek PZLs at Paramythia. The 'Valley of Fairy Tales' as it became known to the RAF, was to become of increasing importance in the weeks which followed. Flg Off. *Curly* Fabian, the New Zealand-born ops officer, had earlier visited Paramythia to assess its potential use for Blenheim operations:

Fabian had the task of planning the layout of the camp in Paramythia, south of the Albanian frontier and almost midway between Yannina and the Island of Corfu. There was only the stony flower covered bed of the valley just south of the little village of Paramythia for Fabian to work on with sheer peaks rising on all sides. A solitary saloon car comprised the entire transport section and this was used to carry water, petrol, fetch rations or to bomb up aircraft. A tremendous ridge rose to 5,000 feet to the east. A mountain road followed the Kalamas River to the village of Yannina where was stationed No. 80 (Gladiator) Squadron. Communications were bad. There was one road to the north, and that narrow, and one single track railway. [23]

Ten miles long, 3,000 feet above sea level, and surrounded by mountains reaching to the dominating Mount Korillas, the valley was accessible only by the air, or by foot and mule. It was approached by following a dried-up river bed which meandered for many miles until a break in the mountains appeared. This was wide enough to allow an aircraft the size of a Wellington to fly through—with caution—to reach the airfield, which was a mere 30 minutes flying time from the front. There were no buildings, only tented accommodation, but despite many reconnaissances, the Italians had not been able to locate the base. The Blenheims would use the airfield as an advanced landing ground, and the crews light-heartedly discussed the use of their secret weapons on further raids—empty beer bottles and full latrine buckets! Nine of 84 Squadron and three of 30 would arrive on detachment a few days later. Sqn Ldr Wisdom was offered a flight in Sqn Ldr Dudley Lewis' aircraft:

We floated high over the blue and green of the Gulf of Corinth, the three Blenheims keeping nice formation in spite of the tremendous down-draughts that rocketed us over the turbulent little sea. I was in the observer's seat. We struck north over the mountains—snow-capped Olympus could be seen in the far distance—and crept between two towering peaks. What a view opened out before us!

Five thousand feet below, down cliffs that fell sheer from those peaks, was a narrow valley, almost surrounded by mountains. It was an unforgettable scene, so much wild beauty crammed into one valley. This was Paramythia—its ancient Greek name means 'the place of fairy tales'—south of the Albanian frontier, and almost midway between Yannina and Corfu. There was no aerodrome there—we circled the valley and came down on the stony, flower-covered bed of the valley, just south of the little village perched perilously on the side of the mountain.

He added:

Paramythia was an attractive, dirty little village, more Albanian than Greek, but inhabited by tough peasant families—lovely people. The Italians had occupied Paramythia for three hours at the end of October, but the farmers and their sons—and their daughters as well—had descended upon them during the night, and before volleys from ancient fowling pieces and rook rifles, and much shouting, the Italians had beaten a hasty retreat. The Italians were never the match for these sturdy mountain folk.[24]

The 211 Squadron detachment flew its first operation from Paramythia on **10 February**. Bombs were seen to fall in the vicinity of Tepelene, Sqn Ldr Gordon-Finlayson, Flg Off. Buchanan and Plt Off. Pearson all reporting hits on buildings. The CO led another raid in the Tepelene area next day (**11 February**), reporting:

First Flight bombed first target, bombs were seen to fall east of target. Tepelene and an enemy occupied village were machine-gunned. Second Flight bombed Duki and bombs were seen to score direct hits on two large buildings. Enemy AA defences on spur near Tepelene were machine-gunned by leader's rear-gunner. 10,000 leaflets dropped on frontline troops.[25]

Flg Off. Ken Dundas (L8478) led a section of three 211 Squadron Blenheims to bomb buildings and military stores at Duki during the early morning of **12 February**. Weather over the target was fine and bombs were seen to fall among buildings in the southern part of the village, and gunners sprayed the village as they departed. Having flown its first operation from Greek soil two days earlier—a single PR sortie over Durazzo harbour—11 Squadron flew its first raid on this date, nine Blenheims setting off at 13:00 to bomb military buildings at Elbasan. The crews reported that weather was perfect and the snow on the Pindus Mountains was a fine sight. The target was approached at 13,000 feet from the west. Bombs were seen bursting in the target area and some direct hits obtained on the buildings. The results were later confirmed by photographs. Slight AA fire was experienced as the Blenheims turned for home. All returned safely.

During the day a dozen Blenheims of 84 Squadron arrived at Paramythia on detachment, to enable them to carry out operations against troop concentrations on the Kelcyre–Berat road the following day. Flt Lt Tony Plinston recalled:

Refuelling and rearming was a little primitive at Paramythia. Four-gallon cans were manhandled on to the wing and tipped into a large funnel, with a chamois leather filter. Fortunately, tank capacity on the Blenheim was limited to about 50 gallons a side. Bombing-up required somebody with a strong back and legs, being loaded by two others and then getting up to get the bomb high enough to hook on to the release hook.[26]

On **13 February**, at 10:00, a dozen Blenheims from 84 and 211 Squadrons were led by the respective commanding officers to attack targets north of Tepelene, escorted by fourteen Gladiators. Three 395ª **Squadrig**lia G.50s, led by Spanish Civil War veteran Tenente Fernando Giocondi, had taken off from Devoli to escort a reconnaissance Ro.37 over the Kelcyre-**Tepelene, and** were over the target at 12,000 feet when they saw a lone Blenheim over Tepelene. The intruder was attacked and hit several times until it was believed seen to crash into the ground. This was also 'confirmed' by ground observers. All were mistaken, however. Although Flt Lt *Buck* Buchanan's L8541 had been hit in fuselage, wings and undercarriage, a one-wheel landing was successfully made on returning to Paramythia. The gunner, Sgt George Pattison, believed that he had shot down one of the fighters into a hillside, but none was reported lost. Sqn Ldr Tom Wisdom was present in Sqn Ldr Gordon-Finlayson's aircraft (L1481) and he recorded:

> Our bombs were on their way. It was most exciting. I peered out and saw below me, a number of fleecy white puffs followed by great spurts of earth and moving specks that must have been running men. We turned and retraced our course with AA bursting all round us. Then young Gerry [Plt Off. Davies, the observer] turned to me and shouted: "Fighters!" They were on to *Buck's* flight, but I did not see them. Then they came and had a look at us, judging from the way Arthur Geary [the gunner], in the tunnel behind me, was operating his gun.[27]

The Gladiator escort had become separated when the Blenheims had dived through cloud near Tepelene to sight their target, and these did not encounter the G.50s, returning to Yannina where they landed at 11:35.

The squadrons were off again at 15:00, a dozen Gladiators rendezvousing with six 211 Squadron Blenheims (led by Sqn Ldr Gordon-Finlayson) bound for Bousi, and six of 11 Squadron from Larissa heading for Berat. The latter were attacked over Berat/Devoli by 'nine Macchi 200s'—in fact, six G.50s of 395ª Squadriglia led by Cap. Scarpetta, the others flown by Serg.Magg. Antonio Pierani, Sottoten. Giuliano Fissore, Serg. Manfredo Bianchi, Serg. Adrio Gismondi and Serg. Alessandro Triveri. Plt Off. Jim Hutchison's T2237 fell in flames and crashed into a mountainside, killing pilot and air-gunner Sgt Bill Jackson, a Scot. Only Sgt Stan Whiles (the observer) managed to bale out, landing in deep snow. He was picked up by Greek soldiers, who gave him a horse on which he rode to Koritza.

Meanwhile, T2166 was also seen to go down in flames, only Sgt Len Williams, the pilot, and observer Sgt John Adamson managing to bale out, but both Adamson and the air-gunner 32-year-old Sgt Onslow Traherne were killed; Williams survived to be taken prisoner. Sqn Ldr Stevens' aircraft came under attack but his gunner, Sgt Henry Bowen, believed that he had shot down one attacker in flames, identified as a Macchi, and caused a second to go down smoking for his third victory claim. Flg Off. John Berggren's aircraft (T2347) force-landed in a field with one engine shot out, while two of the others got back to Larissa without further incident, followed 30 minutes later by Plt Off. Alan Hewison's badly damaged aircraft, in which the air-gunner, Sgt David Fisher was seriously wounded by shrapnel in his eyes and face, and observer Sgt Pete Griffiths slightly wounded.

The 211 Squadron formation did not escape attack. Serg. Ruggero Ruggieri of 361ᵃ Squadriglia had scrambled from Devoli to intercept bombers that were reported attacking Italian troops and also dropping leaflets. At 15:25 the bombers were discovered, identified as a Lockheed Hudson and Blenheims and Ruggieri attacked and claimed two of them shot down in flames while a third crashed in the mountains. They were claimed as two Blenheims and a Hudson. An additional Blenheim was claimed as probable. For his performance he was awarded a *Medaglia d'Argento al Valor Militare* (Silver Medal for Bravery). In the meantime, at 15:20, a second G.50 of the same Squadriglia, piloted by Serg. Gian Piero Svanini, had taken off from Devoli at 15:45 to join the fight. He claimed one Blenheim before landing at 16:20. All the bombers fell in the front area defended by 4ᵗʰ and 8ᵗʰ Army Corps. One Blenheim—flown by Flt Lt Buchanan—was damaged, while Flg Off. Alan Godfrey's aircraft was attacked by a fighter and sustained damage to the port engine nacelle. The gunner, Sgt Jack Wainhouse, believed he had hit the attacker in an exchange of fire; he also identified the interceptor as a Macchi.

Four Blenheims were claimed shot down, to make eight claims for the day. It is believed that Cap. Scarpetta and Sottoten. Fissore were each credited with one, while Serg. Bianchi claimed two possibly destroyed. All the G.50s were back at base by 17:00. Although the Gladiator pilots had seen four G.50s they had not managed to engage them, and were unaware of the Blenheims' plight, therefore carried out their allotted task of strafing Italian positions in the Tepelene area. AA was intense and several Gladiators were hit by shrapnel. Later, a signal was received from HQ British Forces in Greece, which stated:

General Papagos has asked me to thank all RAF units on behalf of the Greek Army for their magnificent support in today's field operations. The Greek Army have reached all their intended objectives. (signed) D'Albiac, 13 February 1941.

Around this time the weather again proved unfavourable for flying, allowing some of the aircrew at Paramythia the opportunity to return to Eleusis for a bath, as Sgt Geoff Chapman recalled:

We slept in small four-man ridge tents and messed in a marquee. The cooks had to manage on a field kitchen and very well they did, too. Ablutions were definitely cold water, and in that regard Flt Sgt George Fridd [who would be killed during the ground fighting on Crete[28]] set a fine example by bathing naked and unashamed in a nearby mountain stream. He had few followers—hence the need to return to Eleusis for a clean up.

One night we experienced a very heavy rainstorm. The field was soon waterlogged and finally a gust of wind blew away our ridge tents. We were left lying on our backs, staring at the sky, being pelted with rain. Our first reaction was to laugh, but a second later we were on our feet hurriedly getting our tunics and boots on. We repaired to the Mess, which thankfully was intact. In next to no time the cooks had brewed tea and provided us with slices of tinned bacon on hard tack biscuits. The tea and bacon went down all right, but the hard tack biscuits defied even the hottest tea to be made soft enough to chew.

Later, we were transported to the village police station in Paramythia, where we were warmly greeted by the police officers. We were plied with *Ouzo*—a Greek spirit drink flavoured with aniseed—to drive the cold out, and various other Greek delicacies were given us to eat. Our clothes were draped around the wall of the police station and a huge open fire lit to dry out both clothes and airmen. By nightfall our clothes were dry enough and we were conducted to various empty houses in the village to spend the night. I was lucky enough to find a bedstead but many others had to sleep on the bare boards.

The following day we returned to the airfield to find that during our absence the ground crews had put up all the tents and restored order to the place. They had done a wonderful job whilst we were living it up in the police station.[29]

During the night of **15/16 February**, four of five Wellingtons of the 37 Squadron detachment at Menidi took-off for an attack on Brindisi, bombing the airfield where it was believed a floatplane hangar was set on fire, together with one aircraft on the ground. Intense AA was encountered and one Wellington was shot down. A trio of Blenheim IFs of 30 Squadron searched for signs of the missing aircraft next morning, one crew spotting five Z.1007bis which they chased to the Italian coast. Three G.50s then appeared, which they managed to evade. This was undoubtedly the occasion described by Flt Lt Al Bocking:

I thought it was all up. The bullets flew all around as we had the window open, and the tracer and incendiary bullets were flying past. We smelled something burning and thought the ship was afire, but the sergeant observer, sitting as cool as you like beside me, prodded me and indicated the smell came from the Italian tracer shells. I admired the observer's calm, especially when he grimaced and held his nose, and then delicately closed the window tight, as if to keep out both the smell and bullets. I'll say it's grand to fly with such men. There was one time we almost went down on our bellies. We were flying so low.[30]

While 80 Squadron's Gladiators continued to operate from Yannina, those of 21 Mira moved up to Paramythia at this time and here, on **17 February**, they were joined by the six Hurricanes and by four 30 Squadron Blenheims. One aircraft was lost here next day when a 211 Squadron Blenheim (L6662) crashed on take-off, having been caught in the slipstream of the leader. It swung, resulting in the collapse of the undercarriage; Flg Off. Ken Linton and his crew were unhurt.

Although the weather was very bad all over the front, 211 Squadron managed to continue its series of daily raids albeit with unobserved results owing to heavy cloud cover. The Greek Blenheims carried out a rare mission when Lt-Col Averof led three aircraft to bomb Italian positions in the western side of Trebeshina mountains. After the bombing, the three aircraft entered a cumulonimbus cloud and the leader immediately ordered the two other aircraft to break formation in order to avoid a collision. Averof's aircraft, after a very difficult flight managed to land at Sedes, while the second aircraft reached another ancillary airfield at Serres. The third aircraft, however, flown by Flt Sgt Evanghelos Tzovlas lost navigation and the crew found themselves over the Adriatic Sea, west of Valona. With darkness descending and fuel running low, Tzovlas re-crossed the coast and decided to crash-land in a swamp beside Acheron River, near Paramythia. The three crewmen vacated the aircraft without a single scratch.

Two days later (**19 February**), Wg Cdr Patric *Paddy* Coote and Major Sevastopulo arrived at Paramythia to set up an Advanced Operations Wing, to be known as 'W' (Western) Wing. This comprised initially the Blenheim detachment of 30 Squadron, the whole of 84 and 211 Squadrons, and a detachment of 11 Squadron which was due to arrive in a few days; the Wellingtons of the 37 Squadron detachment were also to return, while the six 80 Squadron Hurricanes would shortly be joined by six more from 33 Squadron, which was just arriving that day. The Wing Headquarters was to be based at Yannina, where the Gladiators of 80 and 112 Squadrons would remain. The PZLs were also attached temporarily to the Wing. Flying in that evening at dusk, two of these little fighters collided in the middle of the airfield. Overnight one good machine was rebuilt from the two.

Some slight improvement in the weather on **20 February** allowed a resumption of activity. Eight Blenheims of 84 Squadron and three from 30 Squadron went off to bomb in the Tepelene area, escorted by six of 80 Squadron's Hurricanes on their first sorties over the front. Over the target at 10:25 the bombers split into two formations to attack, at which point six CR.42s appeared. These did not interfere, having apparently spotted the Hurricanes. Early in the afternoon seven Gladiators of 80 Squadron and ten of 112 Squadron flew up to Paramythia from Yannina. At 14:45, these took off in sections of three to escort two Wellingtons of 37 Squadron each carrying about one and a half tons of supplies; they were accompanied by a Greek Ju 52/3m tasked to drop these supplies to the troops near Kelcyre. Low cloud and rain made the flight difficult, and near Corovode five hostile aircraft were seen but these did not approach. The supplies were dropped successfully.

In the meantime, seventeen Blenheims—eight of 84 Squadron, six of 211 Squadron and three of 30 Squadron—were raiding Berat. One of the 84 Squadron aircraft suffered an engine failure and belly-landed, but the remaining sixteen (with an escort of six Hurricanes), arrived over the target, their bombs falling on the town, supply dumps, and demolishing a bridge carrying the main road over the River Osem. AA fire was experienced and a dozen 154° Gruppo G.50s from the 361ª and 395ª Squadriglie were scrambled from Berat airfield. Four of the G.50s were claimed by the Hurricanes, and these claims were verified by the crews of the Blenheims under attack; Tenente Bassi was one of those shot down; seriously wounded he died six weeks later. Serg. Emilio Piva belatedly participated in the defence but a stroke of luck possibly saved his life, as he later recalled:

> The G.50 flew like a brick. It was very easy to enter a spin and crash. Once it happened to me, but I was able to exit the spin at the very last minute, skimming the top of a mountain. I was saved by my self control that permitted me to put the control stick in a central position. Other pilots—surprised and scared—pulled the control stick against themselves and this worsened the spin. At the time I flew the plane with the individual number 13, that nobody wanted because of the superstition. My commander asked me: "Piva do you want it?" and—not believing in bad luck—I answered yes. He [No. 13] didn't bring me misfortune, on the contrary once he saved my life. I was ready to scramble because an enemy formation was arriving. We were three but while my comrades were already taking off my plane refused to start. They were hit on take-off, one fell at the end of the airstrip, hit in the head, the other was so badly wounded that he died one week later [actually, six weeks later] at the hospital. My engine restarted when the enemy's squadron was already departing. I pursued them in the clouds but to no avail.[31]

211 Squadron's designated target was the bridge at Berat; the CO reported

> Bridge was not hit due to an unexpectedly strong south-west wind. Western end of town was severely damaged by our bombs and was enveloped in smoke as the formation turned away from the target. A fierce fire was started amongst the military buildings. The formation was attacked by four Macchis or G.50s over the target. L8542 as badly damaged before Hurricane escort disposed of them, shooting down the four.[32]

Plt Off. Geary, gunner in Sqn Ldr Gordon-Finlayson's aircraft, reported:

> A G.50 came for us and in a flash a Hurricane just shot it off our wingtip. It simply rolled over, went on fire, and dived into the mountain. It was wizard.[33]

Plt Off. *Pip* Cox was the pilot of L8542:

> When I nipped into that cloud to avoid those fighters I could not find [the CO] again when I came out. It was nice and quiet, so I went and had a look. There were some grand fires burning. Then a little green fighter came at me and made a few holes in me. But a Hurricane came out of the blue and just blew the Iti out of the sky.[34]

Cox's aircraft was that probably attacked by Serg. Leone Gambetta, who claimed a Blenheim before being attacked by a Hurricane; on returning to Paramythia, L8542 was deemed damaged beyond repair and was later written off. Cap. Scarpetta claimed a second Blenheim as probably destroyed—possibly Sgt *Jock* Ratlidge's machine that had its starboard engine shot out, but managed to get it back to Paramythia. Sgt Tony Ovens also returned with slight damage to one wing of K7105. As the formation neared the front, the patrolling Gladiators of 80 and 112 Squadrons spotted the pursuing Italian fighters and engaged them, claiming three shot down.

From Eleusis on **22 February**, six of 30 Squadron's Blenheim IFs were sent off in pairs at hourly intervals to patrol. The first pair, Sqn Ldr *Percy* Milward (K7182) and Flt Lt Bob Davidson, were off at 10:15 and sighted a Z.506B floatplane of 191ª Squadriglia, 86° Gruppo near Zante Island at 7,000 feet. The Blenheims dived out of the sun to make successive attacks which drove it down to sea level. Finally it came down on the water with all engines dead, the crew waving a white cloth. Davidson dropped a dinghy nearby, while Sqn Ldr Milward dropped a message on Agrinion airfield, indicating the plight of the crew. For the CO's gunner, Sgt *Lofty* Lord, it had been the fourth successful combat in which he had participated.

At 12:35 another pair of Blenheims flown by Flt Lt Derek Walker (L4917) and Flg Off. *Bud* Richardson encountered five 47° Stormo Z.1007bis some twelve miles west of Preveza. Walker attacked in a dive from the beam and the aircraft in the 'box' formed by the other four dropped out of control, reportedly crashing into the sea south of Levkas. He then attacked the trailing aircraft, seeing oil and smoke pour from the starboard engine whereupon it slowed down. At this point Walker's guns jammed, but Richardson took up the attack, making several passes—and allowing his gunner Plt Off. Kirkman a chance to open fire—the bomber glided down and crash-landed in the sea. Circling, he saw two members of the crew climb onto the fuselage; a few bullets had struck his Blenheim, but no serious damage had been caused. According to Italian records one Z.1007bis actually came down—obviously the second aircraft—but they recorded that it had been hit by AA.

During the day two Lodestars arrived at Athens from Cairo conveying Air Chief Marshal Longmore, Mr Anthony Eden, now Secretary of State for Foreign Affairs,

General Dill, CIGS and General Wavell, for another proposed meeting with the King, new Prime Minister Alexandros Korizis (General Metaxas had died of natural causes on 29 January) and General Papagos, as the AOC recorded:

> Both Dill and Wavell were superficially disguised as civilians in rather worn raincoats and ancient felt hats and, as we landed at Menidi airfield and pulled up on the far side away from the hangars, we were hustled into waiting cars and driven a mile or so to the King's country residence at Tatoi, where accommodation had been prepared for all of us.

They conferred till late that night:

> We were now committed definitely to supporting the Greeks against the Germans and I came away from the conference with the conviction that, whatever transpired in the future, we were right in honouring our moral obligations to this brave little country to whatever extent was possible.
>
> Next day the rest of the party flew back to Cairo, but I remained to stay with D'Albiac at this very pleasant villa and to visit the various RAF units and see what progress had been made with the airfields. Menidi was unaffected by the winter rains and at Eleusis the long runway was nearly completed.[35]

Next morning (**23 February**) at 10:30, a Gladiator was sent off to search for the Z.506B forced down by the Blenheims during the previous morning, which was believed to be on the sea ten miles south of Parga with engine trouble. Obviously the crew had been able to repair the damage inflicted by Milward and Davidson, for as the Gladiator pilot flew south he saw it at the southern end of Antipaxoi Island, trying to take off. Diving down, he fired a burst and it came to a halt, a white cloth again being waved. As he circled overhead it attempted to take off again and he attacked, his fire being returned even though the white cloth was still flying. The stricken aircraft then began to sink, and he flew to Paramythia to report. Later a second Gladiator confirmed that the aircraft was ashore on Akra Novare Island, where the Greek hospital ship *Andros* later rescued four survivors—second pilot Serg. Vincenzo Casiello, Av.Sc. Gambino, Av. Morra and Av. Cutrone—and collected two bodies—those of the pilot, Tenente Alberto Alberti, and crewman 1°Av. Francesco Pupino. Subsequently one of 30 Squadron's Blenheims reported that the aircraft was half submerged, its floats sticking up out of the water.

Over the front little was seen, although 211 Squadron sent a formation of six to raid Duki, near Tepelene. Wg Cdr *Paddy* Coote accompanied Plt Off. *Pip* Cox in L8478 as observer, to 'have a look' for himself. The target was Duki, where military buildings and M/T were bombed. The six aircraft had an escort of five Hurricanes on this occasion but no Italian fighters appeared.

During this period Paramythia was further reinforced. Ten Blenheims of 11 Squadron flew up from Larissa in very bad weather, but four were forced to return, and a fifth (T2388) crashed while attempting a force-landing in a valley, Plt Off. Alan Hewison and his gunner Sgt John Dukes being killed together with passenger LAC Gordon Bevan; two of the other three passengers were injured. Greek peasants brought the survivors back on mules. One of the survivors was Aircraftman *Jock* McQueen, about whom Airman Marcel Comeau later wrote:

> *Jock* McQueen ... still walked with difficulty on his bandaged leg. This leg intrigued the Greeks who pleaded with us to hear the story. It was simply impossible not to line-shoot to these people. So, with the aid of a French-speaking Greek soldier, I commenced with a tale something like this. "One day it was decided to send many *Inglishi* aeroplanes to bomb the cowardly Italians." Thunderous applause greeted this statement. "The *Inglishi* aeroplanes, heavy with bombs flew away from Larissa. They flew towards Albania." Fresh applause. "They flew high and it was cold. There were many black clouds. Ice covered the aeroplanes." A hushed silence fell throughout the tavern. The old men lowered their eyes. "The aeroplane of my friend"—I pointed to McQueen—"fell from the skies. It fell upon the hard rock of the mountain. Some *Inglishi* were killed." The tavern wept and Greeks cried out. "But," I ended triumphantly "some *Inglishi* were alive and came back to fight the *Italianos*. My friend has come back to fight the *Italianos*." My words were drowned in the mighty cheer which followed as, happy once more, they surged around *Jock* shaking his hand and patting his leg.[36]

The Greeks, ever generous to the RAF airmen, no doubt brought out fresh supplies of fiery Greek brandy and pine-flavoured *Retzina* wine—and a good time was had by all.

The remaining five aircraft were attached to 211 Squadron for operations. Rain continued to disturb the flying programme, particularly at Yannina, which remained unserviceable. Paramythia could be used however, Hurricanes and Blenheims continuing to make raids over the Kelcyre-Tepelene road on **24 February**. One aircraft of 11 Squadron accompanied six from 211 Squadron on a raid against Italian M/T concentrations. Low cloud forced the formation to go up the valleys and considerable light AA was experienced though no aircraft was hit. Bombs fell amongst dispersed M/T. The mission was repeated next day (**25 February**), on this occasion two aircraft from 11 Squadron accompanying six from 211 Squadron. Low cloud was again encountered so that the formation was forced to fly at only 2,000 feet above ground level. In spite of intense light AA fire encountered along the way, no aircraft was hit. And, as with the previous raid, bombs were seen to burst amongst dispersed M/T. Sqn Ldr Gordon-Finlayson was not impressed with the choice of target:

Bombs burst in a field near the road [Tepelene-Berat] and probably damaged some M/T though the concentration was not particularly thick at that point. Two bombs burst on road and judging from the black smoke it is probable that either M/T vehicles or some material of an inflammable nature was hit. Target not particularly good but persistent bombing, apart from material damage, will probably force the enemy to effect more severe dispersal or possibly evacuate the particular area. Formation was escorted by three Hurricanes.

The CO added, mainly for the benefit and guidance of crews on future raids to this area:

Owing to low cloud and rain storms only the Argyrokastron valley approach was feasible. This is a tricky gorge. Extreme caution and an exhaustive study and knowledge of mountain contours are vital in the frequently dense weather.

The role of the navigator is to swing a visual plumb line for his side of the aircraft and check and call out each dangerous peak one by one as they appear in the gloom and disappear to starboard. The pilot checks the peaks and crags on his side and decides from second to second just where he will turn his formation if the time comes to turn back. If there is no room to turn, he must lead his formation up into the clouds and ice, watching anxiously until his altimeter shows he is clear of the mountains. A course is then set for the open sea.[37]

On **26 February**, 33 Squadron's Hurricane detachment at Paramythia joined 80 Squadron's six aircraft to escort three Blenheims from 11 and six from 211 Squadrons (led by the CO) to raid Bousi near Tepelene. The weather was considerably improved compared with previous days; however, an early morning mist lay over the valleys so that identification of the target was difficult. Bomb bursts were not observed and no opposition encountered. Later in the day, at 11:45, a Blenheim force of similar composition, again led by Sqn Ldr Gordon-Finlayson and escorted by Hurricanes, raided the Italian GHQ at Fieri near Valona. The formation came in from the seaward, making use of cloud cover, and bombed the target from 5,000 feet; bombs were seen to fall in the town with some direct hits being made on the buildings. Once again no opposition was experienced. The CO noted, however:

Two large fires started in west part of the town. A reconnaissance was carried out over Valona harbour. The Greek AA defences at Sarande opened up at us as the formation returned over Corfu and damaged L8440 [sic].[38]

It would appear that the Blenheim damaged was L8449 flown by Plt Off. Hugh Clutterbuck; neither he nor Sgts Bill Stack and *Tubby* Taylor was injured and the Blenheim returned safely.

The day was marked by a visit to Paramythia by Air Chief Marshal Longmore and Air Vice-Marshal D'Albiac. They were conveyed aboard Flt Lt. Bob Davidson's aircraft:

After some delay due to bad weather I set off on the 26th in a Blenheim with D'Albiac for Paramythia. Near Patras we passed over Araxos and Agrinion, two of the new airfields under construction; water was lying on them and they did not look like being ready for some time. We landed about noon on the airfield called Paramythia and our pilot had to keep the Blenheim moving to the parking place to prevent his wheels sinking into the soft ground. Aircraft had to land up or down this valley with mountains on either side, and more high ground on the third. It was gorgeous scenery but more pleasant to look at than fly around in.

Here we found 211 Blenheim and 33 Hurricane Squadrons; the latter had recently arrived, much to the satisfaction of Gordon-Finlayson, the CO of 211, and one of the most experienced squadron leaders in Greece. His Blenheims could now be escorted on their Valona raids and on our arrival they had all just returned from an attack on that port. Having waded through the mud to the mess tent for a lunch of bully beef and some vegetables purchased from the one and only local village at the head of the valley, I heard some of their stories. Living conditions at Paramythia tented camp were certainly primitive, and supplies arrived irregularly from a small port about 10 miles away along an extremely bad road; it was a three-day journey to Athens by a long roundabout route.

Paddy Coote, who had been one of my under officers at Cranwell 10 years before and was now the Wing Commander of the squadrons, drove us over the mountain road to Janina [Yannina]; the airfield was waterlogged that afternoon and we were thus unable to fly over. For three hours we motored on an atrocious road through wild mountainous country and we were frequently inside cloud. We eventually arrived about six o'clock in the small town perched on a hill where the personnel of 80 and 112 Gladiator Squadrons were billeted. I enjoyed my evening with these two seasoned squadrons and heard many good stories of their exploits. In spite of cold, wet, mud and cloud-covered mountains they seemed to prefer their life here to the sand of the Western Desert.

The Advanced GHQ of the Greek Army was at Janina [Yannina], but the General and his Chief-of-Staff were back in Athens at a conference. One of his staff explained the military situation from which it seemed to me that the Greeks were unlikely to reach Valona, but thank goodness they could not say it was through lack of RAF support, for I heard nothing but praise for the help our squadrons had given them.

Next morning I paid a visit to the very damp-looking airfield outside Janina [Yannina] where the Gladiators of the two squadrons were dispersed; some of them were just taking off and looked like speedboats with a feather of spray behind them. We motored back to Paramythia over the mountains and through the clouds, passing all sorts of peasants on the road, some driving pack ponies or sheep along and others laboriously mending the most indifferent road surface. I said goodbye to *Paddy* Coote, and it was to be the last time I was to see him.

From Paramythia my Blenheim took off down wind carefully avoiding a bogged Wellington that had force-landed and sunk deep up to its axles. On the flight back we passed through some very thick low cloud at the entrance to the Gulf of Patras. My two-day trip to these advanced airfields had given me a good idea of the difficulties and hazards of weather in which our aircrews were operating.[39]

They returned to Athens with Flt Lt. Davidson, whose air-gunner Sgt *Lofty* Lord noted:

Returned in thunderstorm at 0 feet over the sea, visibility 10 yards—D/F all the way back.

More rather heavy over-claiming was to occur on **27 February**, when at 15:00 nine Blenheims, six from 211 Squadron and three from 11 Squadron, set off to bomb Valona aerodrome, escorted by five 80 Squadron Hurricanes and four more from 33 Squadron. An hour later, as the formation arrived over Valona, three CR.42s of 364ª Squadriglia attacked as the Blenheims were bombing. Led by Sottoten. Egidio Faltoni, the three biplanes engaged the Blenheims but were in turn jumped by the escort. First Faltoni, then Serg. Osvaldo Bartolaccini, were shot down and both baled out. Faltoni, wounded, fell in the mountain area of Krionero close to Valona and was recovered, while Bartolaccini fell close to the airfield and was brought back to his base, where he succumbed to his wounds. The third unknown pilot was the only one able to escape. However, the three pilots had inflicted damage on five Blenheims, including all three of the 11 Squadron machines. Two of these crash-landed on return to Paramythia, both having suffered heavy damage to their hydraulic systems, whereupon they (T2399 and N3579) were written off.

A CR.42 of 364ª Squadriglia was destroyed on the ground by the Blenheims' bombs, and seven others were damaged by splinters and blast. A dozen drums of fuel went up in flames, and two airmen were wounded, one of them Av.Sc. Cianti of 365ª Squadriglia. Serg. Bartolaccini was awarded a posthumous *Medaglia d'Argento al Valor Militare*:

During a mission he discovered a strong formation of enemy bombers escorted by many fighters. Together with his leader he jumped the bombers and machine-gunned them but—on seeing his leader falling in flames—he turned his attention to an enemy fighter and shot it down. Overwhelmed by the enemies, seriously wounded himself, he had to jump with parachute but he died after reaching the ground.

Sqn Ldr Gordon-Finlayson's subsequent detailed report of this raid was critical of the Hurricane escort:

Six Blenheims of 211 Squadron accompanied by three Blenheims of 11 Squadron and escorted by nine Hurricanes of 80 and 33 Squadrons left base at 15:15 hours to attack Valona aerodrome.

The sky was fairly clear out to sea but a layer of cloudy haze led up to the target at 6,000 feet. The formation made a covered approach at this height but came out into the open over the target. Bombs were dropped on the aerodrome, and photographs show that an excellent series of sticks were dropped across the runway, and aerodrome buildings. Several bombs have dropped in slit trenches, direct hits were made on various buildings, while two aircraft were left burning.

Fifteen CR.42s intercepted the formation, and an air battle ensued in which three 11 Squadron aircraft were severely damaged and two had to land on their bellies, while the other is badly shot through the spars. One aircraft of 211 Squadron was slightly touched by AA fire, but it is still serviceable. Damage to our formation was heavy, and an analysis of the cause is submitted. On almost all raids carried out by 211 Squadron each Flight takes individual aim. This gives three chances of a hit on the target, and each of the three patterns measures about 80 yards across and some 400-800 yards in length depending on the type of target. However, it has long been an established principle that if there are fighters in the offing, the Squadron immediately and automatically assumes its defensive formation, and bombing is carried out as a squadron.

The point of keeping close formation was particularly emphasised today, and No.1 and No.2 Flights of 211 Squadron held closely together throughout the attack, both leaders having by acute vigilance made themselves aware of the enemy fighters. No.3 Flight leader however did not become aware of the fighters until he was attacked. At that moment he had fallen well behind the formation leader, and was virtually a straggler and particularly vulnerable. Since the formation had attacked in an easterly direction and turned north of the target, No.3 Flight on the port was able to cut the corner and join the leader, with, in the circumstances, the minimum of delay.

This straggling element was one reason for the fate which overtook the 11 Squadron Flight but there was, alas, another. 80 Squadron flight under F/Lt Pattle have worked out in detail various principles of the new science of escorting bombers. It has been decided that a flight of three Hurricanes must provide direct escort, and must at all costs resist the temptation to pursue any enemy fighters except those actually engaged in attacking the bombers; and these they must only pursue until they break away from their attack on the bombers. They must not be diverted from their guard over the tail of the bombers' formation.

Today a flight of three Hurricanes of 33 Squadron were detailed as direct escort, while the remaining six Hurricanes of 80 and 33 Squadrons were free to divert their attentions to the destruction of any enemy fighters who rose to the occasion. This flight did not carry out its task and left the bombers in order to pursue enemy fighters to the kill. My Air-gunner eventually reported that we were left in clear air unescorted while a dog fight was in progress over Valona Bay.

Only one single Hurricane came up and stuck to us faithfully. This was found to be F/Lt Pattle, who, although he was not detailed for direct escort, was fully aware of the principles underlying his type of fighter operation, and was horrified to see the bomber formation without escort at all, and consciously denying himself several exceptional opportunities of shooting down enemy fighters. Had it not been for him, this formation might have been far more severely damaged than it was.[40]

Again, Plt Off. Geary, gunner in the CO's L1481, recorded his impressions of the raid:

I had a grandstand view of the whole affair. It was lovely bombing—direct hits all over the aerodrome and on buildings. A large [*sic*] formation of CR.42s took off to intercept us. One got on my tail, so I put a burst into him, and he fell away. Then two Hurricanes appeared in a flash, and well, he just fell to pieces. The Hurricanes wheeled and proceeded to deal with the others. The sky was full of crashing aircraft—and they were all enemy. We had a most pleasant tour home, and the scenery looked more lovely than ever.[41]

Sqn Ldr Wisdom flew as bomb-aimer (for which he had received instruction) in Flg Off. Alan Godfrey's aircraft; he later wrote a graphic piece for the press entitled *Return Trip Across the Styx*

In graceful threes the squadron of Blenheim bombers leaves the ground, circles our secret valley that still bears its ancient Greek name, 'the valley of the brave,' joins formation and strikes north. The RAF's blitz in support of the Greek army is on—in a very short time an Albanian village, high in the mountains and used as Italian advanced headquarters, will feel our weight in high-explosive bombs.

Twenty-two-year-old Alan, good-looking and the *Beau Brummel* of this crack bomber squadron, is at the controls. Perched on the bomb-aimer's seat on his right hand—a veritable ringside seat for this spectacle to be—I check up on the many switches which come readily to hand. When the master switch is operated our load of bombs will leave on its way to spread destruction.

We cross a gangling, swollen river—a mighty torrent which rushes between high cliffs and has a dark and desolate air. The Greeks call it the Kalamas River—in ancient times it was the Styx, and Charon the boatman rowed his passengers on a one-way journey. We propose to come back. But the three-headed hound in this modern Hades of the Albanian front awaits us in the form of enemy fighters. On up through the narrow valleys, with storm clouds shrouding the mountain peaks, the squadron winds its way. High skill is required to get a squadron through this sort of country and this sort of weather. Some do not come back—the dice are loaded against the wartime flyers in Albania, for the hazards are many.

There is snow on the mountains, tiny villages nestle deeper into their camouflage, it seems, for the RAF visitations are rightly feared. Bursts of AA—orange-red flashes from the tracer and rounded, slow dispersing, black puffs that are the big stuff—follow us up the valleys. We are over the front-line now. Winding along the narrow mountain tracks are motor convoys. They stop suddenly as if someone had touched a switch, and far below can be seen tiny figures—running. The snow mantle of the hills is pock-marked with black gashes—the wounds of bomb and shell. From the hillsides come flashes of flame—the AA guns.

Now the weather is clearing—the blue sky above us with hardly a wisp of that grand fleecy cloud into which the bomber delights to hide when the fighters come. We are gambling that we shall take the Italians by surprise. If we don't, we can merely hope for cloud, and plenty of it. Another thirty seconds and we shall be over our target. Excitement—that sickly, sinking feeling that reminds me forcibly of those dark minutes before the start of a race at Brooklands in pre-war days—has disappeared. I glance surreptitiously at my hands and find them quite steady—far steadier than during that long half-hour before the take-off. You're pleased to find yourself clear and calculating, with no time to be afraid. But, needlessly, you check the position of your bomb switches half-a-dozen times.

Now! From the aircraft ahead suddenly gushes a shower of twisting yellow objects that quickly straighten out and dive on their streamlined way to earth. 'Mickey Mouse'—the lever that is the master switch—is grasped firmly in my left hand; the pilot is concentrating to keep the aircraft on a level keel and in position. I move the lever over its notches to its limit—slowly because that will give us a long stick of bombs that should straddle the target. The machine lurches slightly—our bombs are on their way.

So intent in the cockpit have we been on our job that we have heard but dimly through the inter-com the air-gunner's repeated warnings that the AA is getting 'bloody close'. It is—we realise now; great puffs of black smoke and red flashes that scream pass the cockpit windows. But *The Bish*, leading his squadron, proceeds on his way unhurriedly across the target. There are pictures to be taken and we want to see what damage has been caused.

Flames are coming from a building that looks like a storehouse, there are lorries in the ditch—one has its wheels in the air—and two guns are no longer firing. "Good show," the pilot yells and gives the thumbs-up sign to other pilots in the formation. Then we are busy again, congratulations forgotten. "Fighters coming up astern," the rear-gunner yells, and there is a preliminary burst from his gun. He is pitting .303 bullets against multi machine-guns and cannon. The three-headed hound has found us.

I look back through the cockpit window—a wicked-looking little monoplane, silhouetted black against the blue of the sky, is coming up quickly—fascinating to watch him grow bigger. He is attacking the flight on our right, twisting and turning to get into position for the kill. But the three aircraft are piloted by old hands—they are taking avoiding action and are making for the sheet of cloud ahead. Tiny red flashes come from the airscrew boss and the leading edges of the wings of the enemy fighter.

"They're Macchis, all right," calmly remarks our air-gunner, as he twists and turns in his turret, keeping his sights on the nearest fighter, waiting for it to come into range. It's rather fun watching this battle—more like a form of aerial sport than a duel in which death is intended for someone. Well, it was fun until the flight the fighters were harrying found its cloud cover and one of the Macchis suddenly turned his attention to us. We had almost reached our objective—a nice thick cloud. *The Bish* and our opposite number in the formation had sunk gracefully and gratefully into the enveloping mist. We were quite alone, with the Macchi attempting a beam attack. I looked back once—the Macchi was so close that you could see the pilot's hooded head. Tracer came past the cockpit window, there was a tinkling, tinny sound accompanied by an unpleasant, burning smell as an explosive bullet struck the port engine nacelle.

We take evasive action—suddenly banking and tight turns as the enemy pilot positions himself for the *coup-de-grace*. The air-gunner, blasting away with his single gun the while, is directing the pilot in this exciting game of aerial tag. We've made it! The Blenheim and her crew sink into the kindly cloud. We fly blind for a minute—the hidden mountains are the menace now—then peep out. The fighters have lost us—the sky is ours again.

Touring gently along at 200 miles an hour we admire the scenery, chat of the combat of a few minutes ago, while the crew airily compares it with other duels. "It wasn't bad" is their verdict, and they add "Wonder if they'll get back—we must have filled 'em full of lead." Then we make the crossing of the Styx on our return journey. The three-headed dog that guards this side of Hades has been tricked again. 'The valley of the brave' looks lovelier than ever as the squadron, not a man missing, and with a good day's work done, touches down and taxies into position—ready for tomorrow's job.[42]

On returning from this raid, the remains of the 11 Squadron detachment were ordered to Larissa. Airman Comeau, who had been serving with 33 Squadron now found himself attached to 11 Squadron:

Any regrets that I may have had in leaving 33 Squadron was to some extent offset by the immediate realization that 11 was not just another squadron. Coincidence had thrown together an unusual collection of outstanding personalities. The adjutant, a lovable character, ran squadrons affairs in the *laissez-faire* manner of a colonial administrator. Much of his work fell upon the capable shoulders of an LAC fitter called Duff, who looked every inch of what he was—a tough Irishman who had started life behind a machine-gun in a Dublin back street. Yet, despite his brogue and his unprepossessing appearance, he was organizing genius with a filing-cabinet brain. Between these two extremes of personality there existed a hard core of talented individuals ... two at least of whom had fought in the Spanish Civil War. Many had been with 11 Squadron for many years ... I got the impression that 11 was more than a squadron: it was an exclusive club.[43]

84 Squadron received a new CO at the end of the month, 27-year-old Sqn Ldr Hubert Jones (known as *Jonah*) replacing Sqn Ldr Lewis, who on promotion moved to Air HQ. The new CO had been seconded to the Royal Egyptian Air Force and lacked operational experience; nor had he any experience of flying over such mountainous terrain as that which now faced him.

At the end of February command of 32 Mira was taken over by Lt-Col Karabinis. The Greek Blenheims continued to carry out dangerous missions all over the southern Albanian front and, especially, in the areas of Luzhati and Glava, north of Tepelene.

CHAPTER 5

March–April 1941

We were very evenly matched—the Blenheim had two guns and the Cant had three, two in the rear turrets and one front.

Plt Off. Ron Pearson 211 Squadron

During the night of **28 February/1 March** the Greeks were hard hit from a different source when Larissa was devastated by the most severe earthquake they had suffered in a century. One official report observed:

Along the river Pinios and its tributaries the ground slumped and cracks appeared along banks running for many kilometres liquefaction of the ground was reported from many places in the town as well as the development of high artesian pressures that resulted in the damage of deep wells … At the village of Eleftherion, water ejected from a well. Sand volcanoes were observed at the banks of river Mirou, while at the village of Nesson, water ejection was observed in many places…

Great rifts opened up on the airfield, where buildings and hangars collapsed, many personnel being buried under the rubble. After salvaging what they could, RAF personnel worked all through the rest of the night rescuing people trapped in the debris of the stricken town. Street after street of poorly-constructed houses had collapsed, and many of those dug out were already dead. One of the main features of the town had been a number of mosques, but the minarets of these had all tumbled. Forty-one persons were killed and 10,000 made homeless. Only five RAF airmen required medical attention, the most serious having a fractured arm. 11 Squadron immediately sent aid including its ambulance and medical staff, and next morning, 30 Squadron Blenheims flew in carrying first aid equipment, RAMC doctors and orderlies.

There was no let-up in the war however, and on this first day of the new month the Hurricanes of 33 and 80 Squadrons were out three times to escort Blenheims of 30 and 211 Squadrons to attack Paraboa (to the north of Bousi), Berat and Valona harbour. At the latter target two Hurricanes dropped down through cloud to see what activity there might be in the harbour itself. They spotted a large merchant vessel which was strafed. Sgt *Nobby* Clark, aboard Sgt *Jock* Marshall's L8531, noted:

> As we approached across the bay, an Italian hospital ship was below us, right on our track. Sgt Dunnet [observer/bomb aimer in No. 2 aircraft flown by Plt Off. Herbert] released one 250 lb bomb—it missed. He was 'on the mat' when we returned and sent back to Athens for a week! Punishment![1]

Next day (**2 March**), at 10:45, four Z.1007s flew over Larissa and dropped about 16 bombs, five of which fell on the aerodrome. A direct hit registered on the underground detonator store but failed to do any damage, but another burst near a stack of four-gallon petrol cans, splinters puncturing the cans with the loss of 800 gallons of aviation fuel. Shortly thereafter, a Blenheim of 11 Squadron departed on a photo-recce flight to Valona and Brindisi, but *en route* the air-gunner got frostbite so the pilot landed at Paramythia to take on board another gunner and thus enable the victim to get prompt treatment. Having safely completed its task over Valona, the Blenheim was intercepted by four CR.42s when on its way to Brindisi, forcing the pilot to abandon the reconnaissance and return to Larissa.

Six of 80 Squadron's Hurricanes escorted nine Blenheims drawn from 84 and 211 Squadrons to raid Berat and Devoli in the early afternoon. Bombs were seen bursting amongst parked aircraft of the 72°Gruppo OA, one Ro.37bis being destroyed and three damaged; two of the unit's pilots were wounded, Serg.Magg. Giovanni Mencarelli fatally so. CR.42s of 160° Gruppo were scrambled, claiming a Hurricane probably destroyed and two damaged. The Blenheims escaped unscathed.

The raiding force would have been unaware of the arrival of Italian Dictator Benito Mussolini at Tirana on this date, where his SM.79 touched down following its flight from Bari. He was accompanied by General Francesco Pricolo, the air force chief, and their SM.79 had been escorted by a dozen Mc.200s and two Z.506Bs. Mussolini had arrived to witness for himself the state of the war, and to be present for the opening of the new Italian offensive *Offensiva di Primavera*. In the air, he was satisfied that the Regia Aeronautica maintained ascendancy over the rapidly diminishing Greek air force, and considered there was little likelihood of substantial RAF reinforcements.

Two formations of five Z.1007s of 50° Gruppo Aut.BT from Brindisi carried out another raid on Larissa at 10:30 on the morning of **3 March**, bombs falling on the earthquake-shattered town. Three Hurricanes and two PZL-24s were airborne as they turned for home, two of the bombers falling to their combined attacks. A further four were hit by AA fire. Sqn Ldr Gordon-Finlayson of 211 Squadron went out to drop a dinghy to any survivors of the downed bombers who might be found, but none were seen.

Five Italian warships identified as two cruisers and three destroyers, sortied down the Albanian coast during the morning of **4 March** and commenced shelling the coastal road near Himara and Port Palermo, under cover of a strong fighter escort of G.50s and CR.42s from the 24° Gruppo CT. The flotilla actually comprised the cruiser *Riboty*, the torpedo-destroyer *Andromeda* and three MAS boats. An immediate strike was ordered by RAF units, 15 Blenheims being ordered off. Nine 211 Squadron aircraft and five from 84 Squadron (a sixth failed to start) were led to the area by Sqn Ldrs Gordon-Finlayson and Jones, escorted by ten Hurricanes, followed by seventeen Gladiators, fourteen from 112 Squadron and three from 80 Squadron. Four 80 Squadron Hurricanes flew on the starboard flank of the bombers, with four from 33 Squadron to port, and two more above as weavers. At 15:00 the warships were seen ten miles south of Valona, and the Blenheims went in to bomb in line-astern; several near misses were seen, but no hits were recorded.

A Greek Blenheim flown by 1/Lt Haralambos Papatheou, returning from a mission on **6 March**, was chased by two Gladiators of 80 Squadron (believed flown by Flg Off. Wanklyn Flower (K8021) and Sgt Ted Hewett (K6138) respectively), who were patrolling over Yannina and mistook the Greek bomber for an Italian one. As a result, the aircraft landed safely at base but with a dozen bullet holes, some of which had pierced one of the fuel tanks; the crew was unhurt.

While the main body of 84 Squadron was still operating from Paramythia with a mixed establishment of Blenheim Is and IVs, the HQ remained at Menidi, where a flight of three photo-reconnaissance Blenheim IVs from 113 Squadron from Egypt had arrived on attachment to the squadron, including T2177/AD-V with Flg Off. Lawrence Grumbley/ Sgt J.T. Latimer/Sgt S.W. Lee; and T2168 with Sgt Ken Price/Sgt Doug Woodcock/Sgt James Rooney. A number of clandestine recces would be flown over Bulgaria by these crews. To maintain security, the flight was attached to 84 Squadron for servicing and administration only, the crews being billeted elsewhere.

On **7 March**, operating from Larissa, 11 Squadron despatched two Blenheims on photo-recce sorties, one to Valona but its camera failed to function; the other made for Brindisi on the Italian mainland during which five CR.42s were sighted, the pilot wisely deciding to abort and return. The flights were repeated the following day but again no pictures were secured, on this occasion owing to cloud cover over both targets. The Squadron's diarist noted:

> Another of our aircraft, the third in ten days, receives damage to its undercarriage when landing after a test flight. Strong representations are made to Headquarters to have the aerodrome surface repaired as it is now extremely rough owing to the dry weather. Flying is restricted to operations only.[2]

As a result of the complaint, 11 Squadron was advised of an imminent move to Almyros, about 60 miles south-east of Larissa. The move was fraught with problems, not least of which was a heavy snowfall that temporarily closed the Larissa-Volos road and thus hampering the road party. However, operations from Almyros would not commence until later in the month. During this period 84 Squadron, at Tatoi/Menidi, lost the services of L1392, when Sgt Alex Gordon, who was practising night take-offs and landings, suffered an undercarriage collapse.

Meanwhile, the new Italian offensive began on **9 March**, at once putting the overstretched defenders under great pressure. The Greek Commander-in-Chief at once requested that RAF bombers operate in direct support of his hard-pressed ground forces instead of their usual strategic targets. Although still reluctant to agree to what many in the RAF still considered a misuse of air power, Air Vice-Marshal D'Albiac now had little option but to agree in the circumstances, and for the next four days the RAF at least gave the Greeks the support they really desired, all attacks being directed on tactical targets.

D'Albiac, however was not wrong in his wish to avoid this kind of action. Although RAF bombers did their best, they were to achieve little more than nuisance attacks on the Italian lines. All the raids by 211 Squadron were directed in the area of Bousi, where the Italian heavy artillery supporting the offensive was based. Results were poor. It is a matter of fact that bombing well-camouflaged targets in a mountain area in prevalent conditions of mist and bad weather was always going to be a difficult job.

On setting out on a mission in the morning, a Greek Blenheim flown by Flt Sgt Dimitrios Soufrilas experienced an engine malfunction over Velestino, north of Almyros, just after take-off. The pilot decided to return to base to attempt an emergency landing. After lowering the undercarriage, the aircraft started losing height dangerously, making the situation more difficult. Observer Wt Off. Georgios Sakkis suggested dropping the bombs over the sea and to execute a belly-landing on the field, but Soufrilas decided to make a single-engine landing, which he achieved.

During the next two days there were few operations, although Greek bombers were in action. About mid-morning on **11 March**, nine G.50s of 24° Gruppo (one 354ª Squadriglia and eight of 355ª Squadriglia) were engaged on a sweep over the front line. At their head there was newly promoted Magg. Silvio Valente and Cap. Enrico Candio, both Spanish Civil War veterans. Valente had been sent to the Gruppo a few days before replacing Col. Eugenio Leotta, sent home to command the elite 4° Stormo. Despite his status Valente had seen very little action in his flying career, having arrived in Spain at the end of that war and having since then commanded the Mc.200-equipped 371ª Squadriglia, a unit that had not yet reached an active front.

At 10:50, when at about 14,000 feet, they discovered a formation of Gladiators from 112 Squadron that we were escorting Blenheims—and engaged. At the end of the fight a Gladiator and a Blenheim were claimed shot down confirmed but two pilots were missing: Serg. Luigi Spallacci of 355ª Squadriglia and Magg.

Valente himself. Both were killed. In addition, three more fighters were heavily damaged and two of their pilots were wounded.

The 22-year-old Spallacci was granted an immediate posthumous *Medaglia d'Oro al Valor Militare*. The citation for the award suggested that in his last combat, after shooting down an enemy plane (it was his first individual victory after three shared ones) he helpfully tried to save his commander that was attacked by many enemy fighters but in doing so he was hit and killed by enemy's fire.

The RAF lost no aircraft on this occasion, but 32 Mira did, which suggests that at least one Greek Blenheim, or perhaps a section, were also on this mission. When under attack by a G.50, Flt Sgt Evangelos Tzovlas rolled B263 onto its back, but he was the only member of the crew to escape as it fell to crash at Koukouvaounes, Sgts Matthaios Tsolakidis and Stefano Mavromatidis being killed, possibly the victim of Serg. Spallacci.

Some days later, a Greek Blenheim coming back from a mission and flying over Yannina, lost one of its propeller blades that suddenly detached from the engine. With Lt Michalis Stratis at the controls, the aircraft was seen to break formation, started turning to the left and was lost from sight in cloud. However, Stratis managed to land it safely on a field in the west of Pamvotis Lake, without injury to himself or his crew.

On the night of **12 March**, five Blenheims of 84 Squadron bombed Calato/ Kalathos airfield on the island of Rhodes, each aircraft dropping four 250 lb bombs. Results were negligible. Three Hurricanes and a dozen Gladiators provided escort for 211 Squadron to the Tepelene-Kelcyre area next day (**13 March**), and a large formation of Italian fighters were sighted, variously identified at CR.42s, G.50s and Mc.200s. In addition a mixed formation of 15 Z.1007bis and BR20s was encountered. In the ensuing skirmish, one BR20 and six fighters were claimed shot down (two actual fighter losses) for the loss of a Hurricane and Gladiator, from which both the pilots baled out. The Blenheims escaped interception and carried out their bombing tasks.

From Paramythia, Sqn Ldr Gordon-Finlayson flew to Eleusis to report to Air HQ on 211 Squadron's recent experiences at the forward airfield, from where 30 operations had been flown in 25 days. On his arrival he was advised of his promotion to Wing Commander and the award of the DSO. He was also informed that he was to set up a new Eastern Wing to command units to be established on the Thessalonikan Plain, following on the success of Western Wing in the Yannina/Paramythia area. The new Wing would comprise 11 Squadron at Almyros; the 113 Squadron detachment at Menidi, soon to be joined by the rest of the unit; the Wellingtons of 37 Squadron at Menidi; B and C Flights of 30 Squadron at Eleusis; and the balance of 33 Squadron's Hurricanes not at Paramythia. Sqn Ldr Richard Nedwill AFC flew in from Egypt to take command of 211 Squadron. A 27-year-old New Zealander from Canterbury, Nedwill had been a flying instructor at 4SFTS and lacked any operational experience.

At 13:25 on **15 March**, seven Blenheims drawn from 84 and 211 Squadrons were off from Paramythia to raid Berat/Devoli airfield, where three Ro.37bis of 72° Gruppo OA were destroyed and three 395ᵃ Squadriglia G.50s damaged, and three airmen were wounded. The same two Blenheim units sent out a futher raid at 17:30, eight aircraft attacking Valona airfield, where a 364ᵃ Squadriglia CR.42 went up in flames. During the day, five Blenheim IFs of 30 Squadron were flown up to Paramythia from Eleusis, where they were to join eight Wellingtons and the Swordfish for attacks on Tirana and Valona that night (**15/16 March**). First off, at 20:30, were Blenheims of 211 Squadron, which carried out a diversionary attack for the Swordfish. As on previous occasion, vessels in the harbour had moved around from their earlier locations. Nonetheless, the Swordfish hit the destroyer *Andromeda* (600-tons) during their attack, aboard which 23 Italian sailors lost their lives (see Chapter VI). At 03:30 on the morning of **16 March**, 30 Squadron's Blenheims began taking off at ten-minute intervals:

Flt Lt. Davidson and *Lofty* Lord with Sgt Bill Gair as observer in K7179, were off at 03:50. The raid on the target was successful with a number of enemy aircraft being damaged or destroyed. *Lofty's* logbook states that his aircraft dropped six bombs, made up of 20 lb and 30 lb fragmentation bombs, and made three dive attacks using front and rear guns. The AA fire was heavy and accurate although only one Blenheim was slightly damaged, *Lofty's*, sustaining a bullet hole to each wing and a shrapnel hole in the nose.[3]

Behind the Blenheims came the Wellingtons, their target being Tirana airfield, but CR.42s intercepted in the moonlight and shot down one in flames, and damaged two others.

Later that morning, Plt Off. *Twink* Pearson of 211 Squadron was despatched on a special recce of Durazzo harbour to check on the amount of shipping present, pending an attack on this target by the Swordfish that night. A number of good-sized ships were seen, but during the return flight a Z.506B of 86° Gruppo was encountered over the sea near Valona; Pearson recalled:

We were very evenly matched—the Blenheim had two guns and the Cant had three, two in the rear turrets and one front. We tackled first the stings in the tail, and with my second burst I got the rear-gunner. Just in time, too, for the tracer from the top turret was fairly whizzing past the cockpit—most unpleasant. Then, the rear guns silenced. I went for the cockpit and made a series of head-on attacks to drive him away from home. When the ammo in the front gun was exhausted, we tried beam attacks to give my rear-gunner a chance. It was jolly good fun. Then we had to come back, regretfully, for the Cant, just above the waves, was still flying, though all his guns were silent. So we landed a little fed up.[4]

Observer Sgt *Jimmy* Riddle added:

> I made frantic signs to *Twink* Pearson indicating sharp movements of the
> controls and the firing of the front gun and he reacted spot on. We came up
> behind the Cant at full boost and *Twink* silenced the rear cockpit with the front
> gun and then flew on a parallel course about 200–300 yards abeam on the port
> side and let Chig [Sgt Gordon Chignall] have a go. We did not see her go down
> as we were now too near Valona for safety, but when we got back to Paramythia
> the *Bish* was waiting at our picket and gave us the biggest dressing down I ever
> received in the RAF! He pointed out that we had been on a photo recce of
> an important entry port for the Italians and that the camera could contain
> information much more valuable than the loss of a seaplane, and that we had
> risked getting this back to base.
>
> Suitably abashed we shuffled awkwardly realising how right he was. He then
> offered his congratulations saying that shore units had seen the Cant go in, and
> we all adjoined to the Officers Mess to celebrate![5]

A Greek observer on the ground had apparently witnessed the action and had
allegedly seen the Cant crash into the sea and sink. The Greek contacted Air
HQ and they had passed on the news to Paramythia before Pearson had landed.
He was then torn off a strip by Sqn Ldr Gordon-Finlayson (as noted) for not
returning directly from the special recce he had been ordered to undertake.
A DFC for this action followed in due course. However, the floatplane did not
crash into the sea and, although damaged, made it safely back to base.

A raid was supposed to have been carried out on Valona on **17 March**, but
had to be abandoned owing to low cloud. A section of 211 Squadron returned
after fifteen minutes, but next day 211 successfully raided buildings and the road
north of Bousi. Two days later (**19 March**), Sqn Ldr Jones led six 84 Squadron
machines on a low-level attack on Tepelene, causing Flt Lt Russell to comment:

> Good results but five out of six hit by ack-ack, possibly due to admiration of
> the scenery.[6]

A single Blenheim recced the Bousi-Berat road on **21 March**. Several recces
were flown over the Yugoslavian and Bulgarian borders by the detachment of 113
Squadron PR Blenheims at this time, seeking to check on developments, since
German forces were now known to be in Bulgaria in strength. Four Blenheims
from 11 Squadron were also engaged in this work, all returning safely bar that
flown by Sgt George Bailey, who became ill in the air and diverted to Salonika,
where he was hospitalised.

At last Italian reconnaissance aircraft discovered the airfield at Paramythia, and
at 06:35 on **22 March**, all three squadriglie of 153° Gruppo CT (29 Mc.200s) from

Lecce and Brindisi took off to carry out a strafing attack. Eight Macchis swept in, claiming two Blenheims destroyed on the ground—at least one aircraft of 211 Squadron was actually hit and burnt out, as observer Sgt *Nobby* Clark noted:

> Our L8531 was set on fire and with 4x250 on board, blows up.[7]

Another witness was Airman Bob Livesey, an engine fitter with C Flight:

> A Blenheim was burning pretty fiercely and two 250 lb bombs were on the ground ready to be loaded. Cpl *Mush* Hale, at great risk to his life, ran over to it—and with his feet—rolled those bombs away from under the aircraft.[8]

As other Macchis patrolled overhead they clashed with Gladiators and claimed two shot down and a third damaged, but there were no losses to either side. Five BR20s from 37° Stormo then attacked Paramythia in the face of intense AA, which damaged two of the bombers, but little damage was caused to the airfield. In the afternoon, 27 more Macchis repeated the strafe of Paramythia, while fifteen others flew top cover. This time two Wellingtons were claimed destroyed, one of them seen to explode, whilst a Gladiator was also claimed. Indeed, one unserviceable Wellington went up in flames, as did one Gladiator. All serviceable aircraft on the airfield were now ferried to Menidi.

Under the impression that the attackers had been G.50s from Berat/Devoli, a retaliatory attack on this airfield was laid on for the following morning (**23 March**), thirteen Hurricanes and eleven Gladiators escorting six Blenheims of 84 Squadron to attack this airfield. Approaching at low level due to heavy cloud, the Blenheims bombed from 1,500 feet, receiving only minor shrapnel damage from the AA defences, although Sgt Jim Hutcheson had his elevators badly damaged. Two Hurricanes also sustained slight AA damage before G.50s of 24° Gruppo attacked, damaging one Hurricane from which the pilot baled out near Larissa.

Next day (**24 March**), five Blenheim IFs from 30 Squadron flew into Maleme airfield on Crete in preparation for strike against Calato/Kalathos airfield on the island of Rhodes, and against sister island Scarpanto, planned for the early hours of the following morning (**25 March**). Thus, at 04:10, two Blenheims, led by Flt Lt. Bob Davidson, made for Scarpanto, but Plt Off. John Jarvis turned back with engine trouble; Davidson continued alone but saw no aircraft on the airfield there, and reported:

> Tin huts and buildings were strafed and four bombs were seen to fall away among the buildings causing considerable damage. AA fire did not open up until the attack was made.[9]

At 04:15, the other three Blenheims set off for Rhodes, led by Sqn Ldr Milward in L8466 (with Sgt *Lofty* Lord as air-gunner); the CO reported:

Considerable difficulty was experienced on approaching the target owing to 10/10 cloud and unavoidable warning was given to enemy due to 10 minutes delay in locating target. A low dive attack was made with all guns concentrated on a line of aircraft, five of which were hit, one completely destroyed. All bombs of No.1 aircraft [Milward] were jettisoned in the sea because of an expected attack from one CR.42.

No. 2 aircraft [Flg Off. Andy Smith in K7105] had equal success and observed that four of the He111s were damaged. Four bombs were observed to fall short of the aircraft on the ground, but the remainder hit some buildings and caused some damage to a small factory.

No. 3 aircraft [K7177 flown by Flg Off. *Bud* Richardson] lost the formation in the cloud when approaching Rhodes; however, the pilot—bent on destruction—sought out a target of his own, over the island of Astropalia, where one large [estimated at 7,000-tons] and two small merchant ships were seen at anchorage, and in the ensuing dive all bombs were observed to hit the target.[10]

Only light machine-gun fire was experienced and the only damage inflicted was from bomb splinters in the wings of L8466 and K7177. Apparently the Heinkels were from II/KG26, one being destroyed and a second badly damaged.

The Italians immediately retaliated by despatching three 162ª Squadriglia CR.42s to again strike at Maleme, while four others flew top cover. The unserviceable Blenheim was hit again and set on fire, being completely burned out. AA fire hit one of the strafers, the gunners believing that it had crashed into the sea; in fact it struggled back to Rhodes where the pilot made a successful landing. Two Swordfish were sent out at 18:30 to attack the ships bombed by Richardson, but failed to locate them.

Six Blenheims of 211 Squadron returned to Paramythia on **25 March**, and later in the morning 211 and 84 set out to bomb Berat/Devoli but this had to be abandoned owing to insufficient cloud over the target. Better weather during the afternoon allowed the Blenheims to bomb the Bousi–Berat road, while Gladiators provided escort. A Blenheim reinforcement arrived at Menidi from Egypt during the day, the bulk of 113 Squadron led by Sqn Ldr Rod Spencer. The unit's role was envisaged initially to attack shipping carrying supplies to the Dodecanese Islands, and to maintain the reconnaissance of Rumanian and Bulgarian borders. The new arrivals were amazed to discover that *Lufthansa* civil Ju 52/3m airliners were still regularly operating from Menidi, and at times shared the circuit with their Blenheims.

The renewed use of Paramythia was apparently spotted by an Italian reconnaissance machine, since Macchis of 153° Gruppo returned for another strafe early in the afternoon of **26 March**. They were met by four Gladiators and in the ensuing clash, one of each side being claimed shot down; 211 Squadron's new CO Sqn Ldr Nedwill, who had flown his first Blenheim operation two days earlier, was possibly shot down and killed by the Macchis. He had volunteered to fly one of 112 Squadron's Gladiators on a defensive patrol over the airfield when the Italian fighters struck[11]. During the dogfight two of the Macchis broke away and strafed the airfield, claiming two Gladiators and one Wellington destroyed; in fact, one Gladiator was destroyed and a badly damaged Wellington destroyed. 211 Squadron's Ron Dudman, an engine fitter, wrote in his diary:

> Another glorious day for the Italians—we had eight raids today. On the third raid the Iti fighters came down ground strafing; they riddled three planes and set a Glad on fire, which burnt out. On the sixth raid they got one Blenheim, it also burnt out [possibly L8466]. On the last raid one of the Glad pilots, our CO, dived and never pulled out—killed.[12]

113 Squadron undertook its first major raid on the morning of **27 March,** Sqn Ldr Rod Spencer leading 11 of the unit's Blenheims for a repeat attack on Rhodes' Calato/Kalathos airfield. Nearly 12,000 lb of bombs were dropped, fuel dumps and buildings being left on fire, while it was believed that one aircraft had been destroyed on the ground. This action was associated with activity over Crete and an *Ultra* intercept which indicated an increased level of activity by Italian forces on Rhodes; *Ultra* had also picked up that Bf 110s (from ZG26) had been ordered from Libya to Palermo (Sicily) for 'special operations'—proposed support and protection for the Italian Fleet preparing to challenge the stretched British Mediterranean Fleet, and possibly intercept British supply ships to Greece. The German Naval Liaison Officer in Rome advised the Italian Naval Staff:

> The German Naval Staff considers that at the moment there is only one British battleship, Valiant, in the Eastern Mediterranean fully ready for action. It is not anticipated that heavy British units will be withdrawn from the Atlantic in the near future. Force H is also considered unlikely to appear in the Mediterranean. Thus the situation in the Mediterranean is at the moment more favourable for the Italian Fleet than ever before.
>
> Intensive traffic from Alexandria to the Greek ports, whereby the Greek forces are receiving constant reinforcements in men and equipment, presents a particularly worthy target for Italian Naval Forces. The German Naval Staff considers that the appearance of Italian units in the area south of Crete will seriously interfere with British shipping, and may even lead to the complete disruption of the transport of troops, especially as these transports are at the moment inadequately protected.

It proved to be a most serious and inaccurate assessment by the Germans, which was to cost the Italians dear. Thus, forewarned of Italian plans, the Royal

Navy's 1st Battle Squadron prepared to sail from Alexandria, together with the carrier *Formidable* equipped with Swordfish and Albacores, and Fulmars. A Sunderland sighted the vanguard of the Italian Fleet some 80 miles east of Cap Passero, the south-eastern tip of Sicily. The 1st Battle Squadron and *Formidable* put to sea after dark that same night.

Battle of Cape Matapan

First light next day (**28 March**), found the Battle Squadron 150 miles south of eastern Crete. Sea searches began, with Albacores from the carrier joined by Swordfish operating from Maleme. At 07:20, the first sighting was made by the Albacores, which shadowed the warships until a strike was launched, firstly by three torpedo carrying Swordish from Maleme followed by six similarly armed Albacores from *Formidable*; escorting Fulmars claimed a covering Ju 88 shot down. Although one torpedo hit was claimed, all missed.

During the early afternoon, a Sunderland sighted 'three cruisers and one destroyer'—actually the vanguard of the Italian 3rd Cruiser Division—and signalled Air HQ Athens accordingly. On receipt of this information three Blenheims from 84 Squadron were despatched and these attacked *Vittorio Veneto* at 14:20. Although the bombs fell close, there were no hits and no damage was caused. Thirty minutes later six more Blenheims, this time from 113 Squadron, again led by Sqn Ldr Spencer, made a low-level attack on the battleship, and once more only near-misses were achieved. Ironically, while waiting to take-off at Eleusis airfield, the Blenheims had queued with a *Lufthansa* Ju 52/3m! Observer Flt Sgt Arthur Davis recalled:

> It was a low level raid through heavy AA fire and a number of Squadron planes were hit, including ourselves. Claims were made that we hit a destroyer and a cruiser which had slowed the fleet down enough to allow the Royal Navy to peck at. We couldn't prove it, however.[13]

Even as the Blenheims were attacking, the Albacores' second strike, which had taken off at 12:22, were approaching *Vittorio Veneto* for a head-on attack, while the two Fulmars machine-gunned the bridge and gun turrets to distract the gunners' aim. The leading Albacore closed to about 1,000 yards before releasing its torpedo, but almost immediately the aircraft was hit repeatedly, dipped, and crashed into the sea. The pilot and his crew perished. The two following Albacores dropped their torpedoes, as did the two Swordfish which were coming in from the starboard side. While it was believed that three hits had been gained, in fact only one struck home, hitting the battleship just above the outer port screw with a mighty explosion. The engines stopped as water flooded into the ship and she began to list to port. At this moment the last of the Blenheims attacked, one bomb also scoring a hit when it fell very close to the stern.

At about the same time as *Vittorio Veneto* was under attack, the 1st Cruiser Division was also being engaged by other Blenheims, six from 113 Squadron led by Flt Lt Denis Rixson and five from 84 Squadron led by Sqn Ldr *Jonah* Jones making the attack, as he recorded:

The weather was hazy over the sea, but we soon found the Iti Navy—two groups of ships steaming like billy-ho for home. They started to zig-zag as soon as they saw us, and their AA opened up. We made a dive attack and fairly plastered them. Observers in my squadron registered hits on one big ship, and we think on a smaller one. They were difficult targets, but quite a number must have been damaged or delayed by near-misses.[14]

While Sgt Tom Ingham-Brown (a South African) reported:

Bombed with four 250 lb from 3,500 feet. Intense and heavy ack-ack but not very accurate; no one hit.

Both *Zara* and the smaller *Garibaldi* were near-missed, but not damaged.

Other Blenheims, three more from 84 Squadron led by the Australian commander of B Flight, Flt Lt Donovan Boehm (of obvious German ancestry), and six from 211 Squadron led by the new acting CO Flt Lt *Potato* Jones, found and attacked ships of the Italian 3rd Division, both *Trento* and *Bolzano* being near-missed, but neither suffering any damage. However, one 84 Squadron crew believed that they had scored hits, Flt Sgt Alex Gordon later reporting:

Though they changed formation and zig-zagged violently, and their AA was reasonably heavy, we were able to spend some time taking aim, and made a low-level attack. I saw two of my biggest bombs hit the largest ship amidships. Clouds of black and yellow smoke issued for a long time and the ship stopped.[15]

This was confirmed by his observer, Sgt George Furney, who added:

It was a hefty but agreeable surprise when I saw those bombs hit and just the place they were aimed at—right amidships. At first there was just the normal white smoke of the bomb burst, and then columns of black and yellow smoke shot up into the air to a height of 200 feet or so. For 50 minutes afterwards the rear-gunner had a good view of the ship, and gave us a running commentary over intercom and we proceeded home. She had stopped and was listing when we lost sight of her.[16]

The crews from 211 Squadron were less sanguine as to their results, Flt Lt *Potato* Jones, the acting CO, recalling:

> The enemy fleet appeared to be in great confusion and was zig-zagging violently, and now and then one would cross the course of another, or two would converge, and there were as a result many phenomenal avoidances. We bombed and added to the confusion. I saw no hits, but there were plenty of near-misses, which could have done them no good, and when we left the enemy was busy laying a smoke screen.[17]

Although *Vittorio Veneto* had slowed to a halt, her damage control party soon had two engines restarted, and before long the battleship was making 16 knots. By 17:00 she was heading for Taranto, 420 miles away, by now making 19 knots. The Italian Admiral was bitter about the continued absence of any form of fighter protection, which had been promised by both Luftwaffe and Regia Aeronautica, but at this range very little other than the handful of CR.42s on Rhodes could have reached the fleet. *Formidable* launched another strike of eight torpedo-bombers at dusk, as did Maleme (two aircraft), one of the latter Swordfish gaining a strike on the cruiser *Pola*. The Royal Navy force, its main ships equipped with radar, now closed in. In less than an hour, the cruisers *Fiume*,[18] *Alfieri* and *Zara* were sunk by gunfire, as was the destroyer *Carducci*; the crippled *Pola* was then despatched after her crew had been taken off. It was estimated that 2,400 Italian sailors lost their lives, while about 1,200 were picked up by the RN, 112 by the Greek destroyer *Hydra*, and 160 by an Italian hospital ship.

As for the Blenheims, they had flown 29 sorties, dropping more than thirteen tons of bombs, mainly from medium altitude. Although returning crews claimed two direct hits on a cruiser, one on a destroyer, and probably two more on another cruiser, as well as a number of near-misses, the only success had been the single hit on *Vittorio Veneto*. But this was not surprising—bombers very seldom scored successes against moving ships when bombing from altitude. However considering that there was no fighter opposition to the attacks, and that while at times heavy, the AA fire was generally inaccurate, the results for such a concerted effort seem meagre.

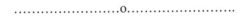

Meanwhile, at 05:35, the six Blenheim IFs of 30 Squadron at Paramythia took off and set course for Lecce airfield on the coast of the Italian mainland, the sections led by Flt Lt Tom Horgan and Flg Off. Ralph Blakeway. The attack was aimed to interfere with possible action which might be launched from this airfield against the RN's retiring Battle Squadron. Arriving over the target an hour later, they dived from 10,000 feet to 1,500 feet, an estimated 80–100 aircraft of all types being seen on the ground. Sgt Geoff Chapman, flying as air-gunner with Flt Lt Horgan (L1239), recalled:

We arrived at Lecce completely unobserved just as the airfield was awakening from its slumbers. As we flew in at a few feet above ground level in line-astern we could see men walking from their billets with towels over the shoulders. The sound of our machine-guns awoke them with a vengeance and by the time we all swung round for a second run the machine-gun posts on top of the hangars were manned.

Apart from one bullet which went through the turret of my aircraft [slight scratch], all three of our aircraft were unscathed, but we reckoned that between 16 and 20 enemy aircraft were either destroyed or seriously damaged by our attack. We flew back to Eleusis across the sea as quickly as we could.[19]

When at last the defences opened up, all three Blenheims of Flg Off. Blakeway's section were hit and slightly damaged, and Sgt Tony Ovens' aircraft subsequently force-landed at an advanced landing ground as a result of damage to its oil cooler. Two Mc.200s were scrambled from Lecce and three more from Brindisi, but they were unable to catch the attackers as they withdrew. 30 Squadron's assessment of the damage they had inflicted was quite accurate; one S.81 was destroyed in flames and 25 other aircraft were damaged, while five airmen were wounded, one of them seriously, as was one civilian outside the base.

At 14:15, an air raid alarm was sounded at Eleusis and four three-engined aircraft were plotted heading towards the Athens area, in presumably a retaliatory strike. Two Blenheims IFs and two Hurricanes were scrambled but the raiders turned away and headed out to sea.

About midday on **29 March,** the Navy requested a recce along the Greek coast for the remnants of the Italian Fleet, which was believed to be escaping northwards. Although air units from Malta had not participated in the action, a Maryland was despatched from Luqa at 11:00 to reconnoitre the area; the Maryland CO recalled:

I despatched the standby crew. They did not return. A few days later Athens advised that the aircraft had crashed in the sea close to an island—Zante. The pilot was killed. The navigator had survived with head injuries but the third crewmember was OK. I signalled to Athens asking them to designate the nearest airfield where I could pick up the surviving crew members.

The local Greek people were magnificent. They were taken to Athens, then to Southern Greece as the Germans advanced. Thence they escaped to Crete. From Crete they escaped to Alexandria. Then they cadged a ride back to Malta on a ship—an ammunition ship. They survived the bombing *en route* and reported back to me as cheeky as ever. And of course wanting to be back on ops.[20]

It seems that the loss of the Maryland was due to friendly fire from a Royal Navy vessel.

On **30 March,** at 11:25, ten Blenheims of 84 Squadron were despatched without escort to raid a military camp at Elbasan, twenty miles south-east of Tirana. Sgt Tom Ingham-Brown's Z5861 was attacked by two fighters but not hit; however, Sgt Jim Hutcheson's L1390 was hit by AA fire and he struggled back to force-land at Neapolis, near Koritza, as recalled by his navigator, Sgt Ken Irwin:

> After both engines failed there was little alternative but to hit the deck. Sgt Jim Hutcheson did a great job and put us down just short of a ravine. I had braced my feet up against the bomb aimer's seat which was just as well as the bottom of the aircraft parted like a piece of cake. Both engines came adrift and there was petrol everywhere. So we got out pronto.
>
> I had always had misgivings about the size of the hatches on the starboard side of the Blenheim but I am sure that I never touched the sides on the way out! We had difficulty getting Sgt Jacky Webb, the air-gunner, out because the hatch was jammed but we eventually succeeded and legged it away before the kite blew up.[21]

The other nine bombers were intercepted by 154° Gruppo CT G.50s which had scrambled from Berat/Devoli, and these took on the Blenheims as they made their attack. L1391 (Sgt George Bailey) was badly shot-up, hit in the nose, fuselage and starboard wing, while T2427 (Flg Off. Ivor Goudge) was also hit—the Fiat pilots claimed two Blenheims probably shot down. Sgt Alan Blackburn, the gunner in Flt Lt Bill Russell's aircraft, believed that he had shot down one of the attackers in return, which was seen diving vertically with smoke pouring from its engine; on this occasion crews identified two of their attackers as Re2000s. 211 Squadron Blenheims were also out, carrying out a raid on Dukati, while another aircraft successfully recced the area. That night five of 113 Squadron's Blenheims bombed an Italian supply convoy off Stampalia Island, but without obvious results. Come daylight and 211 Squadron raided the Bousi-Gualla road.

Three replacement Blenheim IFs were received by 30 Squadron to re-equip its bomber flight, allowing the unit to become entirely fighter-equipped. A Sunderland also arrived from Cairo with six Free French fighter pilots on board for air defence of Athens duty; they were to fly Hurricane patrols over the capital, using the newly delivered aircraft, and thereby relieve the Blenheim IFs of 30 Squadron. However, following a few negative night patrols the French pilots returned to Egypt (where they participated in the defence of Tobruk), and the Hurricanes were handed over to 33 and 80 Squadrons.

April 1941

On **1 April**, 84 Squadron lost its senior flight commander when Flt Lt Donovan Boehm and his crew (Wop/AG Sgt Ken Lee and passenger LAC Harry Jackson) were killed in an accident in T2382 at Kiphissia, north-east of Athens, during a routine flight, possibly an air test. 211 Squadron continued to despatch raids. Next day, Blenheims from the same unit attacked the barracks at Tepelene; and the following day a raid was made on the barracks at Berat. From these sorties all aircraft returned. And then, for the fourth consecutive day, 211 despatched six aircraft on yet another raid.

113 Squadron now moved its Blenheims from Menidi to Larissa, prior to moving again two days later to a newly-constructed landing ground at Niamata. This was situated in an area that was partially bog, between Larissa and Volos. Menidi was required for the return of 37 Squadron's Wellingtons on a further detachment from Egypt. Two replacement aircrew, who arrived during the chaos, were observers Sgt Harry Duignan and Sgt Ewan Brooking, both members of the RNZAF, who were posted to 113 Squadron. They had arrived by sea. Sgt Brooking recalled:

> From Piraeus we were taken to the Greek airforce airfield at Tatoi/Menidi to the north of Athens. We were there a few days, so leave was granted, and Harry and I took advantage to travel into Athens. We visited the Acropolis and some of the sights there, and ended up at the Anglo/Greek Club, where some quite lovely Greek girls were the hostesses, then back to camp. Sightseeing was soon over, so on 1 April, I was temporarily crewed up with P/O Pengelly, and flew in one of our Blenheims from Menidi airfield to Larissa to the north. After landing we were informed that the surface, apart from the landing strips, was too corrugated from earth quakes for taxiing the Blenheims, which appeared to have a weak stern frame. So we took off for Niamata, an airfield to the east of Larissa.
>
> There was a tented encampment already established, and we were told to find and share the four-man tents. Harry and I shared with a part crew of an RAF observer and gunner. One instruction we were given was to dig a slit trench by our tent for our protection, which Harry and I proceeded to do. The RAF duo didn't think much of the idea, so lay on their stretchers instead. Who do you think was first into it when the bullets began to fly?[22]

By **4 April**, British Intelligence had received sufficient *Ultra* intercepts to be fully aware that the German invasion of Yugoslavia and Greece was imminent, although there was nothing that could be done other than warn the Yugoslav Government.

CHAPTER 6

With a Little Help from the Flying Sailors

Swordfish Operations from Paramythia

We were horrified to find what looked like an illuminated buoy in the centre of the harbour, as big as the Albert Hall. It was so brilliantly lit that it had no discernible shape.

Lt Charles Lamb 815 Squadron

The Blenheims in Greece were reinforced by a small but important addition. At the end of February the detachment of Ju 52s providing supply—and troop-carrying facilities for the Italians from Italy to Albania, and evacuating wounded and sick on return flights, came to an end.[1] With the departure of the transports, the shipping routes again bore the brunt and thus became busier, a fact not missed by RAF reconnaissance aircraft. Hence, six Swordfish torpedo-bombers of 815 Squadron, currently residing at Maleme in Crete, were despatched to Paramythia for nocturnal anti-shipping activities in co-operation with the Blenheims.

Led by Lt-Cdr Jackie Jago, the aircraft flew initially to Eleusis, since it would be here that the torpedoes were fitted as facilities were not available at the forward airfield. The CO's aircraft (P4083/A) carried the normal crew of three, but each of the other five were fitted with a long-range fuel tank in the centre cockpit. This increased the range to over 1,000 miles and endurance to nine hours, but the tanks were not self-sealing and represented a major fire hazard if punctured. The main tank was located in the upper wings, but there was also a 'last-gasp' gravity tank that held a few extra gallons. TAG Ken Sims recalled:

The few gallons had to be hand-pumped up. The pilot could use this—the handle was under his seat on the starboard side—but so could the observer, by crawling under the pilot's seat. In 'last-gasp' conditions, obviously the pilot wanted control so the observer was called upon. With the long-range tank, if we got the call, this meant crawling under the tank and under the seat. Not much chance of getting out then![2]

On arrival at Eleusis the aircrews were reunited with some of the unit's ground personnel who had travelled on HMS *Protector* with the torpedoes.

On **12 March**, the six torpedo-armed Swordfish flew up to Paramythia, their arrival coinciding with the full moon period. That same night Lt-Cdr Jago led five off over the mountains to attack the harbour at Valona. Four Blenheims of 211 Squadron went off first at 20-minute intervals from 03:00 onwards, each aircraft spending 15 minutes over the target area to create a diversion and draw off the AA.

Having climbed with difficulty to some 8,000 feet out to sea off Corfu, the torpedo-bombers went into a controlled glide between the 2,750-feet peak of Mount St. Basilios and its neighbour, and arrived over the harbour at about 60 feet. The diffused moonlight made the surface of the water difficult to see, and as the aircraft swept in, their engines throttled back, the AA defences opened up a heavy barrage. At once Lt-Cdr Jago's aircraft (P4083/A) was hit and flew into the water; his TAG L/Air Pat Beagley recalled:

The mountains were fairly tall and we came over the top of the mountain with a great struggle and got caught in searchlights. The CO opened his taps up, and a bloody great flame came out of the exhaust, which made it easy to keep the searchlights on us, but we got away with that. We were doing a run-in with the 'fish' and suddenly the whole of the bottom of the aircraft caught fire, so we went into the drink. I think it may have been a magnesium flare, but it may even have hit the torpedo underneath.[3]

Flying directly behind the CO's aircraft was Lt Charles Lamb in P4080/B. With Lamb was TAG L/Air Ken Sims, who wrote a graphic account of the attack:

The moon sank swiftly behind the clouds on the horizon as our aircraft glided down into Valona harbour. What had been a brilliant silver orb lighting the sea a few moments before, dwindled to a diffused glow and left us peering from the Swordfish cockpit into the darkening gloom. We had planned on that moonlight lasting at least 15 minutes longer. The sing of the wing rigging was clearly audible in the cockpit with the engine throttled back to an eerie hum. It was a memorable moment for a TAG about to experience his first torpedo attack.

We had crossed the isthmus and were down to 1,000 feet when the darkness was pierced by a myriad of menacing lights flickering up to and all around us—so much for our hope of surprise. The engine burst into life as we took avoiding action, and I saw and heard some shells come dangerously close. The gunner, looking back, sees this more clearly than the pilot. A fabric-sided cockpit is no protection, and one feels terribly vulnerable, but it doesn't prevent an instinctive crouching at the first shock of being under fire.

Looking forward for a moment to see where we were heading, I was amazed to see our leading aircraft displaying navigation lights! No wonder we were catching it. They were shooting at him, and with the usual trail we were in the way. Over to our starboard beam I could actually see the pit of a Breda gun with its personnel lit up by the flames. We were close enough to reply with the rear gun, but I didn't wish to offer them a sight of their target with tracer. As we ploughed steadily towards the main harbour the minutes seemed an eternity. They were hose-piping around now from several points, and further jinking was quite pointless.[4]

Following the loss of the CO's aircraft, Lt Lamb took over the lead. He headed towards a large vessel:

We were horrified to find what looked like an illuminated buoy in the centre of the harbour, as big as the Albert Hall. It was so brilliantly lit that it had no discernible shape, and no matter from which direction we approached Valona, we were bound to be silhouetted against it for one or other groups of guns on the banks. Realizing the immediate need to extinguish the revealing glare, the 'tail-end Charlie' Swordfish [P4025/K flown by Lt *Tiffy* Torrence-Spence]— seeing that the aircraft ahead of him were in trouble because of it, very rightly put his torpedo into the middle of it, and all the lights went out almost at once.[5]

Ken Sims, in the back seat, continued:

Then as suddenly as it had started the firing stopped. We were down low on the water, and I fancy the Italians had at last learned that to fire across a harbour does a lot of damage to one's own friends. At Taranto they had done a fair job of bombarding their own merchant shipping. From our point of view, however, it was unfortunately the wrong respite as the night was now as black as ink, and our vision had been impaired by the firework display. We turned towards the jetty area and tried to pick out any shape darker than the rest. At this moment I was jolted by the aircraft checking, and a sudden change in the surrounding blackness as two silvery plumes rose on each side of us. The undercarriage had hit the water.[6]

Lt Lamb's skill, experience and luck saved the day:

Instinctively I held the aircraft steady in case it somersaulted, and opened the throttle wide and pressed the release button, because the water would have activated the pistol on the nose of the torpedo and started the propeller. The sudden deceleration only lasted for about two seconds, then we were airborne again, but they were the longest two seconds I have ever known. Fortunately, we were within fifteen hundred yards of a big ship, right ahead, her hulk a black shape against a searchlight, wavering about from the town behind her, so my fish wasn't wasted.[7]

His victim was apparently the 3,539-ton freighter *Santa Maria,* which was later salved and returned to duty; he continued:

Afterwards on their radio, the Italians claimed that we had sunk a hospital ship which had been 'fully illuminated'... it might have been true; though there were no red crosses [there were, but obviously not observed in the glare], and the ship was certainly being put to military use.[8]

Lt Torrence-Spence's victim was indeed the 7,289-ton hospital ship *Po*; she was beached, sinking later. Twenty-one lives were lost including three nurses. Italian radio claimed that the *Po* had been fully illuminated and condemned the attack, adding that Mussolini's daughter, the Countess Edda Ciano, was aboard and was one of the last to leave the sinking vessel. It seems unlikely that the ship was hit by two torpedoes since only two were launched, the other pair of Swordfish returning to Paramythia with the missiles still attached.

Meanwhile, Lt-Cdr Jago and his crew, Lt John Caldecott-Smith and L/Air Pat Beagley, survived their crash and were able to get aboard their dinghy, as the latter recalled:

We were all right. I had minor injuries, scratched knees and so on, and I can remember bobbing up and down in the water for about four hours, chewing pink signal flimsies and spitting them over the side. The idea had been that after we had finished the attack we were to make a signal to the Fleet that we were attacking destroyers, or bombing, or some thing like that, so consequently we had all the radio frequencies and call-signs of the whole of the Mediterranean Fleet.

Dawn arrived, and some Italian MTBs came and picked us up and took us down in the cabin and dried us out. They were quite good about it. Then Caldecott-Smith, the senior observer, remembered he had a revolver which he had bought in Alex, so he said he thought it better to offer this up to the Italians. They were all crowding round us—I think we must have been in the captain's cabin—but as he pulled out the gun four of them promptly disappeared up the ladder. However, he handed it over by the butt and all was friendly again.

When we got ashore we were taken to be interrogated in Tirana, which was the main Italian fighter base, and some sweet-smelling Italian with long hair and a couple of babes on his arm came along to look at us, and it turned out he was the local ace. About a day later, though, there was a great bang on the airfield, and apparently this chap had gone in. We all cheered when we heard what had happened, which didn't amuse the Italians at all.[9]

Initially well-treated, they were later interrogated by Blackshirts who, angry over the sinking of the hospital ship, threatened them with shooting. However, they were now to begin a long spell as POWs. Meanwhile, command of 815 Squadron now passed to Lt Torrence-Spence, while Senior Observer Lt Alf Sutton, who had been acting as FAA Liaison Officer in Greece, was sent to Paramythia to act as Ops Officer.

The following day (**13 March**), two Swordfish were despatched to Eleusis to collect two more torpedoes. Returning to Paramythia with his torpedo attached, Lt Lamb (with Sub-Lt(A) Jack Bowker in the back seat, returning from a luncheon date in Athens with a girl friend) found himself under attack from two CR.42s of 393ª Squadriglia, 160° Gruppo Aut. Lamb at once jettisoned the torpedo, stood the aircraft (P4080/B) on its tail just as the fighters opened fire, and both stalled and spun away as they attempted to keep their sights on the almost stationary Swordfish. Recovering, they came in again, side by side, but this time Lamb threw his aircraft into a dive beyond the vertical in which his speed rose well over 200 mph. Again the Fiats attempted to keep after him, but in doing so collided with each other and crashed into the sea.

Tenente Ettore Campinoti was killed while Serg.Magg. Maurizio Mandolesi managed to take to his parachute but broke a leg on landing. On reaching Paramythia, Lamb found a jagged hole in the back of his seat and an unexploded 12.7 mm shell lodged in his parachute; and that his passenger, although not hurt, had been violently sick.

That night, at 21:15, three Swordfish were out again after shipping in Valona harbour, again supported by 211 Squadron Blenheims making a diversionary attack on the town. Attacks were made on two vessels, hits being reported on one 10,000-ton liner by Lt(A) Owen Oxley and Sub-Lt(A) Doug Macaulay, but no ships were recorded sunk on this occasion.

Activities on the night of **16/17 March** were opened by three Swordfish that went out at 20:30 to attack Valona harbour again, Blenheims of 211 Squadron once more providing the diversion. As on the previous occasion it was found that the vessels in harbour had been moved around, and the torpedo-bombers had to fly about looking for targets. A small AA vessel opened fire on Lt Lamb's aircraft suddenly, but no damage was done. In Sub-Lt(A) Macaulay's aircraft was gunner Ken Sims:

We were still at 1,000 feet but the fire was sporadic and not particularly close. We soon got underneath it and judging the height was easy. For there in the middle of the harbour, lit up like some glittering crown, was a hospital ship. We skirted by it, picked out the dark shape of a merchant ship and closed in. Mac didn't go for long shots. He seemed to know just how much he needed to get the fish running and primed, and that was the range it was dropped. The shape was looking pretty big when he let go. We banked away and watched. I was expecting something spectacular but the flash, when it came, was quite subdued. It could even have been a reflection from the gun flashes which were spraying around, mostly above us. But we believed we had gained a hit. We skirted the hospital ship again and headed for the harbour entrance, still at no more than 100 feet.[10]

It seems that they hit the destroyer *Andromeda* with this attack. Lt Lamb again spotted the hospital ship, but finding nothing else worth attacking, he released his torpedo at the small AA vessel, which he believed had sunk. Sub-Lt(A) Tony Forde saw nothing warranting an attack, and returned with his torpedo, but could not find Paramythia, force-landing in a field where the aircraft ran into a ditch and overturned.

Bad weather during the night of **18/19 March** prevented a further attack on Durazzo being made, but a reconnaissance on 19 March again showed this port to be the most promising target, and a further Swordfish strike was laid on. Because of the known shallowness of the water, it was decided to arm two aircraft with six 250 lb bombs each, plus flares, and only one with a torpedo. The trio set off at 01:50, reaching the target area two hours later. Recalled L/Air Ken Sims, gunner in the torpedo-equipped aircraft:

It was a long slog up to Durazzo, about 100 miles past Valona. We took a line well out to sea in the hope that the latter place wouldn't notice what we were up to and give warning. After two hours we turned in, came over Durazzo at about 8,000 feet and started dropping flares. The harbour seemed quite full. So was the air -full of anti-aircraft fire. The place was well defended.[11]

Lt Michael Clifford bombed a ship of 3,000–4,000 tons, but did not observe any hits, while L/Air Laurie Smith in Sub-Lt(A) Tony Forde's aircraft L9774/F saw two explosions after an attack was made on a ship in the north-east comer of the bay. Sub-Lt(A) Macaulay searched for a suitable target for his torpedo meantime; Ken Sims continued:

A largish ship which looked like an oil tanker stood out away from a jetty with a fair expanse of water on one side of it. I guessed that was what Mac had his eye on. We did a copy-book attack such as often practised but seldom achieved. A vertical dive with a jink halfway to line up direction and check speed, then down again to pull out and level off on the water close to the target. We seemed terribly unmasked out there in the light of our own flares. But the vertical dive did the trick as far as return fire was concerned. I looked back to see the air full of gunfire above us but we got in close with little visible reaction at our level. By the time they started with the small arms and Breda we had dropped the fish and turned away. There were some moments of suspense before we crossed the harbour wall but much of the fire trailed behind us. I saw no balloons but

I did see a hit on the target lit as it was by the flares. Nothing spectacular but nevertheless a hit. The display went on for some time behind us. I guessed the boys with the bombs had not dropped them all at once and pulled back for a second go. I wished them luck.[12]

The Italian torpedo-boat/destroyer *Aldebaran* was sunk during this attack. Following this raid bad weather over Albania and Greece again frustrated operations. Not until the night of **21/22 March** was 815 Squadron again able to launch a raid, and then just a single Swordfish was sent out to Valona. Two fighters were sighted by the crew and the sortie was aborted, although the aircraft crash-landed on returning to Paramythia. Operations thereafter were curtailed as the weather closed in once again, although allowing the crews to return to Eleusis to collect more torpedoes.

With evening on **5 April**, six Swordfish again arrived at Paramythia armed with torpedoes, but reconnaissance had shown that neither Valona nor Durazzo warranted a strike. At 19:30 therefore the six set out for an offensive sweep over the sea lanes, one aircraft carrying West Wing's Wg Cdr *Paddy* Coote as observer. Two Swordfish flew up the Italian coast to Bari, two to San Giovanni, while two patrolled between Otranto and Valona. Nothing was seen, but as the last pair returned from Valona, Lt(A) Spencer Lea's P4064 developed engine trouble and the propeller flew off. As the Swordfish was too low for the crew to bale out, Lea crash-landed in a dried-up river bed some twenty miles short of Paramythia. Although the aircraft was badly damaged, Lea and his observer were unhurt. They had however come down in a very remote area, and they were forced to trek out on foot, which would take them three days to do. By the time they reached Paramythia again they found a very different war in progress.

With darkness on **12 April**, six Swordfish (having received six replacement aircraft a few days earlier) at Paramythia were serviceable and available for renewed attacks on harbours in Albania and Italy. Five Swordfish flew down to Eleusis to exchange torpedoes for mines, preparatory to a mission to Durazzo. However rumour that the Yugoslavs had possibly captured this port from the Italians led to a last minute cancellation, and the attack was directed on Brindisi instead. At 01:30 Lt Torrens-Spence led off six aircraft, five with mines and one with a torpedo, the formation climbing up to 10,000 feet and approaching within 25 miles of the target. Heavy cloud covered the Italian coast at 6,000 feet, but a break was found and the harbour was located by its flashing lighthouse. Gliding down, the pilots saw before them a large number of ships in the roadstead; it was assumed that these were preparing for a dash across to Durazzo. L/Airman Ken Sims flying in Sub-Lt(A) Martin Rudorf's L9743/R recalled:

With torpedoes we would have had a bonanza. But what to do with mines? There was no point in putting them in the inner harbour entrance as planned.

Instead we selected a largish ship, turned over the harbour entrance and came back at her. As we did so the shore batteries woke up to our presence and opened up. Our ship looked big as we flew over her at about 100 feet. She was anchored and we dropped the mine right alongside. We hoped they would take long enough to get underway that the mine would activate as she swung in the current. We were not to know the result at the time though later I gathered it had not been effective.[13]

However Sub-Lt(A) Macaulay, flying the single torpedo-armed aircraft, launched at a tanker which was claimed as hit, one crew reporting seeing a large flash down on the water as they departed. All Swordfish landed safely at Paramythia at dawn.

On the evening of 14 April, seven Swordfish staged through Paramythia, heading for Valona at 23:50, led by Lt Torrens-Spence; all were armed with torpedoes on this occasion. In poor hazy visibility, the formation climbed to about 8,000 feet before gliding in to attack independently. Only six made the attack, for Lt(A) Spencer Lea had been forced to turn back early due to technical problems. Targets were not found where they had been expected, and all aircraft had to fly round the harbour looking for ships. Torrens-Spence found and attacked one vessel—'there was a big bang and no mistake about it', he noted—which was apparently a 7,000-ton ammunition ship. Sub-Lt(A) Doug Macaulay reported having got a strike on a merchant vessel of some 6,000 tons after Lt(A) Ian Swayne had missed it from astern. In the darkness the attacking crews overestimated the sizes of their respective targets but not the results—the steamer *Luciano*, a 3,329-ton freighter, was sunk, as was the smaller *Stampalia* (1,228 tons). Two crews failed to find targets after a 45-minute search and returned with their torpedoes, but P4137 crewed by Sub-Lts(A) Bill Sarra and Jack Bowker hit the water and crashed; they survived to become prisoners. After landing at Paramythia to refuel, the six remaining aircraft left for Eleusis at dawn on 15 April.

CHAPTER 7

The German Invasion of Yugoslavia & Greece

His [the CO's] last words were: 'The time has come, either to strike as warriors or to die!' We all separated into the night each in the general direction of his aircraft.

Lt Ivan Miklavec 215 Esk.

Throughout the operations of the winter one thought had remained paramount in British and Greek minds—the possibility of German intervention. This threat had appeared a strong eventuality from the first days of British involvement in Greece. For the hard-pressed British, it was a question of when, rather than if. Stretched to the limit, it would be very difficult to deliver and supply a force of sufficient size to counter any serious German thrust into the country. The shortage of airfields made it almost impossible in any event realistically to provide a viable level of air support to whatever force could be assembled. Yet the cause was seen to be just: the gallant Greeks be not deserted in their hour of need.

For the Greeks the situation was even more straightforward. While the Italians were seen clearly as the enemy, there was much goodwill towards the Germans. While Italy might be held at bay, and with British help even beaten, logically war with Germany could end only in one way—overwhelming defeat. Therefore, while British help for the Italian Front—particularly in the air—was of extreme importance, this should nevertheless only be accepted if it did not unduly antagonize the Germans; they obviously hoped that the Germans would not intervene.

In the event, the British appraisal was the more realistic one. They believed that the Germans would find it quite unacceptable to see their Italian allies face defeat in the Balkans. They were right; as early as 4 November, Hitler had ordered a study to be made of the problems involved in sending German troops to Greece—he had already formulated the plans for the invasion of Russia— and nothing would be allowed to stand in the way of this. By late March 1941, Hungary, Rumania and Bulgaria had fallen under German control, leaving just Yugoslavia in the way of the German military juggernaut.

For the British there was just one possibility which might stem disaster—to reach an understanding with the two most powerful Balkan states—Turkey and Yugoslavia. However, Yugoslavia was rife with internal dissent, under political pressure from the Germans, and in no mood to make commitments to lost causes. Turkey, an ally of Germany during the Great War, was anxious not to become embroiled in war either. Her forces were woefully ill-equipped and ill-prepared, and only a massive injection of material aid from Britain might possibly persuade her to consider taking sides; but this was neither available nor forthcoming. Nonetheless, diplomatic negotiations had progressed during the winter although without result.

By mid-March events were beginning to accelerate and for the Germans only one matter remained outstanding for the complete subjugation of the Balkans—Yugoslavia. Consequently, the Yugoslav government was asked to sign the Tripartite Pact. Adolf Hitler, in his speech at the Reichstag on 11 December 1941 explained:

Yugoslavia received from the Three Powers [Germany, Italy and Russia] the solemn assurance that they would not ask for assistance, and were even prepared to abstain from any transport of war materials through Yugoslavia from the very beginning. At the request of her government, Yugoslavia also received the guarantee of an outlet under Yugoslav sovereignty to the Aegean Sea, in the case of any territorial changes in the Balkans. The outlet was to include Salonika.

On 25 March, a Pact was signed in Vienna which offered the greatest possible future to the Yugoslav State, and secured peace for the Balkans at the same time. You will understand that on that day I left the beautiful city on the Danube with a truly happy feeling, not only because eight years' labour seemed to yield their reward at last, but because it appeared as if German intervention in the Balkans would be rendered unnecessary. Two day's later we were deeply shocked by the news of a coup carried out by a handful of hirelings.

I was able to take this decision all the more calmly as I could rely on the constant and immutable fidelity and friendly attitude of Bulgaria, and also of Hungary, now filled with justified indignation. Both these old Allies of the World War necessarily felt this act a provocation, coming from a State that once before had set the whole of Europe on fire and afterwards caused untold suffering to Germany, Hungary and Bulgaria.

On 27 March, I issued general operational directions to the High Command of the Armed Forces, which presented the Army and Air Force with a very different task. The march to new operational bases had to be improvised; detachments already on the spot had to be moved; supplies had to be ensured. The Air Force had to make use of numerous improvised bases, some of which were waterlogged. Without the understanding assistance of Hungary, and the thoroughly loyal attitude of Rumania, it would have been very difficult indeed to carry out the orders in the short time at our disposal. I fixed the date of attack for **6 April.**

From the start of Italy's attack on Greece, border incursions mainly by Italian aircraft had been frequent, the first on 5 November, when southern-most Yugoslav Macedonia was twice bombed with much damage to property, the death of nine persons and injury to 21 more. Yugoslav Hurricanes and Bf 109s moved to Mostar to patrol over the coastal region from Split to the Albanian border. Frequent attempts were made to intercept intruding bombers and reconnaissance aircraft during the next few months, but the only success was when a Hurricane forced a Greek Hs 126 to land near Bitolj, the crew being interned.

The RYAF was secretly mobilized on 6 March, and six days later dispersal to the auxiliary airfields began, being completed by 20 March. However, on 3 April, Major Vladimir Kren defected to Graz in Austria in a Potez 25. He had information as to the location of many of these airfields, and of the codes and cypher used by the Air Force Command, which had to be urgently changed as a result. On 5 April, the British Consul visited General Borivoja Mirković, Chief of the RYAF, to confirm what the Yugoslavs already knew—that the German attack on Belgrade would commence at 06:30 next morning.

On the eve of hostilities, the RYAF could boast in excess of 170 relatively modern bombers—Do 17Ks, SM.79s and including 62 Blenheims, and a similar number of fighters—Bf 109Es, Hurricanes and Fury biplanes—a far stronger force than the combined strength of the RAF and RHAF currently engaged against the Italians, but would prove no match for the Messerschmitts of the Luftwaffe, many flown by ace pilots. The Blenheims were operated by 1 and 8 Bombarderski Puks (Regiments), each comprising two Grupas:

1 Bombarderski Puk C/O Colonel Ferdo Gradišnik
61 Grupa C/O Major Branko Malojčić

201 Esk. (Kapt. Dragiša Nikodijević)	6 Blenheim I	Davidovac
202 Esk. (Kapt. Stevan Filipović)	5 Blenheim I	Davidovac

62 Grupa C/O Major Krsta Lozić

203 Esk. (Kapt. Teodor Pavlović)	6 Blenheim I	Bijeljina
204 Esk. (Kapt. Nikola Ivančević)	6 Blenheim I	Bijeljina

8 Bombarderski Puk C/O Colonel Stanko Diklić
68 Grupa C/O Major Lazar Donović

215 Esk. (Kapt. Vladimir Jovičić)	6 Blenheim I	Rovine
216 Esk. (Kapt. Sergije Vojinov)	6 Blenheim I	Rovine

69 Grupa C/O Major Dobrosav Tešić

217 Esk. (Kapt. Matija Petrović)	6 Blenheim I	Rovine
218 Esk. (Kapt.Vladimir Ferenčina)	5 Blenheim I	Rovine

11 Independent LR Recce Grupa C/O Major Dragomir Lazarević

21 Esk. (Kapt. Živojin Ristić)		
22 Esk. (Kapt. Ljubomir Jančić)	9 Blenheim I	Veliki Radinci

Four Blenheims of the long-range 11 Independent Grupa were despatched to attack Arad and Timişoara airfields in Rumania during the morning of **6 April**; two machines reached Arad and the other two Timşoara as separate sections. Bf 109s of III/JG54 were encountered near Arad and 3523 flown by W/Off Obrad Milićević was shot down by Hptm Arnold Lipnitz, the Gruppenkommandeur. Oblt Günther Scholz claimed the other. This was obviously the Blenheim flown by W/Off Todor Radović, the possibly-damaged aircraft being targeted by Yugoslav AA fire on return; it crashed, killing the crew.

The Blenheim section assigned to bomb Timişoara seemingly escaped damage. Sgt Josip Peršić bombed the airfield, while Kapt. Milovanović dropped his bombs on the railway station. On returning from the mission, in the region of Deta, almost 40 kilometres south from the target, the Blenheim crashed. Whether it had sustained damage during the raid is unclear. An inauspicious and costly introduction to the reality of air war.

Blenheim crews of 1Bombarderski Puk were briefed to carry out an afternoon attack on targets in Rumania. The first order for 62 Grupa was issued at 15:00 by Regiment Commander Colonel Gradišnik:

> Group is to bomb enemy's armoured and mechanized columns in the following directions: the valley of Nera River towards Bela Crkva and Timişoara—Vršac.

The crew in the first section of 203 Esk. included Major Krsta Lozić with observer Lt Velizar Vučković and gunner Sgt Terzić Mladen, first wingman was CO of 203 Esk. Kapt. Teodor Pavlović and second was Sgt Milivoje Jovanović, while 204 Esk. was led by its CO Kapt. Nikola Ivančević.

Since no movement of the enemy was detected at the target location, due to their good cover, the attack was carried out against the German motorized units' camp near Saska Banja and against the railway station in Rakadžija, as well as against several auxiliary targets. The attack was carried out by three Blenheims from 203 Esk. The Rumanians reported that only seven out of twelve released bombs exploded. This was a result of rather unpredictable detonators on 100kg *Stanković* bombs. In his combat report Major Lozić described action against the enemy as follows:

There were no enemy armoured or motorized units in this direction, nor were Germans in Bela Crkva or Vršac until 17:30. Near Saska Banja I noticed large German camp with armoured and motorized units which I bombed with both sections of 203 Esk. I didn't see my bombs explosions, but I saw fire later on. As we executed the surprise attack in one pass and rather low, the success had to follow.

Kapt. Pavlović, who did not eject all of his bombs, separated and bombed Rakidžija railway station. During the bombing itself, we received almost no enemy AA fire from the ground. While returning, we experienced machine-gun fire from our units near Bela Crkva and Vršac. The landing was carried out in dark around 19:00.

Kapt. Ivančević's Blenheim was hit twice by Yugoslav ground fire near Bela Crkva, a bullet piercing its glass nose, half a metre from observer Lt Vladimir Kink's head, while Sgt Dragoljub Stefanović's aircraft was shot twice in the wing.

The 204 Esk. section had similarly not noticed the enemy units right away, so their attack was carried out against one minor infantry/artillery column. The return flight was carried out in large U-turn across Banat. It was already dark when the aircraft, one after another, arrived and prepared for landing. Since there was no equipment for night landing on the airport, bombers arriving from all direction landed with the help of headlights of cars parked on the airfield perimeter. More by luck than judgement, the landing went through without any accident.

Meanwhile, 8 Bombarderski Puk at Rovine experienced a relatively quiet day, as Lt Ivan Miklavec, an observer with 215 Eskadrila, wrote:

Sunday, the first war day passed in take-off readiness just in case we were attacked. We loaded our planes with 100 kg bombs and with machine gun ammo. In the afternoon the first two machines took-off at 13:30 with a recon mission over Graz. They bombed a station in the way back and returned safely.[1]

68 and 69 Grupi each sent a single Blenheim to bomb the railway station at Graz in Austria. The 68 Grupa machine—of 216 Esk.—was flown by Sgt Karlo Murko (with observer Lt Ivan Pandža and air-gunner Sgt Radenko Malešević. Two Yugoslav Hurricanes from 4 Fighter Regiment located nearby provided escort; Murko reported:

Because of the murky weather we didn't fly at the prescribed height of 2,500 m but pressed down to the ground and followed some river courses and rail tracks, which led us directly to Graz. There we must climb to about 500 m for better orientation and, when we discovered the railway junction, I put my

Blenheim in a gentle dive. Three bombs went down amid the tracks and there were only one or two trains, but the fourth was a direct hit on a large two-storey building, obviously some sort of magazine.

We were convinced that no air-raid warning was given before our bombs exploded, as we could see people quietly walking the streets. There was no enemy reaction over the town although I climbed in a large circle to some 700m to observe the damage. In the low flight home I emerged over the aerodrome of Talerhof near Leibnitz crowded with Messerschmitts and Stukas. Some Me109s scrambled after me, but only one was persistent enough to catch me when I was already over our own territory. After one short burst of his guns, this adversary also turned for home, and I returned safely to Rovine, where my mechanics found only two small holes in the tail surfaces.[2]

Lt Ivan Miklavec continued:

At 5 o'clock in the afternoon we received the order for take-off, but regretfully for tomorrow. Kommander Jovičić explained the mission for us, we were to bomb road and railway bridges around Klagenfurt. Jovičić surprised us by saying: "We don't have much ammunition, but we will use the one we got the best we can. To make sure the bombing is accurate and to avoid enemy fighters I suggest that we attack at 300m. Do you agree?" We all accepted the dare suggestion. At 20:30 we were surprised by another mission order, the first was called off. We were to bomb the railway section and station Feldbach in Austria. Take off before dawn; we were to meet at the airfield at 3 o'clock in the morning. So tomorrow is the day...[3]

The next day, **7 April**, witnessed intense action by the Yugoslav Blenheims, with resulting severe losses. The focus of activity on the ground remained in the south, where the Luftwaffe directed most of its attention in support of the northern-most of the columns penetrating Macedonia. During the afternoon these troops would reach the Vardar.

At Bijeljina airfield at 01:00, Colonel Ferdo Gradišnik, commander of 1 Bombarderski Puk, briefed his men:

Attack the enemy's armoured and motorized columns on the route: Kiustendil—Kriva Palanka—Stracin—Kumanovo. The attack is to be executed at dawn.

Owing to the worsening weather conditions, the plan was for one section with three Blenheims to carry out offensive reconnaissance followed by the entire group. The section of three from 204 Esk. was personally designated by Major Krsta Lozić, who took Lt Velizar Vučković as observer and Sgt Mladen Terzić as gunner, while the wingmen were flying instructor and the best pilot in the group, Sgt Živan Jovanović, with observer Lt Branko Glumac and gunner Sgt Bogdan Zečević, and pilot Sgt Milan Pavlović with observer 1/Lt Đorđe Stefanović and gunner Flt Sgt Stevan Vojnić.

When above Vranje, Major Lozić, content with weather conditions, issued the order that others from the group were to be informed of favourable weather conditions and that sections prepared for the attack were to take-off immediately. Of the initial attack he reported:

> When I was at Kozjak mountain above Bojkovica, I noticed on the road from Stracin to Kriva Palanka one armoured motorized column around 15–20 kilometres long. I gave signal to wingmen to prepare for the attack. I continued eastward to Kozjak slopes hiding between some reefs. In front of Kriva Palanka I turned towards the west. I aimed at road. Both of my wingmen followed me in a column by one. I gave command to my observer to drop the bombs on the column. When the observer Lt Vučković ejected the first bomb I was hit from downside. One bullet penetrated the glass in front of me. As I thought that Vučković ejected all the bombs, I abruptly turned away from the road.
>
> While turning I saw the result of my wingmens' bombs, right at the moment when one bomb hit the truck with men inside and blew it up. I didn't see the result of my bombs. In that moment Vučković told me that he hadn't released all the bombs but that he had three 100kg bombs and eight 10kg bombs left. I was very angry with him since now I was expected to turn back to the column, and at that moment under Stracin itself I saw enemy armoured vehicles waiting on a square surface 800–1000 metres left and right from the road. I instantly directed to them and in front of me I saw horrifying AA gunfire which made real firework with all its inflammable flashing bullets.
>
> There was no turning back, I passed that barrage, Vučković dropped bombs from 150 metres altitude, I manoeuvred in terms of direction and slightly in terms of altitude to avoid fire, but still I had almost 50 machine-gun hits and around 10 small grenades [cannon holes] in my plane, when I distanced a bit while turning I saw Sgt Živojin Jovanović shooting with his machine-guns. According to recollections of Sgt Pavlović and late Sgt Jovanović Žika, my bombs fell in the group of tanks and soldiers and caused grave loss to the enemy. When I distanced from the enemy a bit, I ordered to radio-telegrapher to inform my sections on enemy position, and he told me that one small grenade [cannon shell] damaged the radio.
>
> Behind Stracin I noticed seven Ju 87s. These planes didn't notice me, but they dove onto the road, probably on one Yugoslav battery that operated. At around 09:30 I landed on Bijeljina airport. Upon my return, I noticed that our Do 17s operated against this column.

In spite of their efforts, it seems that none of eight crews from 69 Grupa managed to find the target. They returned to the base dropping the bombs on their way on bombing Lonjsko Polje which was one of the heavily bombed targets that day. Many locations were bombed both inside and outside the operational zone of 215 Esk. and 216 Esk., even targets in the area of Hungary bordering with Austria. A railway train was also attacked while moving near Alsószölnök in Hungary, and the locomotive was damaged. The bomber was mistaken by the Hungarians for an SM.79. A railroad in Szentgotthárd, Körmend, as well as a similar target in Kelebia were also bombed, all in Hungarian territory.

The order to attack targets in Hungary—specifically the airfields at Szeged and Pécs, from where the Luftwaffe was operating—had been issued in the evening hours of 6 April, at around 21:00. However, due to sabotage of the Ustaša elements inside 2 Liaison Centre in Zagreb (Croatia), it was not delivered before **7 April**, at about 10:00. The delay resulted in heavy losses to the Blenheims of 8 Bombarderski Puk over Hungarian territory.

Of the eight Blenheims of 68 Grupa that set out for Szeged, four were shot down by Bf 109s of 5./JG54, two by Staffelkapitän Oblt Hubert Mütherick (his 9th and 10th victories), and one each by Ltn Wolfgang Späte and Ltn Josef Pöhs (his 8th). Among the Blenheims lost to fighter attack were those flown by the Grupa CO, Major Lazar Donović, and the CO of 216 Esk., Kapt. Sergije Vojinov. Before his demise, the gunner aboard Vojinov's aircraft, Sgt Ilija Mraković, apparently managed to hit one of the attacking Messerschmitts, since it was damaged and forced-landed a mile from Srpski Krstur in Hungarian territory; the pilot was uninjured. A third Blenheim, flown by Lt Radomir Lazaravić of 216 Esk., also fell to the Bf 109s, as did Sgt Vladimir Ferant's aircraft of 218 Esk. Although his crew were killed outright, Ferant apparently survived his injuries until 13 April.

In addition to the victories claimed by pilots of 5./JG54, the Blenheim flown by Sgt Viktor Grdović of 215 Esk. was shot down by a Bf 110 from I/ZG26 over Szöreg, close to Szeged. Again, there were no survivors. Two more Blenheims fell to AA fire, that flown by CO of 215 Esk., Kapt Vladimir Jovičić (all lost), but Lt Ivan Miklavec and his crew were fortunate. Of this tragic day, he graphically recalled:

> We all woke up at 3 o'clock in the morning. In the dark backyard splashes of water were heard, the well pump was quickly filling the buckets with water for refreshment. A bus drove us from the village to the airfield in pitch darkness carefully following the blackout regulations. At the airfield, Kommander Jovičić repeated the mission, refreshed all agreements and we all started to dress for the flight. We didn't get any meteorological report. At 4 o'clock in the morning we were ordered: "To positions! Start the engines!" A quick salute to the CO. His last words were: "The time has come, either to strike as warriors or to die!" We all separated into the night each in the general direction of his aircraft.

The mechanic with his soldiers was already there. The formation was starting their engines, the noise was tremendous. I checked my aircraft, walking around it with a flashlight. I was stunned; the lower wing surface had multiple bayonet-made holes. So, sabotage ... I didn't notice any other damage, so I didn't report it. I thought that I could do it after the mission. I also checked the four bombs and unscrewed the igniters half a turn each. I presumed we would have to fly low. When I entered the cockpit I found out that somebody broke the clock in the aircraft. I didn't have the time to find out who did it so I borrowed a wrist watch from the first man who walked past.

One by one all of our 28 [*sic*, 23] aircraft took-off in pitch-dark; only a small signal light blinked the take-off command in one minute intervals. I counted the take-offs ... five ... six ... seven ... we were number ten. But where is my pilot? I am waiting. He should have been here minutes ago. Mechanic leans out of the cockpit and asks the closest solider if he has seen him. Nothing ... number eight is already rolling ... I order the mechanic to close the cabin, we will fly alone. I check both engines again, everything is OK. Then I hear knocking on the cabin. The pilot [Sgt Dragiša Baralić] boards the plane in the nick of time. The cabin is closed again. I am looking for the light signal. Here it is! Let's go.

An unpleasant felling of dampness surrounds us at 700m. I quickly notice the first meteorological information-clouds. I order the pilot to climb, because we are flying above 600m high mountains, and my map is telling me we are flying towards even higher mountains. My pencil marks the already flown path of our Blenheim. The pilot asks me where we are. I answer him: Varazdin is to the right. Our altitude is 1,500m. It will be dawn soon, and I think we are flying in upper cloud levels so I order to climb to 1,700m. The success is obvious as we break the clouds. I am scanning the sky to spot the others who took-off before us. Far below us I spot a white dot—it's a plane. We are quickly catching him, I recognize him he is one of ours! We are closing in, I want to see the commander, but the aeroplane signals us the sign.

Watch it! It waggles its wings and makes a U-turn and flies back from where it came from. When he disappears I start to wonder. Did they receive the command for return? Was it the weather? Without the radio receiver I didn't get the answer to any of those questions. Soon after we cross the border my mechanic [Sgt Velimir Grdović] shakes my shoulder and screams. There are two fighters in combat above us, one of them is ours. In a moment we lose sight of them. We have reached our target, far below us, in the valley surrounded by hills but we don't see it, it is hidden by the cloud base, our recon won't do us much good. I calculated another six minutes before we make the U-turn. We start to sink in the clouds; we are waiting for results of our cloud breaking if I miscalculated. We dive to only 400m. Then we break through; first we see something dark brown, then fields, then houses. We fly over a road at 300m. Raindrops are banging on the windshield and are obscuring my sight. I notice some dark transport vehicles driving south; we are going that way too. Feldbach must be somewhere on the right side. I am looking for the railway. I set the bombsight, triggers, electric button. We passed over the road again, we still don't see the railway; then a bright line flashes—a river; a bridge bonds both sides with a road. I show the bridge to the pilot. We fly over the river and make a turn.

Another glance to the bombsight, I press the button, the plane climbs a little and makes the turn. The old bridge is gone only a couple of beams are left. 100m ahead two transport cars stopped, they won't get over the bridge! Then the valley closes in, then opens up again. Look there is the Feldbach station, we fly over the station at 200m, no traffic, no defence, they even removed the station's name. I press the button and the second bomb parts from the aircraft. After the turn we notice a full hit on the tracks and railway crossing. After a while my mechanic screams: "Aeroplane!" and shows me a little dot on the right. When we close in to 300m and recognize the shape, the yellow band, the black cross ... no doubt Stuka!!! "Machine-gun!" a yell to the mechanic who is already in the machine-gun turret. We close in to 30m and they spot us. In that moment our machine-gun sings it's mortal song—three salvos 50 bullets each, and the Stuka rolls over an disappears in the clouds. First victory ... We won't be taken easily. We fly over a 900m high hill, then we spot barracks; lots of them, then a warehouse, then a railway, more barracks. I drop the fourth bomb on this establishment. I later found out I bombed a wings assembly plant in Wiener Neustadt. When I was ready to order the plane back I saw a main road leading to Vienna. I dropped my last bomb there.

Then my mechanic screams—"Enemy fighters!" I turn around, yes four fighters on our tail. I order the pilot to climb into the clouds a turn right then after a minute a turn left to previous direction. I quickly calculate the heading from Vienna to Maribor. We turn our trusty Blenheim in that direction. Then we literally fall out of a cloud and we see the Wiener Neustadt airfield full of aircraft. The temptation was just too great so we made a low pass, our machine-guns spitting death. Then came the flak ... but the worst was yet to come—we had to fly over a hill 900m high and we were flying at 300m. We have to make a circle to gain height over the airfield, and the flak was ready for us. We took multiple hits and escaped in the clouds. It is getting lighter. I suddenly heard the engines coughing and spitting. I check the gasoline level ... 30 litres ... the pilot immediately cuts down the throttle to save gas. What now? We had 400 litres seven minutes ago; the fuel tanks must be hit. The pilot and mechanic ask me: "Shall we jump?" "No! Steer 30° to the left!" I choose to crash-land because our Yugoslavian-made Blenheims didn't have the emergency hatch. Our CO had a simple explanation: "No jumping. These machines cost 5 million dinars each!"

We gave up hope to reach Yugoslavian soil. Only 400m left we break the cloud base and start looking for a place to land. There on the left below that hill, a crash-landing is possible only there. We will plug our nose in, but we have no choice, pilot pulls out the flaps, and I the gears. We are flying with speed 230kmh. The wheels absorb a strong blow, full throttle, the earth bounces. I am not strapped in so I grab for my harness at the last second, a nose blow, the cabin crashes; I am thrown out of the seat. I don't know how long we just lay there, not unconscious but we just lay there. We crawl from our positions and we check if everybody is all right. We climb on the wing and we pet our giant Blenheim N° 25 [3525] which saved our lives with his destruction.[4]

Miklavec and his crew were subsequently taken prisoner. They were fortunate, since there would be no survivors from the other six 68 Grupa Blenheims shot down on this mission. Only one Blenheim returned, that flown by Sgt Karlo Murko, which landed at Rovine with its nose plexiglas completely shattered.

Meanwhile, Blenheims of 69 Grupa were tasked to attack airfields at Pecs in Hungary, had also suffered casualties. The unit commander Major Dobrosav Tešić (flying 3505[5]) was shot down by Bf 109s over Pecs, while the CO of 215 Esk., Kapt Nikola Ivancevič's aircraft fell to AA fire. There were no survivors from either aircraft. Two more forced-landed due to AA damage, Sgt Živan Jovanović of 203 Esk. at Bijeljina, and W/Off Branislav Majstorović in 3544 of 201 Esk. at Davidovac, while two Blenheims of 204 Esk. also crash-landed due to AA damage, each with a wounded pilot: Sgt Đuro Ratković at Kraljevo airfield, and Sgt Dragoslav Ilić at Kosovo, while another (Sgt Rudolf Dunjko) landed at Novi Sad when it ran out of fuel. The returning crews claimed hits on the airfields attacked, but in reality little damage had been inflicted.

Bad weather curtailed much operational flying next day (**8 April**), although it did little to deter the ground intrusion into Yugoslavia and now Greece by elements of the German *12th Armee*, the latter advancing on Thessalonika. But of greater immediate danger to the Yugoslavs was the route taken by the northern thrust, which now swung north from Skoplje through the Kacanik Gorge towards Kosovo Polje, and up a parallel valley north of Kumanovo towards Bujanovac and the Morava river valley.

In spite of the weather conditions, all bomber, and even some nearby fighter units of the RYAF were ordered to attack the intruding ground units including Blenheims of 61 and 62 Grupa joined by those from 11 Independent Grupa, all aircraft tasked to attack eight miles of closely-packed and heavily protected convoys. In the event, the Blenheims of 62 Grupa encountered the severest flak, the first trio being led by Colonel Ferdo Gradišnik, the Puk commander. Lt Branko Glumac, observer in the second aircraft flown by Sgt Milan Simin, later reported:

Colonel Gradišnik, at the sight of numerous tanks on the Skoplje-Kumanovo road, pressed his Blenheim even lower in the drizzle, which obscured visibility to about 500m. I saw one of his bombs going down and exploding, but at practically the same moment violent flames erupted from the starboard wing fuel tank of his Blenheim. A few seconds later, also from the port wing flames erupted and the Blenheim crash-landed beside the road. In the next second we were over it, but our gunner [Sgt Bogdan] Zečević saw the Blenheim explode.

However, although the Colonel and his pilot, Sgt Živan Jovanović, were killed, the gunner Sgt Dobrilo Terzić got out with his clothes on fire and rolled in the wet grass at the feet of some astonished German soldiers as he sought to extinguish the flames. He survived to be taken prisoner. Shortly before the Blenheim hit the ground, 3510 flown by W/Off Vasilije Mirović had fallen in flames—also victim of the guns—with the loss of its crew.

The next two sections from 62 Grupa failed to find the target owing to the cloudy conditions although they attacked with some success, while aircraft of 61 Grupa were even more successful, encountering slightly improved weather that allowed them to attack and escape without severe damage. They were followed by a further four Blenheims from 11 Independent Grupa, which attacked one of the German columns north of Kumanovo. The aircraft flown by Kapt. Živomir Petrović from 21 Esk. (3547) was shot down with all on board being killed, while a second Blenheim from 22 Esk. became lost (Lt Jŕnićije Korać) and landed at 61 Grupa's airfield at Davidovac.

The *12th Armee* column threatening southern Macedonia advanced through Tetovo and Prilep towards Bitolj on **9 April**, this thrust and that on Niš receiving most Luftwaffe support on this date. During the morning snow fell in Serbia and Macedonia, the Blenheims of 61 Grupa at Davidovac being grounded by a ten-inch fall.

Next day (**10 April**), saw German *12th Armee* elements enter Bitolj and the fighting in Yugoslavian Macedonia neared its end. As German aircraft from airfields in Austria, Rumania and Hungary swept over the northern areas, the situation at Davidovac became serious as German forces entered Paraćin, only a mile or so away. Despite fog and soft snow, all Blenheims on the airfield took off. Of ten 61 Grupa aircraft, one crashed at the end of the runway, although the crew survived unhurt. Less fortunate was the crew of the 11 Independent Grupa Blenheim that had landed at Davidovac two days earlier; as the pilot lifted the aircraft off the ground the Blenheim stalled and all four on board were killed in the crash that followed (beside the crew of Lt Korać/Lt Dragomir Dobrović/Flt Sgt DušanVukčević, mechanic Sgt Medveščak died as well). The ten remaining 61 Grupa machines meanwhile successfully reached Bijeljina, some 150 miles away, undertaking the whole flight at an altitude of only 80 feet. At Bijeljina they joined forces with 62 Grupa.

Bf 110s attacked Bijeljina on the following day (**11 April**), destroying several aircraft on the ground including one Blenheim. The attack was repeated next morning (**12 April**) at 07:30, when three Staffeln of Bf 110s of I/ZG26 swept in at low level, undertaking three strafing passes. Ten Blenheims of 1 Bombarderski Puk and five of 11 Independent Grupa were destroyed, as were many trainers. Just two Blenheims remained airworthy, and they were at once ordered off to make their escape to Sokolac airfield in Bosnia; there they were strafed by Mc.200s of 359ᵃ Squadriglia, 22° Gruppo whilst landing at Podgorica airfield in Montenegro. Sgt Ilija Ivanović's aircraft was hit while still in the air, but neither crew was hurt, only shaken. Just five or six airworthy Blenheims of the 8 Bombarderski Puk remained at Rovine and these were ordered to fly to Nikšić, but most of these were destroyed at Rovine by their crews and not a single machine reached Nikšić.

However, three Blenheims did succeed in escaping the destruction, including 3516 of 22 Esk. that defected to Hungary in the hands of Sgt Stjepan Rudić with two mechanics, Sgt Sava Šuković and Sgt Vladimir Molnar. As Croat nationals, Rudić and Molnar were released from internment and later joined the newly founded Independent Croatia Air Force; the fate of Šuković remains unknown.

The other two Blenheims, flown by Kapt. Đorde Putica of 217 Esk. and Kapt. Matija Petrović, CO of 218 Esk. both landed in Croatian territory, the former in a corn field near Auguštinovac, while Petrovic landed close to Zagreb; probably at Borongaj airfield. Both aircraft were pressed into Croat service. Yet one more Blenheim, 3533 of 1 Bombarderski Puk with two escaping pilots on board, Sgt Danilo Dejić and Sgt Dušan Jovanović, was damaged by RN ships over Preveza and crashed-landed near Yannina; the crew was unhurt.

CHAPTER 8

Blenheims' Greek Nemesis

*Preceded by a terrified assortment of stray dogs racing across the landing ground,
the 110 destroyers hit Menidi. Bellies scraping the grass, they flashed past as if
propelled by the rhythmic thumping of their cannons.*

LAC Marcel Comeau 11 Squadron

While the Yugoslavs were staggering under the initial German blows on **6
April**, the first moves against Greece were also underway. There had at least
been a declaration of war, the German Ambassador in Athens, Prinz Erbach-
Schönberg, presenting an appropriate note to the Hellenic government at 05:30
that morning, at which time the first troops crossed the Bulgarian borders to
begin the assault on Salonika and north-east Greece generally. One of the
Hurricane pilots of 33 Squadron at Larissa recalled:

> We heard the news before dawn, got up, washed in freezing water and dressed.
> Everyone was tense; our feelings and thoughts were confused—what was going
> to happen now? Our army was on the retreat in Egypt; the Greeks were only just
> managing to hold the Italians back in Albania; had we sufficient British troops
> to hold the Germans in Greece? What was going to happen in the air? While we
> had sufficient to cope with the Italians, surely we were going to be hopelessly
> outnumbered by the Germans? For weeks past we had heard of colossal German
> air forces forming up in Bulgaria. What were we in for? Little did we know![1]

33 Squadron's first encounter with Bf 109s later that afternoon resulted in
a resounding victory, shooting down no fewer than four Messerschmitts of
8./JG27 for no loss, while further south a Hurricane pilot of 80 Squadron shot
down a reconnaissance Ju 88 of 2.(F)/123. A Blenheim of 113 Squadron was sent
out to search for signs of the crew but without success. 32 Mira carried out its
first operation against the Germans, bombing enemy positions in the area of Lin,
north of Pogradec in order to help the Serbian troops who were moving to the
south, trying to meet the Greek ones. All Blenheims returned safely. As night fell
Blenheims of 84 Squadron attacked a railway station 50 miles south of Sofia in

Bulgaria, and others from 113 Squadron raided Petrich. Two of the latter, L9338 flown by Sgt Vic McPherson, and T2168 (Sgt Ken Price) crash-landed at Niamata on return. The latter aircraft had been hit by AA shrapnel in the fuselage, and all three crewmen were slightly injured in the crash-landing.

Activity over Greece was more limited on **7 April**, as the Luftwaffe continued to concentrate its main efforts over Yugoslavia, but the RAF was busy, formations of Blenheims going out to attack German columns inside Yugoslavia, often bombing with telling effect. One such attack by nine aircraft from 11 Squadron was escorted by a dozen Hurricanes early in the afternoon, three more of the unit's Blenheims returning to attack similar targets east of Strumica later in the day, this time with an escort of two Hurricanes. Only T2342 crewed by Sqn Ldr Stevens, Flt Sgt Frank Mason and Sgt Jim Winslip, found the target and bombed from 3,500 feet; all the others returned due to bad weather.

During the morning of **8 April**, eight Blenheims of 11 Squadron again took off to attack targets in the Strumica region, but T2247 crashed on take-off, seriously injuring the pilot, Plt Off. Coombs while Sgt Randall, the observer, was also hurt. The other aircraft were forced to return by bad visibility. 84 Squadron's inexperienced CO, Sqn Ldr *Jonah* Jones and his crew, survived a forced landing in bad weather when attempting to take a short cut through cloud, thinking that he could fly between two hills only to find no valley. He climbed desperately. Just scraping a ridge before managing to regain control and carry out a force-landing at Kereechori. He and his crew escaped with cuts and bruises but Z5897 was damaged beyond repair.

On the ground all was far from well for the Allies. While the Greeks had again attacked on the Epirus Front on **9 April**, that same day armoured units of the German *XVII Armee Gruppe* had entered Salonika despite sustained resistance by three Greek divisions under General Bacopoulos, and next day all fighting in Eastern Macedonia would come to an end. In Yugoslavia the Panzers were slicing through the defences everywhere. Bad weather again prevented any worthwhile bomber operations and restricted fighter activity. At Eleusis meanwhile a Blenheim IV arrived from Egypt via Crete, together with six new Hurricanes, for which it had been navigating.

By night 30 Squadron Blenheim IFs stood at readiness at Eleusis, one being ordered off at 05:20 on **10 April** to intercept an aircraft held in the searchlights at 8,000 feet over Athens. Identifying it as a Ju 88, Flt Sgt Don Innes-Smith attacked, but his opponent dived away rapidly, the rear-gunner returning fire and obtaining a single hit on the Blenheim. An unconfirmed report was subsequently received that an aircraft had crashed near Scaramanga Bay. A reconnaissance Ju 88 of 1.(F)/122 was reported missing, but recorded as 'south of Crete'.

Shortly thereafter, 84 Squadron's Plt Off. John Eldred and his crew—Sgts Adam Loudon and Jack Acres—were briefed to fly a special mission to Sarajevo in T2164. They were to transport a Greek General carrying secret British

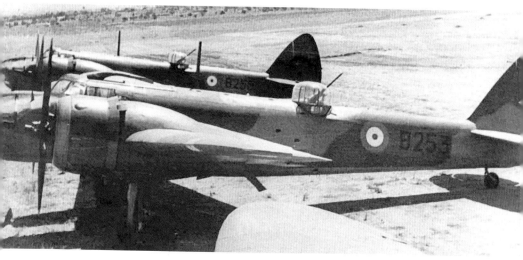

Pristine 32 Mira Blenheims after arrival in Greece, with B253 nearest the camera (B258 in background).

B253's fate, having been badly damaged in combat by three CR42s on 14 November 1940 (air gunner wounded). It was not repaired, and eventually destroyed by strafing Bf109s and Bf110s.

32 Mira's B268.

Capt. Panhayotis Orphandis was killed in B252 following a take-off accident on 30 December 1940.

Observer Sgt Matthaios Tsolakidis was k in action when his B263 was shot down G.50 on 11 March 1941.

Bombs for Mira's B252.

32 Mira crewmembers Touliatos and Vogiatzakis posing with 100 lb bombs. (*via Georgios Sakkis*)

Ground crew of 32 Mira pose for the photographer.

'One of ours?' Probably the observer and air-gunner of a 32 Mira Blenheim.

Major Moschovinos with other officers of 32 Mira (*MISPA*)

Crew members of 32 Mira posing with bombs at Vasiliki airfield. (*via Oikonomou family*)

Tenente Livio Bassi of 395ª Squadriglia was credited with six victories including two Blenheims, one of 30 Squadron, the other 211 Squadron, before he was shot down and seriously wounded on 20 February 1941, and died six weeks later.

A fine study of a pair of G.50s of 372ª Squadriglia.

Cap. Piergiuseppe Scarpetta of 395ᵃ Squadriglia was credited with six victories including two Blenheims in February 1941.

Cap. Nicola Magaldi of 364ᵃ Squadriglia claimed a Blenheim on 7 November 1940, but was shot down and killed later in the month.

Sgt Luigi Spallacci of 355ᵃ Squadriglia was killed in action 11 March 1941 following combat in which he may have claimed a Blenheim. He was granted an immediate posthumous *Medaglia d'Oro al Valor Militare.*

40-year-old Chief Petty Officer (Mechanic) Ruggero Slongo (Ludovico's grandfather) was lost on 28 March 1941 aboard the Italian cruiser *Fiume.*

Plt Off. Dickie Bird and his 84 Squadron crew aboard L1385 survived to become prisoners of war following their forced-landing in a dried-up river bed at Devoli on 28 November 1940.

Z.506B of 191ª Squadriglia RM was forced down by 30 Squadron Blenheim IFs on 22 February 1941, and was shot-up and capsized next day by a Gladiator as it attempted to take-off after repair.

Plt Off. Arthur Geary (standing) with Sqn Ldr Gordon-Finlayson, Plt Off. Curly Fabian (IO) and Flg Off. Alan Godfrey, all 211 Squadron. (*Wings over Olympus*)

Plt Off. Eric Bevington-Smith, Sqn Ldr Gordon-Finlayson, Plt Off. Herby Herbert and Flt Lt Buck Buchanan, all of 211 Squadron, converse with a young Greek friend at Paramythia. (*Wings over Olympus*)

L1391/VA-J *Doughnut Doris* of 84 Squadron at Menidi. (*Scorpions Sting*).

Back from Bousi, left to right: Unknown, Sqn Ldr Tommy Wisdom, Flg Off. Alan Godfrey and Sgt Jack Wainhouse. (*Wings over Olympus*)

Valona—target for today!
And almost every day
when weather permitted.

Two Greek airmen converse with returning 30 Squadron aircrew.

K7095/VT-G of 30 Squadron at Paramythia.

211 Squadron Blenheim being prepared for the next sortie.

Back from Corfu: 211 Squadron's Sqn Ldr Gordon-Finlayson and Plt Off. Arthur Geary. (*Wings over Olympus*)

211 Squadron's L143
Paramythia.

211 Squadron's UQ-▮
at Paramythia. (*Bris*
Aeroplane Co.)

211 Squadron's UQ-▮
at Paramythia. (*Bris*
Aeroplane Co.)

Eric Childs of 30 Squadron was lost on ovember 1940 when L1120 was shot n by a CR42.

Flg Off. Bert Blackmore, a New Zealander with 30 Squadron.

A 30 Squadron observer preparing to board K7095/VT-G. (*Bristol Aeroplane Co.*)

30 Squadron's Flg Off. Bud Richardson, wearing his ice hockey top, with Flt Lt Bob Davidson. (*Bristol Aeroplane Co.*)

USAAF observers in Greece, Colonel G. C. Bower and Major Demas Craw, converse with Flg Off. Bud Richardson, Flt Lt Bob Davidson and Flt Lt Al Bocking, Canadians with 30 Squadron. (*Bristol Aeroplane Co.*)

211 Squadron stalwarts. *Above left:* Canadian Flg Off. Ken Dundas; *Above right:* observer Sgt Cyril 'Nobby' Clark; *Below:* Flg Off. Duke Delaney nursing an Italian dud. (*Wings over Olympus*)

Sgt Herbert 'Lofty' Lord (later Flt Lt DFC) 30 Squadron air gunner.

Sqn Ldr Gordon-Finlayson of 211 Squadron.

Sqn Ldr 'Jonah' Jones, CO of 84 Squadron, with Press Officer Sqn Ldr Tommy Wisdom. (*Wings over Olympus*)

84 Squadron's K7096/VA-0 shortly before take-off. (*Bristol Aeroplane Co.*)

Final checks! (*Bristol Aeroplane Co.*)

New Zealander Flg Off Buck Buchanan of 211 Squadron in the Valley of Fairy Tales (Paramythia). (*Wings over Olympus*)

The Percival Q.6 G-AFMV flown by Wg Cdr Lord Forbes during his 'clandestine' adventures in Greece. (*via Andy Thomas*)

Lt(A) Owen Oxley's 815 Squadron Swordfish P4071/M following a mishap at Paramythia.

19-year-old Plt Off. Travers Allison (known as 'Pee-Wee') of 30 Squadron, shared with a Hurricane in shooting down a Ju88 of I/LG1 over Athens on 15 April 1941.

On 24 April 1941, Plt Off. Lawrence Basan of 30 Squadron shot down a Ju88 of I/LG1 that had previously been damaged by a Sea Gladiator of 805 Squadron off the coast of Crete.

Observer Plt Off. Joe Strong of 30 Squadron saw much action over Greece and off Crete.

British Secretary of State for Foreign Affairs Mr Anthony Eden on his arrival at Menidi on 22 February 1941, greeting a sergeant of 30 Squadron with Sqn Ldr Percy Milward, the CO, in the background. (*Wings over Olympus*)

Flt Lt Tom Horgan had flown Blenheim ops in the UK and Malta before joining 30 Squadron in Greece. Awarded the DFC, he converted to Hurricanes and commanded 80 Squadron before being shot down and seriously wounded in November 1941.

Plt Off Steven Paget of 30 Squadron fell victim to a G.50 while flying L8463 on 18 December 1940

Flt Lt Derek Walker also later flew Hurricanes and gained two victories; later awarded the DFC, but was killed in a flying accident postwar. (*Wings over Olympus*)

Sgt Jock Ratlidge carried out many bombing missions while in Greece, but found his *forte* as a Hurricane pilot in the desert, gaining three victories before his own death. (*Flat Out*)

On 5 April 1941, L4833 of 84 Squadro crashed on the edge of Menidi airfield o return from a sortie to Elbasan. Canadia pilot Flt Lt Bob Towgood suffered fatal injuries when a propeller blade penetrated the cock

The cockpit of Flt Lt Bob Towgood's Blenheim shows where propeller bla penetrated.

Two Blenheims of I Squadron suffered AA damage during raid in the early ho of 7 April 1941, and both crash-landed Niamata. The crew Sgt Ken Price's T21 (nearest camera) w all slightly injured, while those aboard Vic McPherson's LS survived unscathed

Lt Radomir Lazarević's Blenheim of 216 Esk was shot down by Bf109s near Szeged on 7 April 1941; the crew were killed and the wreck displayed in Szeged's central square. (*George Pynka via Aleks Ognjević*)

Sgt Karlo Murko (left) and his crew of 216 Esk. (*Milan Micevski via Aleks Ornjević*)

Burnt-out Yugoslav Blenheim after attack by Bf110s of I/ZG26 on 12 April 1941 (*Milan Micevski via Aleks Ornjević*)

Blenheim 3516 defected to Hungary on 12 April 1941 flown by Sgt Stjepan Rudić of 22 Esk. (*George Pynka via Aleks Ognjević*)

Remains of a Greek Blenheim at Larissa and the arrival of the new occupants—Bf109s of III/JG27.

A Ju88 leaves on a sortie from its new Greek airfield, passing over the remains of one of the Greek Blenheims, which exhibits evidence of a fighter strafe.

Above and below: Sad remains of 11 Squadron's YH-K and YH-R.
(*via Martin Goodman*)

The aftermath—German airmen inspect AD-V of 113 Squadron, and VA-C of 84 Squadron. (*via Martin Goodman*)

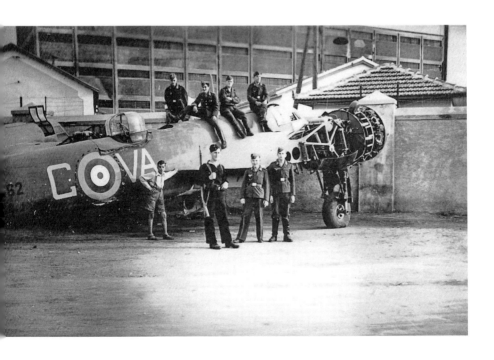

Sgt Tony Ovens of 30 Squadron. On evacuating Crete, he converted to Hurricanes and was killed in April 1942 during the Japanese attack on Ceylon. (*via Bill Gair Jnr*)

Sgt Bill Gair, 30 Squadron observer, loading his automatic in preparation for the defence Maleme against the forthcoming invasion, was evacuated beforehand. (*via Bill Gair Jn*

Sergeants three! Tony Ovens and Bill Gair flank an unidentified pilot as part of Crete's ground defence, though not required. (*via Bill Gair Jnr*)

...quadron's Marcel
...eau, author of *Operation*
...cury and winner of the
...ary Medal.

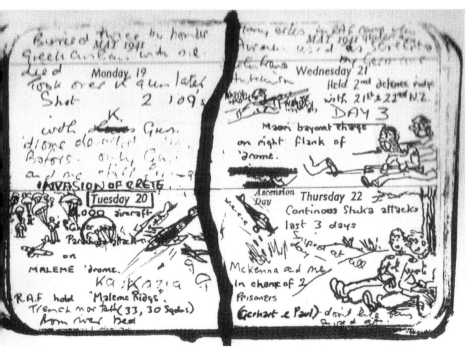

Marcel Comeau retained his sense of humour while at Crete, as witnessed by
pages from his diary.

German troops pile up ammunition boxes in front of the engineless abandoned 30 Squadron Blenheim, K7177/VT-N. Note the wing of a Ju52 immediately behind that of the British aircraft, and another of these transports in the background.

The remains of K7177 were still to be seen at Maleme the following year (1942) together with wrecks and parts of Ju52s.

documents with details of a planned attack by Greek and Yugoslav forces against the Germans. Sgt Loudon later wrote:

We took off at dawn in a snowstorm … when nearing the Albania/Yugoslav border, the weather conditions were so bad our pilot decided to make a landing in a field, which I think was an airfield under construction at a place called Bar in Yugoslavia. Just prior to landing, I strapped the general into my seat and I knelt on the floor of the aircraft in readiness for the landing, but we had failed to see a nine-foot wide water filled trench, covered with green scum. I assumed it had been dug to prevent enemy aircraft landing. On landing the aircraft's undercarriage went into the ditch and all I could remember after the crash, since I passed out for a time, was fighting for breath, a strong smell of petrol, struggling to get out of the aircraft and dropping over the side onto the bank of a ditch. After releasing my parachute harness, I passed out.[2]

Some villagers carried Loudon unconscious to the house of a woman called Madame Kralovic who tended to his wounds as best as she could before arranging for him to be sent to hospital in Cetingji. The General was also slightly injured. An army lorry took them to Saravejo from where a seaplane of 3 Hidrogrupa flew the general and Sgt Loudon to hospital. The General was soon released and was flown to Greece aboard a Yugoslav Do 17K on 14 April. Loudon, however, had temporarily lost the use of his legs, and whilst in hospital he received a visit from some of the British Legation staff from Belgrade; the latter had organised an evacuation by a Sunderland aircraft of 230 Squadron from the Yugoslav Naval Base at Kotor, but when Loudon and Acres arrived they saw the aircraft take off without them: amongst the 44 evacuees only Plt Off. Eldred was on board. Loudon and Acres were given civilian suits and were informed to be prepared to be evacuated the following day on a destroyer. The warship did not arrive—but the Italians did.

Weather yet again prevented much activity, but during the early afternoon nine Blenheims from 84 Squadron got through to attack columns on the Prilep-Bitolj road. One aircraft was slightly damaged by AA fire. At 15:30 five Blenheim IFs of 30 Squadron took off to strafe the same road, while ten Blenheims from 11 Squadron escorted by a number of 33 Squadron Hurricanes headed for this same target, and four more Hurricanes from 80 Squadron made for Bitolj itself. Sqn Ldr Milward led his fighter-Blenheims in a successful attack which was believed to have caused much damage, but the main formation was set upon by a number of Bf 109s and Bf 110s. Cloud provided cover prevented losses being suffered. Sgt Geoff Chapman, air-gunner in Flt Lt Horgan's aircraft (L8398), recalled:

Soon after we reached our operational height we spotted a formation of three aircraft approaching us head-on, or so it seemed. As they got closer we could see that they were Ju 88s. We watched them and they watched us as we passed one another at about 500 yards. Such was the discipline of the RAF and the Luftwaffe, I imagine, requiring the appointed tasks to be carried out regardless of any distractions!

We found the German transports and flew in line-astern to make a long run right down the road and back again. Trucks burst into flames and others overturned into ditches on either side of the road. Soldiers could be seen running for cover across the fields. In attempting to do my part with the gun in the rear turret, I inadvertently fired a bullet through our own tailplane. It was a ghastly moment. This, I thought, is pure P/O Prune! Flt Lt Horgan said very little when I reported what I had done. We carried on with the attack and then returned to Eleusis.

On the ground, Sqn Ldr Milward had a few terse words to say to me, for he feared that the aircraft would be put out of action. Happily, the ground crew found nothing of consequence had been damaged, so that the aircraft was operational for the next day.[3]

The collapse of Greek resistance in Eastern Macedonia now allowed the Germans to begin moving southwards, and over the next five days the British forces facing them began withdrawing to the partly-prepared Servia line. On **11 April**, six 84 Squadron Blenheims set out to bomb the Prilep-Bitolj road, where tanks and lorries were reported hit, as was a nearby train. The Germans were ready for them this time however, and a hail of ground fire hit all six aircraft, Flt Sgt Les Nuttall's Blenheim (L8612) being shot down, the pilot losing his life with his crew, Flt Sgt Arthur Neal and Sgt Gaston Thistle. 211 Squadron also despatched a raid, led by the new CO Sqn Ldr Anthony Irvine; all returned safely. Bad weather prevented further sorties by Blenheims of 11, 30 and 113 Squadrons, all of which were scheduled to operate. However a new detachment of Wellingtons from 38 Squadron in Egypt arrived during the day, and were in action that night against Sofia and Veles.

After dark, 30 Squadron was tasked to fly nocturnal patrols over Athens to hunt for intruders, as recalled by Sgt Geoff Chapman, who was up with Flg Off. Andy Smith in L1239:

Attempted interception of e/a flying at 8,000 feet. No luck. We did not, of course, have any radar or any other sophisticated equipment to aid us. It was just a question of keeping one's eyes open and following the AA fire and searchlight beams.[4]

Sqn Ldr Milward, up on patrol in K7095, was more fortunate in that he actually engaged the Ju 88 in searchlights at 8,000 feet north-west of Athens, but was unfortunate to have been seen by his intended victim. As he attacked, his aircraft was hit by return fire and burst into flames, and while he was able to bale out, his gunner, Sgt John Crooks, was killed; believed by troops on the ground to be a German, Milward was shot at in his parachute; he then narrowly avoided high tension cables and crashed into a glasshouse, escaping this whole catalogue of misfortunes with no more than a severe shaking. Many ground observers reported that a Ju 88 was seen to spin down and crash with an explosion, but this may well have been the falling Blenheim, or bombs. No Ju 88 was reported lost and the only identification of Milward's possible opponent may have been a Ju 88 of 9./LG1 which crash-landed on return from a sortie over Crete.

RAF Blenheims and Hurricanes were again out over the Bitolj-Veles road during the morning of **12 April**. Three raids were undertaken by 211 Squadron against enemy troops advancing north of Valona; one at dawn, one at noon, and one at dusk. All returned safely and each raid was led by Sqn Ldr Irvine. RAF Blenheims were very active throughout the daylight hours of **13 April**, which turned out to be 'unlucky 13' for 211 Squadron. The unit had already undertaken two raids during the morning on vehicles and troop concentrations in the Florina region, both under Hurricane escort; no opposition was encountered; Flg Off. Alan Godfrey recalled:

Long before dawn breaks over the Pindus mountains in northern Greece, I have to get up. I half dress myself in bed. While there is still a vestige of warmth in my feet I put them into my flying boots. Drawing on my suit, I slip a captured Italian automatic into my pocket and am ready. I undo the tent and step outside. Stumbling over the uneven ground I make my way to the ops tent. This warms me up a bit. The crews already there are standing around in groups and talking about the news—remember, it is April 13 and the Germans are rolling down the Monastir Gap and flooding northwest Greece.

In a few minutes the CO arrives. Map in hand he tells us where we are going to bomb. My flight is all present and accounted for. I am thinking, how much longer will our luck hold out? I am a great believer in luck, and our Squadron has done hundreds of raids with less than 3 per cent casualties. We split up and walk over to our machines. I am with my crew, two lads my own age—and one of them is singing 'We Three'. I like it. Besides, as we walk I am thawing out.

Seated in the cockpit, I begin to feel important. The fitter is waiting for my signal to start up: men are at the chocks; everything awaits my order. I look at my watch and set the clock on the dashboard. A minute or so to go. I feel fine. Then I taxi out and take my position at the end of the field, and the other two machines in my flight form up on either side. A wave of the hand, and the three of us start bumping over the uneven field. Circling around, I slide into position in the 'box', directly below and behind the leading flight.

Dawn is just breaking over endless ranges of snow-capped mountains—a wonderful sight, if you go for stuff like that. I take one look and then concentrate on flying in close formation, and as the minutes slip by I begin to wonder how this raid will go. It is too early for enemy fighters, but there is sure to be ack-

ack. And it is sure to be pretty rotten, because the Italians don't know how to
co-ordinate their fire. Presently we turn a bit to run up on the target—a road
junction in a small valley. I fly steady and level and the bomb aimer gets ready
to send a ton of bombs crashing down to the road below. There is a slight jar
and I know the bombs have gone. The bomb aimer is leaning forward to watch
the burst, and I fly on till he gives me the 'thumbs up'. Then I swing away and
head for home. No fighters, very little ack-ack. That's the kind of raid I like.

Back at base between mouthfuls of tinned bacon and eggs, we talk of the next
raid. There is just time for a shave before we are off again. Provided our luck
holds, we may do four raids today—which will be a record for our Squadron.
This one is my fortieth raid in Greece and it's almost becoming a routine. This
time, as before, all our aircraft return safely.[5]

At 15:00, 211 Squadron was briefed for its third raid of the day—to send six
more bombers to raid Prilep. On this occasion no Hurricanes were available.
Only seven Blenheims could be mustered in total, and one was required to carry
out a photo-recce over Valona and Durazzo. Plt Off. Jack Hooper was fortuitously
selected for the task, which was duly carried out. He recalled:

Some of the pilots and crews, including my brother and the only other
Rhodesian on the Squadron, Jack Cox, had been detached … This meant
that there were only seven serviceable. Short-nosed Blenheims on the field at
Paramythia that morning. These were ordered to attack military transport at
Prilep, on the Bulgarian border.

I was standing outside the ops tent, being briefed by Sqn Ldr Irvine for the
third attack, when he was handed a signal from HQ ordering one of the seven
of us to be detached to undertake a photographic-reconnaissance of Valona
and Durazzo, the two main Albanian ports. The CO asked if any aircraft was
not already bombed up … Mine was the only one … I was, therefore, detailed
for the reconnaissance. I remember there were expressions of sympathy from
the others at my ill luck. There were said to be heavy fighter concentrations
around the two ports.

Off I went on that beautiful, clear afternoon—visibility 100 per cent and took
the photographs of the ports from about 20,000 feet. There was a considerable
amount of shipping in the harbour at Durazzo. No hostile aircraft, however,
appeared anywhere near me, and I returned safely to Paramythia. I left at once
to take the films to HQ in Athens. It was there that I heard the dreadful news
that not one of the six Blenheims despatched on that third raid had returned.[6]

Wg Cdr *Paddy* Coote had decided to go along with the raid as an observer
to assess the progress of the German advance, while his deputy Sqn Ldr Leslie
Cryer accompanied another crew. The formation was led by Sqn Ldr Irvine.

A Flight		B Flight	
L8478	†Sqn Ldr A. T. Irvine	L8449	Flg Off. A. C. Godfrey
	†Plt Off. G. Davies		†Sgt J. B. T. O'Neill
	†Plt Off. A. C. Geary		†Flt Sgt J. Wainhouse
L1434	†Flt Lt L. B. Buchanan	L8664	†FlgOff C. E. V. Thompson
	†Sqn Ldr L. E. Cryer		†Plt Off. P. Hogarth
	†Sgt G. Pattison		†Sgt W. Arscott
L4819	†Plt Off. R. V. Herbert[7]	L1539	Flt Sgt A. G. James
	†Wg Cdr P. B. Coote		†Flt Sgt A. Bryce
	†Sgt W. N. Young		†Sgt A. J. Waring

Flg Off. Godfrey commented:

> At two-thirty the raid signal goes yet again. Then we are in the air again and heading for Florina. We leave Yannina on our right, then Koritza on our left. I see hundreds of heavy lorries leaving Koritza as the Greeks evacuate it. I think it's a great pity, after they fought so hard to capture the place. We fly on, and presently, as we cross the last range of mountains, I see the target, and I also see that the road leading into Florina from Yugoslavia is packed with German transport lorries, tanks, guns. That's for us.
>
> I don't look at the target anymore now because I'm too busy keeping in exact formation. I know we are getting close, however, when I see some black puffs of coiled smoke puncture the sky around us. I grip the stick hard and moisten my lips while I wait to see the bombs fall from the leading machine. The seconds go by … maybe a minute, maybe more … and then I see the bombs tumble out of the belly ahead of me, and I feel the jar which tells ours have gone. We fly straight on while the photographs are taken and necks craned to see the bombs strike.[8]

As the diving bombers approached Lake Prespa three Bf 109s of 6./JG27— flying from a newly constructed airstrip between Prilep and the lake—were seen closing rapidly on the rear vic of three Blenheims, the gunners at once opening fire. Hptm Hans-Joachim Gerlach, leading the Messerschmitts, attacked Godfrey's L8449, which caught fire almost immediately, as he later recorded:

> Just then the bomb-aimer [Sgt *Peggy* O'Neill] nudges me and points ahead and below. "Fighters!" he yells. I can see a few Messerschmitt 109s circling around. The leader has also seen them, for the formation goes into a turn to the left and heads back the way we came. I am busy keeping good formation. We go into a shallow dive. Then I hear my rear-gunner [Jack Wainwright] open up and

smell the burning cordite. That tells me the fighters have connected and we are having a running fight. I've had many a scrap with Italian fighters and am not worried about it, so I don't get the wind up just because these happen to be Jerries.

We are diving pretty fast now, and I am still under the leader's tail. We turn slightly and head for a valley leading down the other side of the mountains. I hear the bursts of our guns as the rear-gunner keeps on firing, and I am wondering how he is doing. Then the bomb aimer points to my port engine and I see streaks of tracer and incendiary bullets passing under it. I think that it is pretty good shooting, but I am not worrying. The rear-gunner stops firing, and I'm just about to ask him if his gun has jammed when the bomb aimer again points to the engine. I start to do things throttle back, switch off engine, undo safety belt—but we just haven't got a chance, in a few seconds the aircraft is blazing and sheets of scorching flame shoot forward from the well into the cockpit. Through the intercom I yell, "Jump!"

I raise myself up to get out through the roof. I see the bomb aimer beside me, fumbling with his pack. What can I do? I don't seem to be afraid—although God knows, another ten seconds in here and I'll be roasted alive. As it is my gloves are burning and I can't keep my eyes open for more than a second at a time. In a flash I realize we must jump now or never. The heat is terrific as wave after wave of red flame sweeps through the cockpit. I look down to earth—we'll never make it ...[9]

The pilot of the victorious Messerschmitt, Hptm Gerlach, recalled:

I took off in the afternoon with my air combat-experienced Staffel comrades, Feldwebel [Herbert] Krenz and Unteroffizier [Fritz] Gromotka. At our destination we cruised in about 400 m above ground with special observation to south and southwards from where, if at all, hit and run attacks had to be suspected.

We had cruised about 20 minutes, in a loose line, when in the distance and about 500 m higher, emerging from behind the cumulus clouds, a compact group of bigger planes appeared heading direct towards our track. The silhouettes of the six aircraft were recognized as Blenheim bombers, which we already knew from Channel [operations]. The squadron leader must have recognized our sun-lighted Messerschmitts at the same time and immediately broke off with the whole squadron to port. I cannot remember if the Blenheims released their bombs. We climbed quickly to the same height and closed up to the unexpectedly descending Blenheim squadron which now deployed two by two trying to escape in the direction of the Prespa Lake and the behind rising mountains.

On reaching firing position I gave the order to attack and sighted myself as usual with a burst of fire (every fourth round a phosphor bullet) of the correct line. The Blenheim on the right wing which was then attacked by me quickly showed smoke followed by fire after I used my gun. I saw a crew member baling out at very low height and landing on the ground with already opened canopy next to a sheep or goat flock. I didn't see the burning aircraft anymore. It must have crashed while I was closing up to Krenz who had shot down the Blenheim flying left of me on the same heading. He was now chasing the two other further left, and close to the ground, was just attacking the one closest to him when I reached the fourth Blenheim. I hit her but had to turn away and fly a second attack because of my jammed gun. This one resulted then in a hit. Both aircraft crashed as far as I can remember just short of the lake. Gromotka who had followed the two far left off flying aircraft was far ahead out of my sight. His shot down fifth aircraft fell into the lake and the sixth Blenheim crashed due to his report at the very south corner close to the beach into the lake. The whole air battle must not have last longer than 10 minutes.[10]

Amidst the carnage overhead, Flg Off. Godfrey was drifting down in his parachute:

I feel no sense of falling. I am suspended in mid-air, rolled up in a ball, and looking down at the earth about three hundred feet below. I pull the ripcord good and hard, and I feel a little jerk as the pilot chute springs away from the pack. When the main chute opens there is only a gentle firm pressure around my thighs and crotch. A great silence seems to be descending with me.

Then I hear a crackling and the sound of shots below, and I see my machine blazing on the ground about half a mile away, with all the ammunition going off. I am only fifty feet from the ground so I don't have many torturous moments wondering if I am going to be machine-gunned. I land on my left side in a ditch. For a moment I just stand there and thank God I'm alive. Then I undo my harness and take off my helmet, hide the chute in the ditch, start walking south. I don't go over to my machine, because I know that no one could have lived through that crash.

Presently I see some soldiers. And am I happy! They are Greeks. There are only about six of them and when they see me they raise their rifles. I take no chances and raise my arms above my head. Very cautiously they close in on me. I keep on saying, "Anglica" and "Inglese", but they search me and take that Italian automatic! They find my wallet with my pass in it—but I am out of luck: they can't even read their own language. So they march me off with a rifle stuck in my back. Soon we meet a group of peasants. An old man questions me with his few words of broken English, but we don't get very far. Just then a Greek officer rides up, and fortunately he speaks French. He is soon satisfied about my identity.

Transport is very scarce, but the Greeks help me all they can, and I get a lift down the line to a small town north of Larissa, where I find an advanced RAF unit.[11]

Godfrey's aircraft crashed near the village of Karia, where it was joined almost immediately by L8664, in which Flg Off. Tommy Thompson and his crew perished. The only other survivor of the ill-fated raid was Flt Sgt Jimmy James, the Welsh pilot of L1539, who was able to bale out, breaking his ankle on landing near the village of Mikrolimni, while his aircraft crashed near the south-west shore of the lake. The injured James joined Godfrey at Karia, and buried those of their dead comrades that they could find, before making their way by foot, mule and Greek lorry to Larissa.

On his return, Godfrey reported on what he had witnessed regarding the missing Blenheims:

> While on the end of my parachute I saw No. 2 of the leading flight spinning down in flames over the lake. I have every reason to believe that this was the machine in which S/L Cryer was flying, and that certainly there can be no hope of any of the occupants being alive. I also saw the other two machines of A Flight flying on with the enemy fighters firing at them from behind. I wondered at the time if they would manage to escape but as they did not return I feel sure they were brought down immediately after I lost sight of them and that they therefore must have crashed between the south and south-west shore of Lake Ohrida.[12]

It transpired that Sqn Ldr Irvine's aircraft crashed into the hillside of Tumbitsa mountain, its demise witnessed by local partisans Pantlis Alexciou and Constantine Marcos, who reported seeing a single undamaged aircraft coming up the valley very low, before clipping trees with one wing. It would seem that Irvine had seen the mountain, but too late, as mist and fog were present. When villagers went up the next day, the aircraft was reasonably intact. They removed the bodies of Sqn Ldr Irvine and Plt Off. Gerry Davies from the cockpit without trouble, but that of Plt Off. Arthur Geary, the gunner, was trapped in the wreckage and took time to recover; all three were eventually buried in shallow graves. The following day two Germans arrived on a motorcycle to see the site, and ordered the locals to refrain from visiting.

Even as this slaughter was taking place, nine more Blenheims from 113 Squadron had set off fifteen minutes later, at 15:15, heading for the same target, but with an escort of six Hurricanes. The Blenheims were led by Flt Lt Denis Rixson:

> We were going up the line to bomb enemy forward troops. In the valley as we went north we suddenly saw far more aircraft than we had ever seen in the air before, going down the other side of the valley to attack our forward troops—later confirmed as a Luftwaffe bomber formation. I remember our Hurricanes fussing around us like bees, but obviously both formations had the

same instructions—do not leave the bombers—because although only a few miles apart none interfered with the other.[13]

It was on **14 April**, as the British army completed its withdrawal to the Olympus-Servia line, that improving weather and reduction of effort over Yugoslavia, allowed aerial activity over Greece to show a marked increase. Early in the day six Blenheims from 84 Squadron, escorted by four Hurricanes, attacked vehicles and troops north of Ptolemais. Intense flak was experienced and two Bf 109s also attacked the Blenheims, four being damaged, one of which was believed to have crash-landed in Yugoslavia. Some five hours later, eight more Blenheims, these from 113 Squadron, set off with an escort of ten Hurricanes. Returning from attacking targets north of Ptolemais, Ju 87s were seen dive-bombing Allied troops near Servia and one of these was claimed shot down by a Hurricane pilot; a Blenheim gunner also fired at one of the dive-bombers, reporting seeing smoke and flame pouring from the aircraft, but this is believed to have been the machine attacked by the Hurricane. Several Ju 87s were shot down in the area during the day.

Over Athens three Hurricanes and four Blenheims of 30 Squadron scrambled to intercept Ju 88s and Bf 110s attacking Piraeus early in the afternoon. The Blenheims failed to make contact but one Hurricane was believed to have been hit and force-landed.

Elsewhere, a Blenheim crew of 113 Squadron—Flt Lt George Green, Sgt Bill Gingell with Sgt Ken Jamieson as air-gunner—was tasked to deliver unfused bombs (by airdrop) to New Zealand sappers at Grevena during the day, who were to use these for demolition purposes. However, the Blenheim (T2177) was hit in the port engine and undercarriage by friendly AA fire before being intercepted by a Bf 109 and further damaged. Nonetheless, Flt Lt Green was able to return to Niamata, where the Blenheim was force-landed, its mission uncompleted. Their assailant was possibly Uffz Wilhelm Schneider of 1.(J)/LG2, who claimed a Blenheim destroyed.

The retreat was in full swing by now, Wg Cdr Dudley Lewis from Air HQ flying into Paramythia with instructions to disband Western Wing. He was also to arrange the evacuation of both Paramythia and Yannina. The last five Blenheims of 211 Squadron were to move to Agrinion to continue operations. Next morning they began ferrying ground personnel—nine to an aircraft; this operation would take three days to complete. Before the airfield was abandoned, however, more aircraft arrived. At Paramythia during the afternoon, a Do 17K flew in followed by a Savoia, which was flying a white flag, escorted by six Gladiators, and carrying King Peter of Yugoslavia and members of his staff. The Royal party was not expected and, according to one source, the Swordfish CO, Lt *Tiffy* Torrence-Spence was the first on the scene:

… the new CO of 815 Squadron wrenched open the machine's door, thrust his revolver inside the cabin and yelled that everyone should put their hands up. However when he checked the cabin, Torrens-Spence found just three passengers, all of them smartly dressed. One of then stood up and introduced himself. "I am King Peter of Yugoslavia and that gentleman," he pointed, "is my prime minister." "And I am Father Christmas," said Torrence-Spence. "Now come on, get out, with your hand up." As the three men stepped into the evening sunlight, onlookers immediately recognised the King's face.[14]

The young monarch and his prime minister were hastily provided with an impromptu guard of honour composed of airmen of 211 Squadron. The King commented that it was the smartest guard he had seen, and almost certainly the first on a battlefield. One of those involved in the guard was Cpl Tom Henderson:

What His Majesty didn't know was that 90 per cent of the gear we were wearing was borrowed from our comrades, such was the dire shortage of decent uniforms and equipment at the time. One piece of luggage unloaded off the SM.79 was reported to contain the Yugoslav Crown Jewels! It may have been true, but true or not it brightened up our lives at a time when our luck appeared to be running out.[15]

A somewhat chastened Lt Torrence-Spence then invited the King and his retinue to visit the officers' mess where a copious supply of gin was on offer. Allegedly the prime minister had succumbed to the gin and by the time the aircraft was refuelled, he had to be carried back to the machine for onward flight to Athens. The King's SM.79 was escorted to Menidi by a Blenheim (L8533) flown by Sgt *Jock* Marshall, with Sgt *Nobby* Clark as observer:

L8533, the only flyable Blenheim available, had been shot up and had no turret, and a piece of plywood covered the hole. Our outline was distinctly odd—i.e. for aircraft recognition—we had quite a time with 30 Squadron—me firing the colour of the day all over the sky but they were not convinced. *Haggis* [Sgt Baird] got on the radio to Menidi to get them to warn them off, which they do as we cross the Corinth Canal. Then the SM.79 fails to follow us round the circuit—goes straight in against the 'sock', leaving us to flounder.[16]

The 30 Squadron Blenheims were flown by Flt Lt Bob Davidson and Plt Off. John Jarvis, as the latter recalled:

When we arrived over Eleusis [Menidi] there were three SM.79s in the circuit, so we started an attack. Bob Davidson suddenly shouted to hold fire, and I could see a bowler-hatted gentleman in the rear turret doffing his hat to us. It turned out that the aircraft were carrying King Peter of Yugoslavia and his court to safety. It was rumoured that the entire gold reserves of the country (nine tons) were packed in the aircraft, so it would have been an expensive splat.[17]

More Yugoslav aircraft began arriving at Paramythia, mainly Do 17Ks, SM.79s and Lockheed 10s, but also a large number of smaller biplanes of many types. Cpl Henderson continued:

As far as I can remember, the Yugoslav boys began arriving over a period of about three days and kept trickling in—I saw no Furies or Hurricanes but an odd Lockheed twin-engined aircraft was present. I have never seen such magnificent uniforms as some of the Yugoslav chaps wore—and such marvellous moustaches![18]

By the end of the day the number of Yugoslav machines present at Paramythia had reportedly reached 44 (unlikely), and others were landing elsewhere, including two at Corfu. Before the mass of Yugoslav aircraft had been refuelled, Mc.200s of 22° Gruppo swept in to strafe, claiming six bombers and one fighter destroyed and a further ten damaged. At least one airman was killed on the airfield. Meanwhile, a force of G.50s from 24° Gruppo attacked Larissa but were engaged by RAF Gladiators. Two G.50s were claimed damaged and one Gladiator was forced down, but only one Yugoslav SM.79 was destroyed on the ground. During the afternoon six more Yugoslav Do 17Ks and four SM.79s arrived at Paramythia, all but four Dorniers flying on to Agrinion as ordered.

At 06:50 on the morning of **15 April,** eight Bf 109s of 4./JG77 swept over Larissa airfield in threes, the second section catching three Hurricanes as they scrambled, shooting down two for the loss of two. The other Messerschmitts meanwhile strafed the many targets including several Hurricanes (one source stated fourteen were damaged beyond repair) and a Gladiator and several Greek aircraft. One of 11 Squadron's pilots, Sgt Vernon Hudson, had a lucky escape during one of the morning strafes. He was flying the unit's Magister from Alymos to Larissa to collect orders from Wing HQ, when several Bf 109s appeared and attacked the tiny communications machine. Although not hit he was forced down short of Larissa. Ten minutes later he took off and reached the airfield shortly before another of the heavy attacks, which rendered most aircraft unserviceable, although the Magister survived with a few holes in the port wing.

Paramythia was also attacked with the destruction of the four Yugoslav Dorniers. During the day, II and III/JG77 pilots claimed a total of 19 aircraft destroyed in the Larissa area. Immediately these airfield attacks were over, two Lysanders took off from Larissa to convey the two 211 Squadron survivors, Flg Off. Alan Godfrey and Flt Sgt *Jimmy* James, to Athens, as Godfrey recalled:

I ask the pilot [Flg Off. Don Waymark]—who is going to fly me down—what he will do if we are attacked by enemy fighters. "Dive to the deck and outmanoeuvre them," he replies. "Besides you will be the rear-gunner, so you will have plenty to do." We take off. I look back over the tail as we climb, and watch Mount Olympus in the distance. In the afternoon sun it looks so quiet and peaceful. Yet in its shadow a grim action is being fought, and—suddenly the machine goes into a dive. I look up and see five Me 109s peeling off for a stern attack. For the first split second I am neither surprised nor frightened—I don't know why not; I should be. I try to fire the gun, it doesn't work. I see that I haven't pulled the cocking handle safety catch. I fix that and aim again.

Bullets come crashing into the machine and tear through the port wing. I go on firing but we are diving like hell and it's difficult to aim properly. Each time a fighter closes in over the tail I see bullets coming at us. They look like silvery pencil lines drawn on blue paper, all converging on us. They look terrible. What's it going to feel like when a burst comes tearing into my chest or stomach or some place? I'm still wondering when I feel a blow on my right hand and it is pulled away from the gun. I go to grab the gun again, when I notice my hand is a mass of blood. The two middle fingers are missing—shot away. Now this does shake me a bit. I hold my arm tight against my side and go on firing with my left hand. But not for long. With a sudden colossal thump, we hit the ground and go somersaulting across a field. I am thrown all over the place. The aircraft has broken into two pieces and I am in the tail half. The noise is terrific.

Finally the wreckage comes to rest and I am thrown forward on my face. I hear the pilot shout, "Are you alright? Run like hell." I try to, but my left leg just collapses, and I see that the knee is all wrong. I start crawling, and the pilot comes to my aid. He was thrown clear and is uninjured. Then with a roar, the Messerschmitts come sweeping down, spattering bullets. Flinging ourselves flat on the ground, we manage to crawl about fifty feet without being hit. I look at my hand. "Handkerchief—left-hand—tourniquet," I say between groans, and the pilot gets busy. He tightens up the tourniquet, and I hold the pencil to keep it tight. Groaning seems to be the only thing that eases the pain.

The German fighters have gone now, and the pilot runs over to find the first-aid kit. Some Greek peasants try to carry me to the main road, but my leg hurts like hell and they have to put me down. For hours I sit back, keeping a firm hold on the tourniquet. Finally an RAF car arrives to pick me up. As we reach the next town an air raid starts, and the driver pulls the car into the side of the road. Everyone gets out and shelters under a wall. But I stay in the back of the car and just don't care anymore. The bombs make a loud 'crump' as they land all over the place, and I can feel the blasts rock the car. This is the first time I have ever really been in among the bombs in a raid, and it's not as bad as I thought.

Some hours later we halt at an emergency aerodrome. When the doctor comes, he says "Alan, I'm going to send you off in an aircraft to Athens."[19]

Meanwhile, the aircraft carrying Flt Sgt *Jimmy* James was also shot down. Its pilot Plt Off. John Stewart recalled:

I formated on Waymark and we had barely turned onto our course when Waymark dived steeply; I following him as best I could. We could not have been more than a few hundred feet up. The air around my Lysander seemed full of tracer and I was aware of Me109s coming out of their dives. We crash-landed in an olive grove. I had been concussed, and when I came to I was being helped out of the aircraft by Greeks. Thank heavens the aircraft hadn't caught fire, because I was soaked in petrol and this caused the second-degree burns for which I was later treated, so I must have been there for some time. Eventually I was taken in a taxi by a Greek doctor to a Casualty Clearing Station, No.33, I think, at Larissa. I was told that my passenger was dead and was led to believe that he had been killed by bullets, not the impact of the crash.[20]

The two Lysanders were the victims of Oblt Berthold Jung and Oblt Gerhard Rahm of 5./JG77.

Larissa and Paramythia were not the only targets, however, for at 07:50 waves of Bf 109s attacked Niamata, home of 113 Squadron, where crews were breakfasting prior to taking off on a raid. The first attack by eight Messerschmitts destroyed six of the unit's Blenheims and wounded four airmen. Newly arrived New Zealand observer Sgt Ewan Brooking recalled.

We hadn't been up that long when the Luftwaffe struck. The camp was on the south side of the road that led to the airfield, and the approach path of the two Me109s was on the north side parallel to the road, but not too close. The gunfire that scrambled us into the slit trench was the 109s opening up on the planes on the airfield. Our 16 planes were the targets. Twelve were bombed up ready for an op later that day, and four were in the workshops. Though the camp was not that close to the airfield, we had a reasonable view of the damage that was being inflicted on the Blenheims.[21]

Two hours later three Bf 109s from II/JG27 swept over the airfield and several more Blenheims were rendered unserviceable, two more airmen being wounded. Bofors fire was fairly accurate and two of the attackers were hit but both got back to Bitolj, where one crash-landed. At 11:00, four more Bf 109s appeared over Niamata and proceeded to destroy four more Blenheims; they were followed by another quartet some 45 minutes later, these damaging one more Blenheim and a Magister communications aircraft. An hour later came the final attack on the day on this airfield, all remaining Blenheims being shot up and rendered unserviceable. Sgt Brooking continued:

About every half hour, another pair of 109s would arrive, make their strafing run and depart, back to their base. As the attack developed, another plane would be set on fire, with a column of smoke rising up, and the 109s doing victory rolls through the plumes. The bombed-up planes eventually blew up. The only anti-aircraft fire seemed to be coming from a red-headed Syrian Jew airman, in a slit trench on the other side of the road, opposite the Sergeants' Mess, firing a .303 rifle at the 109s. Without much luck it seemed, until, in the mid-afternoon, he appeared to hit one. This evidently annoyed the 109 pilots, so the next and last run was at the camp. This resulted in what was possibly our only casualty. An airman dived under the petrol tanker for shelter, but the tanker was a prime target, and he was killed. When the 109s left, one of them was trailing a thin streamer of white smoke.[22]

During these attacks all motor vehicles on the airfield were also destroyed, as was much tented accommodation. 113 Squadron had ceased to exist as an operational unit: ten Blenheims had been destroyed or damaged beyond repair. Flt Lt Denis Rixson recalled:

There was very little, if any, early warning. I have a vivid recollection of my air-gunner crouching under a little bridge firing off a .38 revolver at the Iron Crosses![23]

Further south, at 08:45, some 25 Ju 88s from I/LG1 and I/KG51 had appeared over Athens to target shipping at Piraeus, where three large merchantmen were severely damaged by their attack. Hurricanes intercepted the bombers and claimed six shot down (in fact two crash-landed and two more were damaged), while four of 30 Squadron's IFs were also scrambled, Plt Off. Travers Allison, the unit's youngest pilot known as *Pee-Wee*, sighting a dozen Ju 88s at 12,000 feet over Athens. These were probably aircraft of I/LG1 and, as he approached, they dived to attack shipping in the harbour. He caught up with one and carried out a starboard quarter attack, but broke away as the bomber was diving too steeply. Another Ju 88 was sighted by the gunner, Sgt Jock Connors, and the Blenheim closed to 75 yards, allowing Connors to fire 1,250 rounds at it, following which it was believed to have gone into the sea. This was possibly L1+SK flown by Uffz Karl Stütz that failed to return with the loss of the crew (Gfr Helmut Frege, Gfr Erich Wolfenkammer and Gfr Karl Scheidhammer); a second aircraft from this unit crash-landed at Kozani and was completely destroyed. L1+SK was probably the same aircraft as claimed by one of the Hurricane pilots, who saw three crew bale out of his victim.

Following the attacks on the airfields, Air Vice-Marshal D'Albiac was flown up to Larissa in a Lysander to see for himself the extent of the damage and losses. As a result an evacuation of Paramythia, Yannina, Larissa, Kazaklar, Niamata and Almyros was ordered. Flt Sgt Arthur Davis of 113 Squadron recalled:

Later that day the Squadron received instructions to get rid of all personal clothes—in fact, we put them into the trenches we had dug for our own safety. Following this, we then climbed into our lorries and, moving by night, we made our way to the main aerodrome in Athens. Along the way we were strafed and bombed twice, but I can not say if there were any casualties. Upon our arrival, to our surprise, some Blenheim Is arrived, and we aircrew (mostly) were crammed into these aircraft and flown to Crete.[24]

Sgt Ewan Brooking, also of 113 Squadron, wrote of this period in greater detail:

Later in the afternoon, a little RAF high wing monoplane [a Lysander] flew over at low level. It dropped what was evidently a message, in a ball with streamers attached. It appeared that the message was to evacuate immediately. Orders were given to pack the kitbags and throw them and ourselves onto the back of our trucks, and be ready to move off. The camp and all gear and equipment was to be left as it was. Not long afterwards we moved off.

To reach the road south, we had to pass through Larissa, which had suffered considerable damage from the three air raids. We passed through the Olympus Pass safely, and moved on, spending the rest of the night in a field off the road, sleeping where we could. Off again next morning, still heading south but by now things were getting a bit blurry. We passed through a town, possibly Volos, and then Daphni, and on to Piraeus. There we were put on a train, which left at night and headed northwards. The train stopped in the middle of a plain later in the morning, and we took shelter in the small trees and scrub on the small hills nearby. This was in case of an air raid on the train. Later on in the afternoon, we boarded the train again which carried on to Corinth and the Canal.

The bridge across the Canal was a rail bridge, so we walked across in the dark, treading from sleeper to sleeper, very carefully, as the Canal was hundreds of feet down. On the other side of the Canal, we dossed down where we could on the side of a small hill. Sleep was fitful as I was trying to sleep on a narrow path where one side fell away down the slope of the hill. Next morning early we were marshalled to a small clearing in the trees, where some army trucks were waiting. All aboard, and off we went to the south, through Argos to the little port of Nauplia.

We didn't get to Nauplia but the hills a few kilometres away, where we took shelter in an apple orchard. There was a ship in the harbour, with a load of ammunition. It had already been sunk, and was resting on the seabed, but the Stukas kept dive-bombing it until it finally blew up. Then they turned their attention to all the Aussie troops and us sheltering on the hillside. There were eight of us sheltering under a small old apple tree, so we tried to hide behind the trunk the opposite side to where the attacks were coming from. There was a fresh cow pat on one side but, fortunately, nobody landed in that. Somehow, along the way we seemed to have lost our kit-bags. As for food, the Sergeants' Mess was not operating, and nor was the Airmans' or Officers' messes. I don't know [can't remember] what we did for food or drink—it was probably bully beef and biscuits somewhere along the way. When we were under the apple trees, the CO somehow managed to scrounge a demi-john of rum, so all the Squadron personnel got a tot of rum to cheer us up. This was Anzac Day.[24]

The party eventually boarded a commando landing ship at Nauplia and reached Crete, from where Sgt Brooking was flown by Lodestar to Ma'aten Bagush.

Meanwhile, 11 Squadron's Blenheims were still at Almyros, and that evening a Hurricane was despatched to drop a message bag containing instructions to withdraw to Menidi. Unfortunately the drop was made in the wrong area, on an airstrip still under construction. As a result the canister was not located until next morning, the withdrawal not taking place until the following evening. The unit's eight Blenheims joined forces at Menidi with nine aircraft of 84 Squadron, while 211's remaining five bombers joined fourteen Blenheim IF fighters at Eleusis. Early in the day Sgt *Jock* Marshall had attempted to ferry L8533 to Agrinion, as *Nobby* Clark recalled:

> Aborted—not able to get out of valley. Port engine develops a mighty mag drop after take-off. *Jock* has a great struggle to get us back, turning on the starboard only. We have enough power in port engine for flaps and undercart—a very shaky do![26]

They were instructed to ferry another aircraft, L1486, but that night it—and the crew—remained at Paramythia:

> The aircraft (L1486) was damaged but flyable. We [with Sgts Marshall and Baird] had a night out in the village of Paramythia. At the taverna the natives kept the brandy flowing, and we found beds for the night with the doctor.[27]

Next morning they flew L1486 to Agrinion where Sgt Clark, being the eldest member of the crew received a 'bollocking' on behalf of the crew from the flight commander—"I expected better of you at least, Clark"—thus, little more than a mild rebuke.

With the German advance now approaching the Olympus-Servia line, and threatening to outflank the defenders, the decision was taken to begin withdrawal of the Imperial force to Thermopylae. The reason for this latest move was again an *Ultra* intercept, which indicated that German armour would be operating to the south of the Olympus line by this date. All was going badly for the Allies. Whilst the Imperial forces were still managing to withdraw in good order across the Plain of Thessaly, improved weather now brought them under constant and heavy air attack just at the point at which the cover afforded by the mountains ran out. To the west, the advance of the German *XL Korps* units from Skoplje threatened to outflank the gallant but exhausted Greek Army of the Epirus. The offensive against the Italians had already been broken off, whilst the evacuation of the airfields close behind the front—particularly that of Paramythia—denuded the Greek soldiers of the residue of air cover that they had been enjoying.

To ensure the security of these forces, a rapid withdrawal southwards was required, but to give up territory captured with such sacrifice from the Italians would be quite unacceptable to the troops on morale grounds. All looked hopeless, and during the day General Papagos explained to General Maitland-Wilson the plight of his army and suggested a British withdrawal to save the country from the full devastation of war.

Eleusis received two more Yugoslav SM.79s and two Lockheed 10s from Paramythia during the day, all carrying government officials. That evening a Yugoslav Do 17K flown by Lt Peter Todorović came into land at Menidi but met an unexpected reception, as Airman Comeau of 11 Squadron wrote:

> Its occupants, surviving the blitz on Paramythia on 15 April and the two more heavy bombing and strafing attacks while their aircraft underwent repairs, did not take kindly to the volume of small-arms fire which now greeted them from trigger-happy erks at Menidi. The aircraft circled the aerodrome for a full half hour, kept aloft by airmen pea-shooters. When it eventually landed and discharged its voluble cargo of irate, fist-brandishing Yugoslavs, the erks made themselves scarce.[28]

Next day (**16 April**), a Yugoslav SM.79 carrying General Mirković to Greece was fired on by Greek AA near Preveza, and was hit. The aircraft crashed, the fuselage breaking into two, and Mirković was severely injured, the government minister travelling with him losing his life. During the day Mc.200s of 150° Gruppo scrambled from Valona to intercept aircraft identified as Yugoslav Blenheims, two of these being claimed shot down and a third probably so, between Cap Linguetta and Saseno. The aircraft attacked were in fact Ca.310s of 603 Training Eskadrila attempting to reach Greece, at least one of these aircraft being lost in such circumstances, all six persons aboard being killed in the crash on Corfu.

30 Squadron at Eleusis was ordered to despatch half of its Blenheim IFs to Crete for convoy patrols and sea reconnaissances on **17 April**, seven aircraft leaving for Maleme next day, as remembered by Sgt Geoff Chapman on board L4825:

> A really beautiful spring day—we were given orders to evacuate to Maleme in Crete. By 12:40, A Flight was ready and led on this occasion by Flg Off. [Andy] Smith. Unfortunately, our landfall was a little off course and we came out over

Suda Bay, which was the Royal Navy anchorage in Crete. Not surprisingly, our sudden arrival at low level through the haze evoked a torrent of RN AA fire. Mercifully, the haze enabled us to depart almost as swiftly as we had arrived, so no harm was done. We were, however, a little miffed to learn when we arrived at Maleme a few minutes later that the Royal Navy claimed they were buzzed by three Ju 88s and that they had shot one of them down![29]

The last of the Wellingtons detached to Eleusis also departed for Shallufa (Egypt). En route, when north-west of Crete, the aircraft was attacked by CR.42s but not hit. The rear-gunner believed that he may have hit one in return.

Due to the rapid advance of the German army to the south, the 32 Mira was forced to move to the airfield of Tanagra, north of Athens. With all RAF Blenheim bombers now concentrated at Menidi, it was decided that all crews would operate under the control of 11 Squadron. Consequently, 14 Blenheims—six each from 11 and 84 Squadrons, and two from 211 Squadron—were off individually during the afternoon of **18 April** to make bombing and strafing attacks on German columns in the Kozani, Katerine and Lake Kastoria area. During one such sortie, the Blenheim flown by Sqn Ldr *Jonah* Jones, CO of 84 Squadron, was attacked by two Bf 110s of 8./ZG26 in the Larissa area, and was chased to the coast near Mount Mavrovouni, where he was obliged to ditch L1391 in the sea after being hit by Ltn Ferdinand Glanz.

Local villagers saw the crew climb into their dinghy and start paddling towards the shore, a local motor boat starting out to meet them. At this juncture the Messerschmitts dived on the dinghy and strafed it—Sqn Ldr Jones, Sgt Harry Keen and Flt Sgt Jacky Webb were all killed, their bodies being recovered and buried in the nearby village of Keramidi. A second Blenheim—T2348 of 11 Squadron—was intercepted in the Kozani area by two Bf 109s of 9./JG77 flown by Oblt Armin Schmidt and Oblt Kurt Lasse, after it had attacked a German troop column in which eight soldiers were killed an fifteen wounded. Plt Off. Pat Montague-Bates and his air-gunner 36-year-old Sgt Henry Murphy were killed, but the observer, Canadian Plt Off. Roy Edge made his way back to Allied lines.

32 Mira carried out its last mission during the day. Three Blenheims flown by Capt. Tsallas, Capt. Vogiatzis and 1/Lt Touliatos took off loaded with biscuits, tea and sugar packaged in sacks to the Albanian front in order to drop them by air on the cut-off 17 Division of the Greek Army. This was nothing more than a symbolic mission as the amount of the goods was not enough for all the men of 17 Division. Moreover, the sacks falling from the sky hit the ground in high speed and the goods dispersed over the area as observer 1/Lt Savoulides remembered:

What was really bad was that when the sacks hit the ground, they exploded like bombs and their content was broken in really small and, practically, useless pieces. Thus, we could not feel the joy and relief after this mission.

Some of the Greek aircrew now requested permission to fly the remaining Blenheims to Crete or Egypt, but permission was denied under the threat of court martial.

Following the capitulation of the Yugoslav armies, rumours were rife in Greece that surrender was imminent. The King of the Hellenes was determined that his country should fight on, and resolved to stay in Athens until the last possible moment, although others counselled that he and his government should evacuate to Crete forthwith. All available Hurricanes flew low over Athens to strengthen morale amongst the population, but in the city martial law was declared. Prime Minister Alexanderos Korizis was against a retirement to Crete, since he considered that pro-German elements would then seize power on the mainland and seek an armistice. Following an emergency meeting at which no decision was reached, Korizis shot himself, having learned that the commander of the Army of Epirus had initiated negotiations with the German *12th Armee* for its surrender, which would take place on 21 April.

With the abolishment of the two RAF Wings, Air Vice-Marshal D'Albiac took personal command of the remaining units from his HQ in Athens. While 19 April proved a quiet day for the Blenheims, the Hurricane pilots experienced much action. A similar scenario awaited the fighter pilots on **20 April**, culminating in the so-called Battle of Athens. In fiercely contested engagements during the day, a total of eight Hurricanes were lost (including Sqn Ldr Pattle who was believed to have shot down his 50th aircraft before his own demise) against some 20 claims (fourteen actual losses).

Odd Blenheims had been despatched to attack specific targets after dark, including V5424 crewed by Sqn Ldr Stevens, Flt Sgt Frank Mason and Sgt Jim Winship of 11 Squadron; Observer Mason noted:

> Arrived over target area 04:40, located village, roads and river, but not target. Low ground mist, and 7/10th cloud, poor moon. Dropped bombs and dived on road ... might be drome.

The Blenheims did not escape attention, however. 211 Squadron's Sgt *Jock* Marshall (L8501), returning from a solo night sortie to Kozani airfield, was apparently followed back to Menidi by a *Schwarm* of Bf 109s from III/JG77, as Sgt *Nobby* Clark recorded:

> On landing back at Menidi (06:40) we discovered it was a first for all of us!! We found we had been followed back by Me109s. Halfway between aircraft and the operations building the fun began. There were 109s everywhere we ran like hell [but] they were for [after] aircraft, however, not three little airmen— and they sure gave the place a going over. First floor of HQ was a marvellous grandstand.[30]

The Messerschmitt pilots claimed five Blenheims destroyed; several indeed were badly hit, and an ancient RAF Valentia biplane transport went up in flames. About an hour later a formation of Bf 110s from II/ZG26 made a second strafe of the airfield, their arrival coinciding with that of an 11 Squadron Blenheim flown by Sgt Vernon Hudson, who managed to get down and taxi to safety seconds before the Messerschmitts hit the target. Airman Comeau graphically described the attack:

> Preceded by a terrified assortment of stray dogs racing across the landing ground, the 110 Destroyers hit Menidi. Bellies scraping the grass, they flashed past as if propelled by the rhythmic thumping of their cannons. Suddenly the aerodrome was alight with Bofors and small-arms fire. A Greek Junkers burst into flames on the hangar apron. A Blenheim collapsed suddenly on a broken oleo. The noise was terrific. So low were the Messerschmitts flying that a nearby Bofors sent a burst into another Bofors across the aerodrome, killing the officer in charge. Then they were diving back for a second run in ... Out in the open a bunch of Aussie soldiers having a late breakfast alternated between taking mouthfuls of tinned sausage and rifle-potting the passing aircraft. A dozen columns of smoke arose among the Blenheims.[31]

LAC *Paddy* Duff, an 11 Squadron mechanic, was seen to grab a Lewis-gun from an unserviceable 84 Squadron Blenheim and walk up the centre of the airfield, blazing away from the hip at the oncoming Messerschmitts. Miraculously he was not hit. During the two raids four RAF Blenheims had been totally destroyed, two each from 11 and 211 Squadrons, one more from 84 Squadron had been seriously damaged, and another five from all three units had been less seriously hit. A Yugoslav SM.79 had also gone up in flames, as had the Greek Junkers and the RAF Valentia.

At least two Blenheims of 30 Squadron were sent from Maleme to Eleusis on special duties, L6672 flown by Flt Lt Horgan to collect some stores and then lead five Hurricanes to Crete. Sgt Geoff Chapman was on board as air-gunner:

> My pilot parked the Blenheim and went off to arrange for the stores to be loaded, leaving me to guard the aircraft. I got out of the turret and decided to relieve my bladder behind the tailplane, out of sight of the control tower. Whilst performing this act, an Army officer suddenly appeared from the other side of the aircraft and said 'That's a good idea" and so we urinated side by side. The officer was none other than General Wavell himself! I did not consider the situation called for standing to attention and saluting, and obviously neither did he. We then exchanged a few words and he went on his way.[32]

At 15:35, Eleusis came under attack by Bf 109s of II/JG27, their fire destroying several aircraft including two Hurricanes and two Greek fighters. Six RAF personnel were slightly wounded. Sgt Chapman continued:

Soon afterwards a squadron of Hurricanes landed for refuelling and rearming. As they taxied to the hangars I spotted a number of aircraft in line abreast approaching the airfield at high speed. I recognised them immediately as Me109s and shouted out the news to the ground gunners, simultaneously jumping into a nearby ditch. The ground defence was swift and accurate enough to bring down a Me109, but the enemy did considerable damage to our depleted fighter force. The captured pilot of the Messerschmitt was quite arrogant, confident that he would be rescued very soon since the Panzers were about 50km from Eleusis at the time!

Not surprisingly, there was a change in plan; instead of stores we took aboard about a dozen RAF tradesmen in the bomb bay and flew off back to Maleme. It must have been very uncomfortable for them but I know they appreciated the lift! [33]

The Messerchmitt pilot brought down was Obfw Fritz Rockel of 4./JG27, whose shin had been shattered by a bullet. One of the Hurricane pilots wrote:

Then there was chaos. The Greeks around us raised a shout and jumped on to the fire tender and headed out towards the crashed German aeroplane. At the same time more Greeks streamed out from every corner of the airfield, shouting and yelling and crying for the blood of the pilot. It was a mob intent on vengeance and one could not blame them.[34]

Fortunately for the German pilot RAF personnel reached him first and he was lifted from the cockpit and driven to the Medical Officer for treatment. Meanwhile, the second Blenheim, flown by Flt Lt Bob Davidson also had a narrow escape; as he arrived over Eleusis he was cheered by the sight of many Hurricanes in the air:

It was a grand show—I didn't think we had so many. I flew round with them, and then, to my horror, realised that they weren't Hurricanes at all, but 109s. There was a cloud of smoke in the corner of the aerodrome, so I put down in a flash and hid in the smoke.[35]

Amongst those sheltering at Eleusis was Flg Off. Len Bartley, a Canadian Gladiator pilot of 112 Squadron, who had not been allocated an aircraft when his colleagues had evacuated:

I hitch-hiked my way [from Yannina] to Athens—to see if by any chance I could get out of Greece in a Blenheim. All that night we sat in a blacked-out mess at Eleusis, carefully disposing of the bar stock, and when dawn arrived, so did the Me109s and Me110s.

After their first attack, six of us crawled aboard an aged Blenheim that had miraculously escaped serious damage. We were taxiing out at high speed when—wham!—we heard a heart-breaking crack. The tail had fallen into a hole in the grass field and the stern post had broken. So there we were, a sitting duck right in the middle of the airfield.

I thought I'd had it that time for sure. But just then another Blenheim—the last one on the field—taxied out for take-off. When he left we'd be on our own. But I was determined to get out at any cost. I charged across the airfield, and, just as the pilot was opening up, I grabbed his port aileron and waggled it frantically. The engines closed down momentarily and a head poked out of the pilot's compartment.

I recognised Bob Davidson's bushy moustache and beaming smile. "Get your men aboard" he yelled. We needed no second invitation. As six more chaps—in addition to the seven already there before us—climbed in an aircraft built to hold a crew of three. Bob looked a little worried for a moment. Then he said, "What the hell, let's go! Either we all make it or we all won't!" I don't like to dwell on that take-off. Suffice to say that at last we brushed through the olive groves at the end of the airfield and were on our way to Crete. Twelve people owe their lives to Bob's superb flying. Our overloaded aircraft broke its back as we landed on the short runway at Crete, but we were down.[36]

The last seven Blenheims of 32 Mira had also been ordered to Eleusis. Shortly after they had landed, the Messerschmitts struck, as Wt Off. Georgios Sakkis recalled:

The German aircraft burned half of our squadron's aircraft and some British, as well. I just managed to fall on the ground in order to cover myself. From my personal effects, I only saved a small suitcase containing my war diary, my flight logbook, my photographs and my letters, which I never parted with.[37]

B253 and B255, at least, were badly damaged during the strafe; while B268 was later captured on the airfield by the Germans more or less intact. That night, the RAF attempted to hit back, all remaining Blenheims at Menidi going off at ten-minute intervals, from 03:00 onwards, to bomb Kozani and Katarine airfields, and any motor transport that might be seen. All returned safely.

The Germans pressed home their advantage next morning (**21 April**), starting at Eleusis which was attacked between 07:00 and 07:30 by 20 Ju 87s and escorting Bf 109s, which strafed. It had become apparent from previous attacks that the Luftwaffe hoped to take the aerodrome for their own early use, and whilst strafing, no bombs had been dropped. Only the hangars were targeted by the Stukas, two damaged Hurricanes now being destroyed and several others further damaged. A Messerschmitt of I(J)/LG2 was hit by the light defences and later crash-landed.

Menidi was next to be attacked, a dozen Bf 109s strafing at 11:00, followed by Bf 110s. 211 Squadron's Sgt *Jimmy* Riddle noted:

The 109s knocked hell out of us at Menidi, during which I sustained a slight flesh wound to the arm from a ricochet, but I don't think there were any serious injuries to personnel.[38]

Several Blenheims were damaged, one beyond repair. The fighters also attacked Agrinion, claiming two aircraft destroyed there—presumably abandoned Yugoslav machines. At 14:45, it was Eleusis' turn for a repeat visit when Bf 109s strafed whatever targets found. It is believed that the day's attacks on both Menidi and Eleusis were carried out by II and III/JG77, a total of eight aircraft being claimed by the German pilots.

During the day the Luftwaffe had been involved in an incident of rather different character. A Ju 52/3m of II/KGzbV.172 was carrying a dozen paratroops to the Balkans when it strayed across the Bulgarian frontier into Turkish airspace near Edirne. Turkish AA at once opened fire and the aircraft fell in flames on Bulgarian soil at Otopeni, all on board being killed. Alarmed that some form of invasion might be threatening, the Turkish armed forces were put on immediate alert, two squadrons of Vultee V.11GB attack-bombers and one of PZL-24 fighters at once being moved to forward airfields in the area. Nothing further transpired, however.

Meanwhile, other Luftwaffe units hunted down the many evacuation ships, both large and small, with very little hindrance from the RAF. The full evacuation of troops from Greece commenced under the codename *Operation Demon*. Six beaches had been selected for the main embarkations. Many thousands of troops were now gathering at these points, and all roads leading to them were becoming heavily congested with British, Australian and New Zealand motor transport, Greek ox-drawn wagons and thousands of fleeing refugees. The first evacuations were scheduled for that night, and during the afternoon the ships began approaching, one being attacked and damaged *en route* and a second ran aground. Amongst those at Nauplia were a party from 113 Squadron, who had made their way from Niamata, led by Flt Lt Denis Rixson:

It was particularly galling and humbling to see the very poorly equipped Greek peasants going north to war, armed perhaps with old-fashioned rifles, when we were running away. After crossing the Corinth Canal, we found a railway train which we fired and drove to, or near, the port, which was a gathering place for people like ourselves, and other military support units who were hoping to get away. There was a fair amount of general disorder, but the Squadron was extremely well disciplined and received praise from the Irish Guards staff-major who was endeavouring to co-ordinate the evacuation as there was considerable unruliness amongst the various nationalities and arms being evacuated. We were evacuated with many others, getting to a variety of naval ships, using landing-type barges. The Navy looked after us very well, although the RAF was not all that popular as naturally the German air force had control of the air, and there was very little protection for the naval ships.[39]

That evening Greek forces defending the Larissa area surrendered, while on the Albanian Front, the Greek Army of the Epirus capitulated to the Germans also. Following the surrender of the Army of the Epirus and the damaging air attacks, the British forces prepared to leave Greece as quickly as possible, but in good order. Among those making preparations to leave was Capt. David Hunt, an army intelligence officer seconded to RAF HQ Ops Room, who recalled:

One of my last acts before leaving Athens was inspired by memories of what had happened after the surrender of France. A fair number of German pilots and other aircrew had been shot down during the [Greek] campaign, almost entirely by the RAF, and were in a prison camp very close to Athens. I had interrogated a number of them in the course of my normal duties. It seemed likely that the Greek government, if not the present one than at least its successor, might find it useful, for the sake of getting better terms, to hand these prisoners back [to the Germans] and put the RAF under the tedious necessity of having to shoot them down all over again.[40]

Following the fall of France the previous year, at least 400 Luftwaffe aircrew who had been shot down and captured by the French—including 43 Messerschmitt 109 pilots[41]—were handed back to the Germans, much to Prime Minister Churchill's anger; some were probably fighting the RAF here over Greece. Capt. Hunt continued:

I accordingly got hold of a number of lorries from the nearest RASC depot and picked up a platoon of Australians who had turned up in Athens claiming to have lost all touch with their unit. With these I drove to the cage and went in to see the commandant. He knew quite well what my motives were and though he felt he would get into trouble for it, he readily agreed. The German airmen, who were confidently expecting that their captivity would soon be over, were very upset at being moved out at short notice. I had them loaded on to the trucks, handed them over to the Australian subaltern and told him to take them to Piraeus and put them on a ship that was sailing in a few hours' time for Egypt. Later that afternoon, but after the ship had sailed, the inevitable row began; someone in a senior position in the Greek services was demanding the prisoners back. I never heard the final stages because I took care to keep out of the way.[42]

By now 11 Squadron had only four Blenheims still serviceable, and two of these were Mark Is that had been returned by the Repair & Salvage Unit after previous damage had been made good. Between raids these, together with those remaining in 84 and 211 Squadrons, began evacuating personnel to Crete. Each aircraft carried nine passengers at a time, but not without cost. On landing at Heraklion, 11 Squadron's N3560 burst a tyre, swung violently and suffered the collapse of an oleo leg. The pilot, Plt Off. Alex Darling, broke his arm but there were no other casualties. One of those to reach Heraklion was 11 Squadron's T2342 flown by Flt Lt Lawrence, which carried Sgt Jim Winship in the turret plus seven others squeezed into the fuselage including Sgt Frank Mason, the observer.

Next day (**22 April**), while flying back to Menidi from Heraklion for another load of passengers, 11 Squadron's Sgt Vernon Hudson experienced another amazing escape. His Blenheim (L1481) was intercepted by five CR.42s from Rhodes—probably from 163ᵃ Squadriglia Auto CT—and was badly shot-up; he just managed to carry out a ditching near a small ship and was soon rescued. Hudson's ordeal was far from over however, for as the vessel and another which was accompanying it approached Nauplia harbour, they were attacked by Ju 87s. Since both ships were carrying munitions, this was more than usually dangerous. Both caught fire, one blowing up on reaching port, while the one that rescued Hudson, was abandoned. As he and the crew swam for shore they were machine-gunned by the Stukas, which swept low over the burning ships. Nonetheless, Hudson managed to get ashore safely. He subsequently hitched a lift on another Blenheim heading for Crete. Soon after take-off this was attacked by a Bf 110 and badly damaged, but managed to reach Heraklion. He had certainly earned the soubriquet of *Lucky* Hudson.

All eight of 84 Squadron's Blenheims now left for Crete, led by Flt Lt Tony Plinston. A/Sqn Ldr Bill Russell, who as senior flight commander had taken over command, remained behind with an unserviceable aircraft (L1872):

> Plt Off. Shand was detailed to fly out in L1872, which had been undergoing repairs. I think it was a replacement of the outer panel of the wing, which was not quite finished. He made one of the quickest circuits ever, saying that the aircraft was uncontrollable in its present state, lacking fairings and other parts. So I let him have T2340, which was my aircraft.[43]

Sqn Ldr Russell remained at Menidi with three groundcrew working on L1872. After surviving a strafing attack at dawn on **23 April**, the Blenheim was considered fit for task and Russell flew the three airmen to Fuka. Their only navigation aid was an Admiralty chart of the Eastern Mediterranean.

Among those hoping to get away from Menidi were a group of 113 Squadron airmen, including LAC *Robbie* Robinson:

The 23rd dawned with Fred Archer, Corporal Dickenson, *Porky* Blyth, a small flight sergeant fitter (I can't remember his name) and myself, left as a sort of demolition party. The Jerries completed the job for us and left only a very much shot-up short-nose Blenheim: port cowling missing, oil leaking out, and some cockpit instruments missing, as well as a very flat tyre full of holes. Also, the cockpit hood would not slide shut. As time went on in between Me109 raids, we seriously considered trying to get this kite into the air. During a lull in the proceedings, a pilot appeared, who had previously been shot down, and said that if we could service the Blenheim up to a point, he would get it and us into the air.

Late in the afternoon we all scrambled into the Blenheim, now capable of flight. *Porky* Blyth was in the turret, Fred Archer in the bomb well and [the others] somewhere in the nether regions; myself in the nose compartment with instructions as to the course and colours of the day (which I made a complete balls of). We ran up the engines that grunted and groaned, the wing flapped. One thing I remember very clearly is a great hoarding carrying a poster of 'Vote for General Metaxas' slap bang in the line of take-off and it presented a problem. We charged at the image of the General on the hoarding. I swear to this day that we passed through his left ear-hole!

We took-off during a raid on the port of Athens, but they were too busy to bother with us. We wallowed along at sea level, partly from choice and partly from circumstances, and as the shipping was pretty active, I fired the colours of the day at a destroyer—and was greeted by a very fine burst of naval ack-ack and some unprintable abuse from the pilot (I had got the colours mixed up!) We steered by visual map-reading, by spotting the islands *en route* and by the sun (the compass was u/s), and finally we located Crete—with a very much over-heated engine owing, no doubt, to the oil leak.

After cruising around for a little time we spotted Heraklion strip and prepared to come in—downwind, I think—only to see a perishing clot in a steam-roller systematically rolling the surface. When he saw us he nipped away smartly, leaving us and the roller to fight it out. We got down after a fashion, churned off the runway and came to an ungraceful stop in the grass and shrubs at the end of the runway. After getting out gingerly we dashed off into the rocks as some flipping Huns decided to have a look more closely at the strip.

Robbie added:

One thing I always think about: not one of us had the faintest idea whether we had enough petrol for the trip. It wasn't even checked as far as I know! The pilot and I, some time later, set fire to the aircraft [possibly L8444] as it was u/s, and Jerry was now obviously in charge of the situation.[44]

Of the remaining Blenheim-occupied airfields, only Menidi suffered further heavy attack, on **24 April**, as Marcel Comeau again recorded:

Messerschmitt fighters over Menidi put on an aerobatic display which would have drawn a crowd in times of peace. Yellow-nosed 109s skimmed around the perimeter, making daisy-cutting turns, chasing stray airmen down the trenches, and firing at everything and everybody. Twice forming line-astern they roared flat-out across the grass towards the hangars, stood on one wing, and sped like letters through a letter-box through the gap between the sheds. Messerschmitts appeared suddenly from below hedges, among tents, and round hangar corners. Airman in tree-tops and trenches, firing at them, stood in admiration of their flying skill.[45]

Elsewhere, the remnants of the RAF fighter units were moving south, most occupying the small airfield at Argos in the Peloponnese, prior to flying onwards to Crete. Even at Argos, to where many Greek aircraft had evacuated, there was no respite from the strafing Bf 109s and Bf 110s. Following the latest attack on Argos, thirteen of the remaining Hurricanes had been destroyed. Almost all the Greek aircraft had also been destroyed. Air Commodore Grigson, AOC Greece, now ordered all flyable Hurricanes—just seven—to make for Crete, while spare pilots were to follow aboard an RAF Rapide, that had narrowly avoided being shot down by a Hurricane on its arrival at Argos. After dark three Lodestars arrived to collect key personnel. At 04:30 on **24 April**, the Lodestars, the Rapide and the Hurricanes departed for Crete, followed by four Greek Avro Tutor trainers, the sole remaining PZL-24, and five Ansons of 13 Mira that had arrived from Eleusis.

Originally there had been eleven Ansons about to evacuate to Crete via Argos, but only five arrived. Due to a lack of Greek pilots to fly them, Wg Cdr Lord Forbes offered his services[46.] He was asked to take the wife of a member of the Greek government but, in the event, she failed to turn up. For the flight he co-opted his Intelligence colleague Capt. David Hunt, who had been expecting to board a vessel at Nauplia for a sea journey to Crete; the latter wrote:

The suggestion was … I would go along to man the single machine-gun with which these slow and antiquated machines were equipped. As a matter of fact I would much rather have gone by sea but I could not think of a way of putting this delicately. The idea was that we were to take-off at first light in order to be under way before the usual German fighter patrol turned up. After a reasonably peaceful night we turned up at the appointed time with the usual pre-dawn qualms. The Greek pilots proposed to take off first so we had to wait. The tenth had just gone and we were about to taxi off when the siren went.

For some reason the Germans were early. We would have had little chance either of escaping notice or avoiding being shot down so we tumbled out of the plane and into a slit trench close beside it. It was the deepest slit trench I have ever been in, being a good six feet deep in hard soil. This turned out to be a good thing. The six Messerschmitt 109s lost no time in shooting up our Anson, which roared and crackled some 20 yards away from us, but they also machine-gunned our slit trench.

After they had gone away, fortunately without shooting-up the car we came in, we took breakfast with the aerodrome commander and considered the next move. Fortunately Lord Forbes, who had retained his diplomatic connections, was aware that the British Legation had been provided with a steam yacht which was sailing that evening; and he had been promised a berth if all else failed.[47]

The intrepid duo soon found themselves aboard the yacht HMY *Calanthe* and set course for Crete, sailing under cover of darkness. To avoid becoming a target for any prowling German aircraft, the yacht pulled into a bay on the uninhabited island of Polygos during the hours of daylight. However, it was soon spotted by a pair of Messerschmitts—probably from III/JG77—the leading one scoring a direct hit with one of four bombs it dropped. Two people aboard the yacht were killed and others injured. Lord Forbes had been on board and had to swim ashore with nothing but a pair of trousers. After dark two motor launches arrived from the nearby island of Kimolos, evacuating one and all. Here, Forbes and Hunt located the only tailors shop on the island, where an off-the-peg suit was purchased for his lordship—mauve in colour! Luckily for the stranded party, a caique soon arrived from Crete. The sequel to Lord Forbes' adventure was recorded by Sqn Ldr Tommy Wisdom, an old acquaintance, whom he met when he arrived at RAF HQ Crete:

One afternoon two bedraggled and queerly dressed figures presented themselves at Headquarters. It was difficult to recognize the dapper Lord Forbes, with a smear of oil across his face, torn trousers, and a jacket that looked as if it had been filched from a scarecrow. Willie [from RAF HQ in Athens], with a cut across his forehead, was attired as a sort of Ruritanian sailor. They told the story of their adventures since leaving Athens.[48]

CHAPTER 9

Retreat to Crete – and Defeat

[Jock Ratlidge] opted to carry the maximum number of men rather than equipment. In his aircraft there were 11 passengers. We could hardly breathe, so absurdly tightly packed were we.

Cpl Bob Lawrence 30 Squadron

Ultra intercepts had by now indicated to the British Command that Crete was likely to be the next German objective, although Cyprus also seemed to be at risk to provide a stepping-stone to Syria and Iraq if the situation in those countries warranted further involvement.

Even as the RAF remnants were arriving in Crete, Air Chief Marshal Longmore and Air Vice-Marshal D'Albiac flew in on a short visit to assess the requirements of the fighter defence. They soon realised the impossibility of defending the island against the Luftwaffe soon to be installed a mere 50 miles away in southern Greece. Their conclusions were: 'No intention of reforming RAF Greece HQ.' The Hurricanes and Gladiators evacuated from Greece would remain, mainly for morale-boosting purposes but reinforcements, even if available, would not be sent. Also to remain were the Blenheim IFs of 30 Squadron, mainly for protection of the evacuating vessels from Greece and also for convoy protection. The surviving bomber Blenheims of 11, 84 and 211 Squadrons—a motley collection of about twenty aircraft of dubious serviceability—were to return to Egypt, conveying those military personnel lucky enough to be selected for evacuation. Airmen Jack Clarke and Len Cooper of 211 Squadron's A Flight found themselves left behind to service any more Blenheims arriving from Greece, as the latter recalled:

A few aircraft came in. I can remember a Lysander blowing a tyre, which we changed and a Hurricane which we refuelled; I can't remember any others. There was a Blenheim abandoned off the runway at the bottom of the airfield. An officer, don't know where the hell he came from—it must have been Hooper—told us to go and see what is wrong with the Blenheim. I got in the cockpit and tried to start the engines, just got a lot of banging and popping. We took off the cowlings and took all the spark plugs out, cleaned them and put them back, adjusted the mag contact breaker points which couldn't have been moving they were so badly worn; we cowled up; I ran the engines; they were spot on.

I had just got out of the cockpit, when Hooper and a Sgt Navigator came along. Hooper asked me what the engines were like. I said they were fine; he asked us where out kit was; we had it with us, he said, "Get in, we're going to Egypt." I was told to man the gun turret. I hadn't a clue how to use it. I can remember that I nearly froze to death; I just had a greatcoat on, no hat or gloves. At 10,000 feet it gets a bit chilly. We landed at Heliopolis to refuel, then went on to Ismailia.[1]

30 Squadron's Blenheim IFs had already opened their scoreboard for Crete. At 13:05 on **18 April**, the Canadian Flg Off. Andy Smith set out from Maleme to patrol over Convoy *AN-27* as it approached Suda Bay. After 30 minutes on station he saw two SM.79s approaching from the south-west of Melos. These were torpedo-bombers of 279ª Squadriglia AS from Rhodes led by Tenente Umberto Barbani. Smith closed in and opened fire on the leading aircraft. Black smoke poured from its starboard engine, the undercarriage dropped down, and he believed that the aircraft had fallen into the sea; it had indeed come down, Tenente Barbani ditching near Kamali Rock, all the crew sustaining injuries; they were later rescued by a Z.506B. Meanwhile, Smith attacked the second aircraft, flown by Tenente Angelo Caponnetti, seeing sparks from its starboard engine, but the Blenheim was then hit by return fire. As Smith returned to Maleme, one of his engines began to burn as he went into final approach, but the fire was swiftly extinguished by the observer, Plt Off. Joe Strong.

A steady flow of aircraft was now coming in and out of Crete between Greece and Egypt, via Crete. On this date, a Sunderland alighted in Suda Bay from Greece *en route* for Alexandria, carrying King Peter of Yugoslavia, his prime minister and other members of the Yugoslav Royal Family and of the political and military staffs. Two days later another Sunderland staged through on its way to Scaramanga, returning with sixteen RAF passengers and the AOC's wife, Mrs D'Albiac, complete with her pet canary. Another arrival soon after was a Sunderland carrying King George and Crown Prince Paul of Greece, Sir Michael Palairet, the British Ambassador to Athens, his wife and daughter. They were followed in by yet another Sunderland with 50 RAF personnel on board.

Lt Alf Sutton, 815 Squadron Senior Observer and FAA Liaison Officer in Greece—who had just navigated a motley collection of ten Yugoslav floatplanes from Patras to Suda Bay—arrived at Maleme with orders to direct construction of an underground operations room, but already the first three Swordfish of 815 Squadron were ordered to leave for Egypt. This was a 300-mile flight to Mersa Matruh, Lt Lance Kiggell taking off to lead Lt Lamb and Sub-Lt(A) Rudorf. After about an hour's flight Rudorf's engine began to play up, and sighting a convoy through a gap in the clouds, he headed down, intending to ditch near one of the ships. On emerging into clear air directly over the vessels, he spotted a section of Fulmars (from *Formidable*) climbing towards him, and fearing that these might consider his aircraft to be hostile, he climbed back into cloud, thereby losing sight of the convoy. As a result he decided to head on for Mersa Matruh, landing there safely after some four hours, ten minutes over the sea with a faulty engine. Kiggell and Lamb had already arrived, though both had experienced engine misfires.

During **20 April**, the day of the big air battle over Athens, Blenheim IFs of 30 Squadron were again out on convoy patrols. Some 35 miles south of Gavdhos Island, Flg Off. Andy Smith spotted an SM.79 approaching Convoy *AS-26*. He carried out a stern attack, but after one attack his guns jammed and he was forced to break away. He had nonetheless been successful in causing the bomber to break off its intended attack, and believed that his short burst had killed the rear-gunner. On **22 April**, seven Blenheims of 30 Squadron were tasked with evacuating ground personnel of 33 and 80 Squadrons from Eleusis, and each aircraft carried up to nine men.

During an attack on Suda Bay on the morning of **23 April**, a patrolling Blenheim IF of 30 Squadron flown by Flg Off. Ralph Blakeway intercepted two Ju 88s without obvious results. Meanwhile, other Blenheims of this unit flew up to Eleusis to pick up a group of stranded personnel. 30 Squadron's Cpl Bob Lawrence recalled how he escaped from Eleusis aboard his friend Sgt *Jock* Ratlidge's Blenheim:

Jock bade us all to jettison our rifles, tin helmets and all luggage, because he opted to carry the maximum number of men rather than equipment. In his aircraft there were 11 passengers. We could hardly breathe, so absurdly tightly packed were we. I was pressed hard into the front cockpit, my back pressed in the curved shape of the perspex nose panel, facing the pilot's knees, with other men squashed close to me so that breathing was slightly restricted and *Jock* had difficulty in operating the controls.

Knowing every inch of Eleusis aerodrome as I did, I twisted my head round to watch our hoped-for take-off. We all thought little of our chances of reaching our destination, the island of Crete 450 miles away, and I watched *Jock* frantically trying to get the aircraft off the ground. As it dragged its weight towards the windsock I felt convinced we could not clear the hedge on the perimeter, which appeared all too swiftly. Miraculously, we just scraped over it with wheels up. We made no circuit of the airfield but were on our way at low level across the Aegean Sea, ever watchful for German fighters.

Jock seemed the most unconcerned of us all, smiling and joking between spasms of tuneless Scottish humming. Somehow we made it. We lobbed down heavily on Maleme airstrip after approaching at almost sea level, despite German fighters dancing about above us hoping to destroy all evacuees on arrival. *Jock* bundled us out of his aircraft in great haste, keeping the engines running as we were in the middle of the small airfield. We ran for cover as he flew back to Eleusis for another load of men, and I certainly didn't envy him.[2]

Another who was kept busy at this time was Sgt *Jock* Marshall, who made twelve evacuation flights from Greece to Crete, as noted in his DFM citation:

This Senior NCO has done 52 raids over Libya and Greece and has always shown the greatest determination. On one particular raid to Durazzo, Albania, his aircraft was hit very badly and he managed, by skilful handling, to out-manoeuvre fighters in the vicinity and land safely and unharmed at Larissa. On another raid to Valona, his aircraft was badly hit in the tailplane by an anti-aircraft shell, but he again arrived safely back at Menidi. During the evacuation from Greece, he did several evacuation trips (12) from Menidi to Crete in the face of enemy danger always around Menidi.

Of the chaos prevailing at this time, Sqn Ldr Wisdom wrote:

Just before we said goodbye to Eleusis, one of 30's Blenheims smashed a tail-wheel. The pilot was told to come aboard a Bombay. We landed at Herkalion. Our men were getting out. Little *Pee-Wee* [Allison] and *Bud* [Richardson] had gone back to Eleusis to see if the wrecked aircraft could be saved. The smashed tail-wheel was placed on a wheeled trolley which *Pee-Wee* pushed down the runway as *Bud* wrestled the tail into the air and took off. He got into the air, *Pee-Wee* jumped into the aircraft in which they had come from Crete, and the two landed at Maleme. The salvaged machine was operating next day.[3]

In a subsequent letter to his family in Canada, Flg Off. Richardson recalled his own version of events on that day:

I had the pleasure of being the last person to bring an aircraft out of Athens. Had to go back and fly a damaged plane which had been left there. I flew a plane back with another pilot to bring it back. When I landed, a wing commander rushed out and proceeded to lay me low: "What the bloody hell are you doing back here?" I told him I was going to try and take the damaged kite back, whereupon he said I couldn't possibly get it off.

Well, I knew if we could find a battery trolley (a small cart for carrying batteries), we had a good chance of getting off by lifting the tail up by itself before it dropped off. After the fifth try, with the aircraft dropping off with a crash, got a couple of chaps to push the trolley down the runway after me until

I got up speed to hold up my own tail. Off I went in a crazy take-off with the kite swinging about 60 degrees from the direction of starting. Just managed to skip through a couple of hangars before I got it straightened. At that time the Jerries were dive-bombing and machine-gunning everything in sight, so was pretty lucky to get away with it. I guess, if they had ever caught me fooling around with this plane, I sure would have picked up a bit of trouble.

Bringing this crock back over a couple of hundred miles of water was quite good fun too. The bloody rudder had been bashed up a bit and she didn't control very well, but after the take-off, it managed to stagger to Crete OK. The landing was easy. Had a strong wind and did a long wheel landing.[4]

Next day (**24 April**), Lt Tom Winstanley flying Sea Gladiator N5535 of 805 Squadron from Maleme encountered a Ju 88, one of several attacking the Greek freighter *Kyriaki* in Suda Bay. He made two attacks but without observed results. However, a 30 Squadron Blenheim (K7179) encountered a Ju 88 at 17:35 while on a shipping patrol. Approaching apparently unseen, Plt Off. Lawrence Basan (with Sgt Bill Gair as observer) put four bursts into the aircraft—L1+KH of I/LG1 flown by Fw Walter Zucker—which made off to the north-east, pouring black smoke. It eventually ditched in the sea but only the pilot survived to be rescued; his crew—Gfr Hans Kieser, Gfr Adolf Balkenhol and Gfr Fritz Rubsam—were lost. Zucker claimed that he had been shot down by Gladiators, his crew claiming to have shot down one of the attackers. It would seem that they did not see the Blenheim, as surmised by Basan.

More Blenheim fighters—IVFs of 203 Squadron—now arrived to support the handful of 30 Squadron machines. The five aircraft landed at Heraklion and were led by Sqn Ldr James Pike DFC (T1821); another four would arrive next day led by Sqn Ldr John Gethin DFC, a 23-year-old Irishman from the Republic, in L9174. Each aircraft carried ground crew and a supply of spares, including tail wheels—frequent victims of Heraklion's rutted landing ground.

At dawn on **25 April**, six Blenheim IFs of 30 Squadron and three IVFs from 203 Squadron were sent off to cover evacuating vessels from Greece, but Air HQ had failed to advise of each other's involvement—hence Blenheim pursued Blenheim, fortunately without effect. Meantime, some bombs were dropped on the convoy by unseen aircraft. However, at 08:00, Flg Off. Andy Smith spotted two Ju 88s at about 4,000 feet and attacked both, claiming hits on one that dived away, pouring black smoke. The other was believed to have been hit by ships' AA fire.

With many of the escaping vessels now approaching Suda Bay on the morning of **26 April**, including a convoy loaded with troops from the Megara beaches, a number of small-scale air attacks were made. First came two Ju 87s, then a pair of bomb-carrying Bf 109s, then a few Do 17Zs. Three Blenheims of 203 Squadron were airborne but were fired on by one of two north-bound convoys seen, one aircraft sustaining slight damage.

At 11:00, enemy aircraft were seen approaching convoys, which became mixed up when passing each other, and shortly before midday, a dozen Ju 87s attempted to attack, but their formation was broken up by the escorting warships, while three 203 Squadron Blenheims, which were in the vicinity on patrol, attempted to engage. Sqn Ldr Gethin (L9174) attacked a formation of eight Stukas, hits being observed on several from both front and rear guns (air-gunner Sgt Neale). Observers on the ships reported that at least one was seen to be shot down, but no German losses are known. Gethin continued his pursuit for ten minutes but could not gain on the fleeing aircraft. Another Blenheim, L9335 flown by Flg Off. Ernest Lane-Sansam, was attacked by a reported five Bf 109s and one Ju 87, his aircraft receiving some hits on the wings, but he escaped by diving away and leading his pursuers over the naval barrage.

At 11:50, three Ju 88s attacked the ships but gained no hits, while a further attack by three more at 13:15 achieved no more success. As the vessels approached Suda Bay, Hurricanes, Fulmars and Sea Gladiators from Maleme, and 30 Squadron Blenheims from Heraklion appeared overhead. At 18:00, the convoy put in to Suda Bay; one troopship had six feet of water in her hold due to damage to her plates caused by near misses, but there were no casualties amongst the 3,500 troops she carried.

Luftwaffe assaults on the convoys and other shipping fleeing the Greek mainland continued unabated on **27 April**, including one evacuating troops from Kalamata. At 08:00, a single Do 17 carried out an attack, this being claimed probably shot down by gunners on the destroyer HMS *Defender*, but unfortunately their fire also hit a pursuing Blenheim of 30 Squadron, K7177/VT-N flown by Flt Sgt Don Innes-Smith. He managed to get back to Maleme, where his aircraft was deemed irreparable. Some twenty minutes later a dozen Ju 87s appeared, six taking *Defender* as their target, gunners aboard the destroyer believing they shot down one and damaged another.

Three Blenheims of 203 Squadron then arrived on the scene, reporting 20 dive-bombers, six Bf 110s and some Bf 109s. Sqn Ldr John Pike (T1821) fired three bursts into one Stuka but was then attacked by several other aircraft, his own machine suffering severe damage. Meanwhile, Flt Lt James Whittall (L9237) and Plt Off. John Wilson (L9215) chased a Bf 110 (of I/ZG26), but after being observed to close in and fire a burst from the starboard quarter, Whittall's Blenheim disappeared in a steep dive and was not seen again; in addition to the pilot, Sgt Stan O'Connor and Sgt Tom Air were lost. It was presumed that the Blenheim had been shot down by the aircraft it was chasing, or by another. While Sqn Ldr Pike returned to Heraklion with his damaged aircraft, Wilson maintained a lone patrol over the ships. Observers aboard the destroyer HMS *Hero* reported seeing a Blenheim shoot down a Ju 87—obviously Pike's combat—and this was probably Oblt Harry Lachmann's F1+MN of 5./StG.77, although allegedly falling to AA fire. Lachmann and his gunner Obfw Werner Merten were lost. Further sections of Blenheims continued to patrol over the various small convoys throughout the day, but there were no further engagements although attacks on the vessels continued.

With dawn on **28 April**, three more 203 Squadron Blenheims approached to escort the vessels, lowering their undercarriages and flashing the letter of the day, but were nonetheless fired on by one of the destroyers. No damage was initially reported, but a few minutes later Plt Off. Peter Gordon-Hall in L9044 advised his leader that his starboard engine was on fire, and that he was returning to Crete.

> We set course for Crete but agonizingly we could not hold our precious 1,000 feet of height, despite jettisoning all we could. I think our poor Blenheim had endured too much harsh wear and tear in the desert! Eventually we sighted the coast and willed our aircraft on but it was not to be. Three miles out we were down to sea-level and I had to ditch. The gun-tray under the belly caught the surface and pulled the front end down under the sea. Cliff Poole [the observer] got out only after a struggle but I felt that my seat harness had jammed. There followed one of the worst half minutes of my life while I fought to get free which I did, coming to the surface badly in need of air.[5]

The three crew members managed to get into their dinghy that the gunner Sgt Ivor Oultram had released, and watch their Blenheim slip beneath the waves. They then paddled towards land for an hour-and-a-half where, a quarter-of-a-mile out from the town of Retimo, a Greek soldier swam out to them and towed them in to shore. However, the incident did not finish there as the locals thought they were German:

> In a last desperate effort, I took a deep breath and shouted all of the basic Anglo-Saxon obscenities I knew; this registered! This is recorded in the official history of the RAF—a unique achievement to be mentioned by virtue of the use of bad language![6]

Subsequently, a signal of protest was despatched to the navy by AOC Crete, Grp Capt. George Beamish. Meanwhile, Blenheim L1098/M of 30 Squadron flown by Flt Lt Derek Walker and carrying Sqn Ldr Tommy Wisdom, took off to search for 'strays' on the beaches of southern Greece; the latter wrote:

> We are looking for ships. We glance at Antikythera; we scour Kythera. We dive low and look into the little fishing boats. None of our chaps are there. We pass over Cape Matapan, that most southerly point in all Europe, which gave its name to the great naval victory of a few weeks ago. We scan Kalamata, where so many of our chaps have come away from the beaches. All is quiet. But some of our men were hiding in the woods, as we learned afterwards. They had

been incessantly hunted by German aircraft through all the hours of daylight. They thought we must surely been another Heinie. We had already gone when someone realised that our plane was a Blenheim.

The tiny islands are emerald green, and the deep blue water is flecked with gold as the sun comes up. We scour the southern Peloponnese; every creek and inlet is searched for our men. We look into each tiny caique. Then we search the coastwise tracks, and the olive groves beside them. We go to the entrance of Argos Bay. We turn southwards, for there are more islands to be examined. Then, a mere speck in the distance, we spot a white flash on the surface of the sea. We speed towards it, lose, then find it again. A few minutes ago we were bemoaning the fact that our search was fruitless; but now we are keyed up. The air-gunner in the rear turret has been warned.

Friend or enemy? Then, as we dive down out of the sun, the ship answers the question. Above her, diving down repeatedly, and sweeping her decks with machine-gun fire, are two great black craven birds of war—Me110s. The little ship, zigzagging furiously, is doing her puny best with her few machine-guns. We take the Messerschmitts by surprise. Our guns send a blistering burst of lead and tracer into one. They make away at speed, their prey forgotten. Both rear-gunners are firing their vicious twin guns at us; we can see the little red flashes coming towards us. Suddenly one of those rear-gunners stops firing.

Those Me110s are certainly fast—they disappear in a flash. We circle the tiny ship, and someone on deck waves a hand. But the disappearance of the German fighters is ominous; they are probably getting into the sun for a stern attack on us. And the inter-com has packed up. I look back through the fuselage. The air-gunner is strangely still—has he got a packet? [the gunner was unhurt]. But we must have warning of stern attack. Our hatch cover is gone—I push my head out into the slipstream. I can see nothing as I stare into the sun. We are flat out: all the knobs are in their most forward position. An anxious 10 minutes passes. No sign of the Messerschmitts; we hope they've had enough and have made for home.

Our island comes into view. We touch down, taxi to our position, climb out and pass the aircraft to the fitters for inspection. They call us over, and the flight sergeant asks: "What have you been doing, sir?" as he points to two great rents. A bullet has torn a hole through the main plane, two feet from the cockpit—and my seat. Others have blasted their way through the port engine nacelle. Phew![7]

Following a German attack on the island of Melos the previous day, a report was received that four Ju 52/3ms had landed there. Two 30 Squadron Blenheims were despatched at dawn on **29 April**, but no aircraft or troops were seen. Its job done, 203 Squadron was now ordered to prepare to return to Egypt, the vanguard (four aircraft, each carrying three groundcrew) departing Heraklion at 17:00 on the afternoon of **30 April**, led by Sqn Ldr Gethin. Obviously, Ops Room at Maleme was unaware what was going on at Heraklion, since a patrolling Hurricane pilot reported:

> While returning to base I saw four aircraft in line-astern, very low down. I went in very close and recognised them as Blenheims with what appeared to be English markings … I reported this and was informed that no Blenheims were airborne.[8]

Fortunately for the Blenheim formation, the Hurricane pilot was returning from combat and therefore low on ammunition so did not attack. However, *en route* to Egypt, the Blenheims approached the Royal Navy's Battle Squadron and were intercepted by two sections of Fulmars of 803 Squadron from the carrier *Formidable*. Orders—which had not been conveyed to Sqn Ldr Gethin—required aircraft approaching the Fleet to do so in line-astern, with the leader firing the colours of the day.

PO(A) Arthur Theobald, with L/Air Freddy de Frias in the rear cockpit in N1912, was first to attack, as de Frias recalled:

> With our Ju88 complex, they were fair game … fortunately we only damaged them on our first run, and realised as we turned for another go that they couldn't be 88s if we could have two goes at them![9]

Leading Airman de Frias, who always carried a Tommy-gun in his cockpit, added:

> At our speed of just over 200 knots you only got one pass. I couldn't see much—there was practically no forward vision from the rear seat of a Fulmar, and in any case I was looking for other 88s. You didn't last long if you forgot to do that.[10]

The Blenheim attacked, Plt Off. John Wilson's L9215, was only slightly damaged. The other Fulmars pulled away when Very lights were fired, and the Blenheims continued on their way. On return to *Formidable*, both Theobald and de Frias were grounded pending possible court martial, but this was apparently soon forgotten when action intensified in the weeks to follow.

With Crete increasingly under attack, a number of 30 Squadron's more experienced pilots volunteered to take turns to fly the Hurricanes, thus relieving the handful of RAF and FAA fighter pilots. These included Sqn Ldr Milward, Flt Lt Davidson and Flg Off. Richardson[11] who each undertook patrols, though they failed on encounter raiders during their sorties.

In the early hours of **1 May**, a Sunderland departed Suda Bay for Alexandria. Aboard were Air Vice-Marshal D'Albiac[12], General Maitland-Wilson, and several members of the Greek Royal family including Prince Paul, his wife and two children. From the other direction a Lodestar arrived at Maleme bringing General Wavell to the island. He brought with him the enlightening, if disturbing, news that the plans for the German invasion of Crete had been decyphered (by *Ultra* intercepts, to which General Bernard Freyberg VC, the garrison's newly appointed commander was not privy), which revealed that an airborne invasion was highly probable.

The few remaining Blenheims of 30 Squadron continued to carry out reconnaissance sweeps, one flying to Piraeus harbour on **3 May** to check on the number of ships present, but no movements were observed. Before retuning to Crete, the Blenheim overflew Hassani airfield where a number of well-dispersed aircraft were seen. Next day (**4 May**) Flt Lt Horgan (L4825) undertook a recce in the Athens area; his gunner Sgt Geoff Chapman commented:

> We were surprised to see so many aircraft, particularly Ju52s, parked at our former airfields. Little did we realise that they were being assembled for what was to be the first [*sic*] and most successful [*sic*] airborne invasion of the war.[13]

The next few days' operations over and around Crete continued in a desultory fashion, daily patrols by the Blenheims and fighters netting no engagements for a week. With the Blenheims now in urgent need of servicing, the decision was taken to send them back to Egypt, thus on **7 May**, five unserviceable 30 Squadron Blenheims were sent back together with several Fulmars and Sea Gladiators.

> *Lofty* Lord was one of the lucky airmen to leave Crete for the relative safety of Egypt prior to the island being besieged by the might of the German Luftwaffe. Five of 30 Squadron's aircraft were ordered to return to Egypt for complete overhaul as they were operationally unfit. He took off from the island for the last time on 7 May, and made his last flight in Blenheim K7099 with Flt Lt Davidson and Sgt Bill Gair.[14]

L4825, with Flt Lt Horgan, Plt Off. Strong and Sgt Chapman on board, departed five days later. Flg Off. Richardson followed next day in L4917 with four passengers. There remained just three serviceable Blenheims, but one of these was badly damaged in a bombing raid directed against Maleme at 05:00 on **15 May**. The airfield was now becoming too dangerous for these aircraft, and about an hour later the last two Blenheims left for Egypt. Sqn Ldr Milward was approached by Cdr George Beale, the Naval OC of Maleme, who asked if he would accompany an 805 Squadron Sea Gladiator that was also returning to Egypt. Reluctantly he agreed. Half way to Mersa Matruh the Gladiator's engine failed and its pilot Lt Peter Scott was obliged to ditch. The Blenheim circled the position but could see no sign of the pilot. A Sunderland was sent out but similarly could not find him. "Another unnecessary waste of life" remarked Sqn Ldr Milward.

In his subsequent report, Air Vice-Marshal D'Albiac noted:

In Crete, Blenheim fighter patrols were organised to cover the ships evacuating the troops from the beaches. These escorts were maintained throughout the evacuation without respite, and I consider it was due largely to their efforts that such a large proportion of the total British forces in Greece were evacuated.[15]

During the afternoon of **16 May**, the defenders were encouraged when nine Beaufighters arrived at Heraklion, having flown from Malta, following an appeal from Grp Capt. Beamish to ME HQ for a strike to be made on southern Peloponnese airfields where the Messerschmitts were assumed to be located. Before dawn next morning (**17 May**), the Beaufighters set off in three sub flights to attack the airfields at Hassani, Argos and Molaoi. At Hassani only Ju 52s were seen and although some 20 of the transports were believed hit, actually only one was destroyed and four others badly damaged; one Beaufighter was shot down by AA fire and the crew killed. Better success was achieved at Argos, where three Bf 110s were destroyed and 11 damaged, while at the coastal strip at Molaoi, a number of Bf 109s and He 111s were believed damaged. After refuelling at Heraklion, the eight surviving Beaufighters returned to Malta.

The Luftwaffe blitz intensified over the next few days, destroying on the ground and in the air the RAF's remaining fighters, but not without cost. Bombers and dive-bombers escorted by Bf 109s and Bf 110s took a heavy toll of gun sites and other ground defences. Soldiers, sailors and airmen all became targets, even before the air invasion commenced. 11 Squadron's Airman Marcel Comeau, one of many RAF ground personnel left behind, and a comrade were buried in their gunpit by one bomb burst, but were dug out by others before suffering any serious effects. With the attack still in progress, Comeau headed for the shelter of a nearby slit trench just as two elderly Cretan civilians reached it, and just as another bomb landed close by. Again he was buried but this time managed to free himself, but he could no longer see the Cretans. Digging frantically with his bare hands, he managed to locate and free them, although one died shortly afterwards. He would later receive the Military Medal for this action.

At 08:00 on the morning of **20 May**, the first of almost 500 heavily laden Ju 52/3ms began disgorging their paratroopers over the island, preceded by bombing and strafing, and followed by glider troops. The battle for Crete had begun.

CHAPTER 10

Airmen Soldiers

Appropriately wild poppies now grow among the olive groves where Ken Eaton,
Tubby Dixon and many others met their death. Nearby, there is a small shrine
and Cretans continue to lay fresh flowers beside it … I felt that the RAF would
ever be present in that peaceful olive grove.[1]

Airman Marcel Comeau 11 Squadron

The Luftwaffe's initial and priority target was Maleme airfield, the capture of which would provide a landing ground for the troop-carrying Ju 52s and gliders. But before the paratroopers came an intensive bombing attack by Do 17s and He 111s, followed by Ju 87s and strafing Messerschmitts, against the defenders of the airstrip and gun positions among the slopes of the overlooking Kavkazia Hill (known as Hill 107 to the British). Due to the effective slit trenches that had been dug by the soldiers and airmen here in recent weeks, casualties were relatively light. At the airfield were the rear parties of 30 and 33 Squadrons—229 officers and men—together with 53 FAA officers and men. 30 Squadron's party was commanded by their armament officer Plt Off. Richard Crowther, who was responsible for a total of 115 airmen.

Then came the Ju 52s disgorging hundreds of paratroopers and soon fierce fighting was developing at the eastern end of the RAF camp where groups of airmen were being cut off as the Germans infiltrated. One small party of six airmen from 33 Squadron held out in their trench until their ammunition ran out, and then attempted to retreat as paratroopers approached over the iron bridge. Only three made it. An urgent call went out for medical aid on the airfield and 30 Squadron's ambulance, driven by LAC *Ginger* Betts, with LAC Norman Darch as medical orderly, ventured out across the open area under fire. Although wounded in the back by two bullets, Darch helped rescue a number of wounded and got them to comparative safety (he was awarded the MM). LAC Betts was killed—the first of 30 Squadron's 30 fatalities over the ensuing days.

The RAF men were congregating mainly on the lower slopes of Hill 107 in small parties, trying to reorganize and formulate some plans for defence and survival. It had been proposed that in the event of invasion, officers and NCOs of the two units (30 and 33 Squadrons) would defend allocated sections, and would each be responsible for small groups of airmen. Following the landings, 33 Squadron's CO Sqn Ldr Edward Howell made his way to 22nd NZ Battalion HQ where he discussed events with Cdr George Beale and Colonel L. Andrew VC. Coming under sniper fire, the three carried out a reconnaissance of the forward area to inspect troop disposition, Col Andrew expressing his satisfaction with these before returning to his command post. Beale and Howell, accompanied by a handful of airmen, continued to the area where gliders had landed when suddenly a shot rang out and Beale fell, a bullet in his stomach. At about the same instant Howell was hit by machine-gunfire, one bullet smashing his left shoulder, a second striking his right forearm; an airman was also hit in the ribs.

Ill-armed and in a hopeless position, the various groups of airmen were now led away from the vicinity of the airfield by their officers and NCOs; most headed inland for safety. Fighting side by side with them were FAA personnel. When the attack on Maleme commenced, 30 Squadron's MO, Flt Lt Tom Cullen, was attending to the sick and then the wounded as they were brought in. He remained at his post until the Sick Quarters was overrun and he was taken prisoner. Flt Lt Cullen recalled:

We were overrun by a group of paratroopers, one of whom was a doctor. Later in the day we were moved back to the village at the western end of the Tavronitis bridge. The wounded were gathered together in buildings on the opposite of the road from a German casualty clearing station. German medical staff were helpful in supplying some instruments, dressings and chloroform. They thought their attack had failed and we would be released.[2]

Even then he carried on alone, without sleep for three days, until more captured MOs joined him. Over 1,000 wounded would pass through his hands before further aid was made available. Among those brought in were Sqn Ldr Howell and Cdr Beale, both of whom had survived the initial assault, and a 33 Squadron Hurricane pilot whose leg had been shattered; another Hurricane pilot was killed in the ground fighting. Those most seriously wounded were soon flown to Athens aboard Ju 52s. Meanwhile, Plt Off. Crowther was shepherding his men:

At the beginning of the attack I reached the prearranged position [on the hill near the airfield] at the rear of the New Zealand troops and remained there during the morning. Those of our men not occupied in defending the lower slopes were withdrawn to this prearranged position to act as support troops. It was here that I gathered a handful of men and proceeded to the far side of the hill, where I heard parachute troops were obtaining a hold. The men in the deep dug-out on that side had not been warned of the approach of parachute troops. After mopping up the parachute troops here I discovered that the enemy had obtained a foothold on the eastern side of the aerodrome, actually above the camp. I gathered 30 New Zealand troops who appeared to be without any leader and with my handful of RAF I made three counter-attacks and succeeded in retaking the summit. Throughout this period we were subjected to severe ground strafing by Me109s; the enemy's armament being very superior, namely trench mortars, hand grenades, Tommy guns and small field guns. One particularly objectionable form of aggression was made by way of petrol bombs. These burst in the undergrowth and encircled us with a ring of flames.

At this time I was trying to obtain contact with the remainder of 30 Squadron personnel cut off at the bottom of the valley by the side of the camp, in order to withdraw them to more secure positions on the slopes overlooking the aerodrome. The time was now about 14:00 hours. The enemy drove our men who had been taken prisoner in front of them, using them as a protective screen. Any sign of faltering on their part was rewarded with a shot in the back [30 Squadron's Sgt Max Hoyes was killed in such a manner]. Our men were very reluctant to open fire and gradually gave ground. A small party of RAF led by Corporal [Bill] Harrison succeeded in out-flanking them on one side, and I and a handful of New Zealand troops on the other were able to snipe at the Germans in the rear and succeeded thereby in releasing at least 14 prisoners.[3]

Sadly, about half of those who had been captured were killed in the cross-fire. Following the initial confusion, the FAA Liaison Officer, Lt Alf Sutton, found himself in charge of a party of RAF men:

Left by myself on the hillside, I hurried off to find a position where I could fire at the parachutists … one man landed very near me—a matter of four yards or so—and I remember shooting him as he rolled to disengage himself from his parachute. At about this stage I heard a call from behind me. I turned quickly to look back. I spotted a RAF fellow who was shouting and beckoning. He was outside the olive grove so I hastened away from the trees to join him. In next to no time, others linked up with us and before long we had formed a group of around a dozen or so men. I found myself in a duel with a particular sniper. I knew where he was, although he had made a decoy which he hoped I would aim at. Every time he fired, I fired back

I gathered together quite a group of airfield personnel. As the only officer, the men would follow me. They knew me; I had been working with them at the airfield for about a month.

We heard the sound of more marching feet at which point another contingent of airfield men appeared. The group was under Flg Off. [*sic*] Crowther, an armament officer who I knew to be a very effective man. He was a tough, rough individual who was a very good fighter.[4]

One party of about a dozen RAF men who had become separated from the main body included LAC Ken Stone of 30 Squadron:

We encountered a group of severely wounded men being nursed under the trees as best those who stayed with them could do. It was one of the saddest moments, for I knew some of them. We carried on up the hill in single file … travelled all night and when dawn came took shelter under a wall. We had no idea where we were, but soon found that we were in the centre of fierce cross-fire. Any hope we had of joining up with our forces or of sleep we so badly needed was impossible.[5]

Morning on 21 May, found the Germans most favourably placed at Maleme, where daybreak attacks by Bf 109s and Ju 87s prevented the New Zealanders launching any organised counter-attack against the critical Hill 107. Apart from the constant strafing however, it was relatively quiet here and around Canea, with only skirmishing activity occurring. Amongst those 30 Squadron personnel captured was LAC *Micky* Walker, who with others found himself at Maleme helping to recover and evacuate wounded German troops:

A German shouted for us to go over to where the wounded were lying. While we were sorting ourselves into parties, we heard the roar of aircraft, this time coming from the sea. Suddenly they came into view—Ju 52 troop carriers, flying almost at sea level and presumably coming in from Greece. As they drew close to the landing ground, they broke formation and the leading aircraft made a circuit preparatory to landing. For a time we watched them. The landing ground was pitted with bomb and shell craters, and each time an aircraft landed all eyes focused on it. Would it land safely or end up in a crater? The first five succeeded in avoiding trouble, but the sixth touched down on the very lip of a huge crater and went straight over on its nose. A moment later there was a muffled explosion, followed by a cloud of black smoke.

The sound of tearing metal drew my attention back to the landing ground. Another Ju 52 put down, and as it ran along the ground, brakes full on, one wheel ran into a crater. The machine swung violently around, breaking part of the undercarriage. Then it keeled over and one wing hit the ground. The wing buckled and broke off, then crashed into the side of the capsizing fuselage. There was a dull explosion, and almost immediately the aircraft was hidden from sight by smoke and flame.

While I was watching it burn, there was another crash. Smoke rising from the first wrecked aircraft partly hid it from view, and another troop carrier had landed right on top of it. I strained my eyes to see if there were any survivors but saw none. Soon it was burning fiercely and I could hear the crackle of exploding ammunition. Within minutes the landing ground was enveloped in a thick cloud of black smoke. The chances of the remaining aircraft making safe landings was practically nil. The pilots could see neither craters nor wrecks, and every few minutes a crash told us of another casualty.[6]

The various RAF and FAA parties still at large, mainly without weapons, were gradually being led away from the forward areas. Permission was granted for them to head for Canea. For the best part of the week the party, now numbering about 120 men, travelled southwards, guided by Cretan shepherds. The group in which Airman Comeau was travelling, commanded by a Canadian flight lieutenant of 33 Squadron, had only reached the outskirts of Suda Bay by the afternoon of 25 May, as Comeau recalled:

Then, in the afternoon, a Blenheim dived low over the Bay with three gun-blazing Messerschmitts on its tail. It was the first British aircraft we had seen that week and we felt enraged frustration that we could do nothing to save it. The bomber did not stand a chance and crashed into the water.[7]

The doomed aircraft, in which the whole crew perished, was one of three 14 Squadron Blenheims shot down that afternoon (see Chapter XI). Comeau's party was now ordered to make its way over the central mountains, since an evacuation was taking place from Sphakia, although the Canadian officer himself was to be air evacuated that evening. For the remainder of the party, now under the command of another 33 Squadron officer, two trucks were provided and with all crammed aboard set off along the winding mountainous roads that night. They eventually reached Sphakia, from where they were evacuated aboard the destroyer HMS *Kelvin*. Meanwhile, LAC Ken Stone's party was also on its way to Sphakia:

Passing through the gorge of Samaria some of us were able to get a little food from the monastery, although the monks had little for themselves. Weary as we were, we kept going day and night to reach the evacuation beach. There, we were told to wait in a rocky clearing with hundreds of others, and to appoint one man in charge of a group of fifty, all of whom must be of the same units. There were not a dozen RAF men, let alone fifty, so I made up a list of odd bods and waited for the call that never came.[8]

As the sun rose, a German officer appeared and ordered the men, now numbering several thousand, to display on the beach anything white they possessed to signify surrender to the German pilots flying overhead. Sadly, the Luftwaffe was not aware of local events, as wave after wave of Ju 87s dived on the helpless mass:

Down came the bombs, and the strafing carved visible paths through the mass of men caught in the open. How many died I don't know. I dived behind a rock with another man at my side. He was not fully protected by the rock and a hail of bullets took off his arm at the shoulder, and he died at my side. Finally they flew off, and the German officer apologised through his loud-hailer, explaining he had lost contact with the Luftwaffe.[9]

As fortune or luck would have it, Lt Sutton's party had reached Spahkia a few hours earlier, as had Plt Off. Crowther's 30 Squadron party, about 30 strong,:

Our men were the last to leave the beach for the ships, and at 03:00 we set sail. During the early hours of the morning we were treated to our last dive-bombing attack, which luckily proved abortive.[10]

As the battle and the evacuation drew to a close, some 12,500 troops had been left behind, of whom 226 were RAF personnel. Many of these had already been captured, but those still at large were given discretion to surrender, fight on, or escape if they might. The majority did surrender, but many attempted to evade and escape. Indeed, by the end of 1941, over 1,000 escapees from Crete—as well as from the Greek mainland and the Aegean islands—had arrived back in Egypt by various means and routes. In the fighting, 30 Squadron had lost twenty men killed—the majority of whom have no known burial places —with a further 58 taken prisoner. Total RAF casualties numbered 71 out of a total 1,751 British and Commonwealth fatalities, not counting Royal Navy losses amounting to 1,828 killed.

CHAPTER 11

Blenheim Sacrifice

... the cost has been very heavy in relation to strength. Especially in Blenheims—
Blenheim dawn and dusk raids in particular have been expensive, both in Crete
and on return to the Desert.[1]

Air Chief Marshal Sir Arthur Longmore AOCME

In Egypt, based at Fuka, was the Blenheim Wing that comprised 14, 45 and
55 Squadrons, all with Mark IVs, as part of 204 Group commanded by Air
Commodore Raymond Collishaw, the Canadian World War I fighter ace. He
also controlled a Wellington bomber wing with three squadrons, a Maryland
bomber squadron and four squadrons of Hurricanes.

To the north of Crete on **21 May**, a Maryland of 39 Squadron on a reconnaissance
from Egypt, encountered a single Ju 52/3m making for the island, which
was promptly despatched into the sea. An important discovery by another
reconnaissance aircraft, on this occasion a Blenheim of 45 Squadron, was made
when Flt Lt John Dennis and his crew spotted a number of small craft escorted
by destroyers making for Crete from Melos. It was the reinforcement convoy
with heavy equipment, arrival of which was critical to the success of the German
invasion. One of the Blenheim Wing's units, 14 Squadron suffered a disastrous
mission on this date, losing five aircraft and crews (all killed) during a mission
along the Capuzzo-Tobruk road.

With darkness on the night of **22/23 May**, three Wellingtons from Egypt arrived
with urgently needed supplies of ammunition and medical equipment, which
were dropped from 200 feet to the defenders of Canea, Heraklion and Retimo;
at the latter location the stores fell into the sea. The Wellingtons were followed
by five Blenheims of 45 Squadron led by Sqn Ldr James Willis (V5022), which
departed Fuka at 03:00. Becoming separated in the darkness, two failed to reach
the target, Maleme, while the other three bombed individually. The crew of one,
flown by Lt Enock Jones[2] SAAF (V5592), reported seeing their bombs straddle
the airfield. Apparently a Ju 52/3m of KGrzbV.60 was destroyed by the bombing.

Air Commodore Collishaw was anxious to strike at Maleme by day, and on
the morning of **23 May**, five Blenheims of 14 Squadron with an escort of three

Hurricanes fitted with non-jettisonable long-range tanks, set off. Observer Plt Off. Geoffrey Whittard recalled:

We were ordered to attack Maleme landing ground in daylight. We welcomed the change of target, which would entail a flight duration of more than five hours, leaving little reserve on our Blenheims' maximum range; and as the majority of the flight would be over the sea, other factors, especially on the navigation side, would have to be calculated from a new angle.[3]

However, shortly after take off the leading Blenheim developed a fault, all turned back and the raid was aborted. Seven SAAF Marylands carried out a successful attack on Maleme during the early afternoon, and all returned safely. This attack was followed by four Blenheims of 45 Squadron, which dropped 20 lb and 40 lb fragmentation bombs, but the leading aircraft flown by Plt Off. Paul Vincent (V5624) failed to return. It had in fact been intercepted by two Bf 109s, one flown by Obfw Georg Bergmann of 9./JG77 and the other with Ofhr Günther Hannak of 2.(J)/LG2 at the controls. Vincent and his crew (Plt Off. Stuart Niven RNZAF and Flt Sgt Ossie Thompson) were lost. Finally, two Beaufighters, which had just arrived in Egypt from Malta, swept in to strafe Ju 52/3ms that were seen disembarking troops. During the course of these raids, ten Junkers transports were believed to have been destroyed or badly damaged; records show that six were destroyed, mainly aircraft of KGrzbV.106 and I/LLG.1. Among those on the receiving end of the raid on Maleme were the 30 Squadron captives, LAC *Micky* Walker recording:

I set off in the direction of the tent. I was over half-way there when I heard a series of high-pitched whistles coming from overhead. "Bombs! Run for it!" I heard someone shout. I turned and ran for the building, but before I reached it the first bombs had exploded. I threw myself to the ground, clawing at the earth with my hands and feet in an effort to dig myself in. The ground all around me began to quake and erupt; the noise was deafening. I grew frightened, and angry. Frightened because I though I was going to be killed; angry because I would be killed by British bombs!
    I continued to claw at the earth. If only I could get closer to it and surround myself with it, I would be safe. But the ground was too hard and my fingers made little impression on it. Then I tried to resign myself to the end. No one without shelter could hope to live through this more than a few seconds. Then suddenly the bombing stopped. It was all over and I was still alive! Getting to my feet, I shook myself. Yes, I was still in one piece and uninjured![4]

Earlier in the day, six Hurricanes had been despatched from Sidi Haneish airfield to fly to Crete; the fighters were to land at Heraklion from where they would combat the Ju 52/3m troop-carriers. That was the plan, but soon after setting course for Crete with a Blenheim guide, the aircraft overflew a number of British naval vessels which put up such a tremendous barrage of fire that the formation became scattered. While one Hurricane reached Heraklion, the other five headed back to Sidi Haneish to report on the aborted flight including the belief that the Hurricane and Blenheim guide had been shot down. The same five pilots plus one replacement were sent off again at 15:20, shortly before the 'missing' Blenheim returned. The pilot explained that after the formation had become separated he met up with a lone Hurricane and escorted it to Crete, where he presumed it had landed at Heraklion.

Meanwhile, the second flight of Hurricanes reached Heraklion, there to find their 'missing' comrade, whose aircraft had been damaged, only to be advised to leave next morning at first light since Heraklion held only a limited amount of fuel and no ammunition for the Hurricanes. On the return flight, two of the six aircraft ran out of fuel and crash-landed on the Egyptian coast and two others failed to return, believed shot down by British naval forces.

On the night of **23/24 May**, nine out of ten Wellingtons despatched to bomb Maleme released their bombs over the target area, one having returned early with technical problems. Three failed to return, one of which belly-landed at Heraklion; another ditched in the sea on the return flight, its crew rescued, but of the third nothing more was heard. During the daylight hours of **24 May**, two Blenheims of 45 Squadron flown by Sgt Eric McClelland (V5766) and Sgt Sam Champion (T1823), acted as guides to four Hurricanes that carried out another strafing attack on Maleme. On the return flight, Sgt McClelland's Blenheim suffered an engine failure when it entered a sandstorm, hit a ridge south of Sidi Barrani and force-landed; none of the crew (Sgts Vipond and McGurk) was hurt. The Wellingtons were out again that night (**24/25 May**), but only two actually reached and bombed Maleme.

On **25 May**, 204 Group's involvement in the battle over Crete was much increased. However, due to the inexperience of some navigators, who had learned their trade over the desert, and were therefore not competent to fly long distances over the sea, a trawl of more capable navigators was made. Thus some crews included a navigator from another squadron. At dawn, first strike was carried out by six Blenheims from 45 Squadron led by Sqn Ldr Willis (V5422) and four Marylands that bombed and strafed Maleme. Three Blenheims of 55 Squadron then followed, experiencing only light flak; and were followed by six 14 Squadron Blenheims led by Sqn Ldr Deryck Stapleton. These approached Maleme low from the east and bombed from 2,000 feet. The crews saw a number of Ju 52/3ms already on fire as a result of earlier attacks, and added their light bombs to the carnage. An estimated 24 aircraft were considered to have been destroyed or badly damaged, although many of those hit were almost certainly already wrecked. One Blenheim, that flown by Flt Lt John *Buck* Buchanan, was slightly damaged by flak, the gunner of which, Sgt Ball, was wounded in the foot from small-arms fire.

A second raid by another five of 14 Squadron set off at 10:45, but turned back when the leader's aircraft developed engine trouble. A third raid, comprising three aircraft of 14 Squadron, took-off during the afternoon but, over Suda Bay, they were intercepted by patrolling Bf 109s of II/JG77. Within minutes, Flt Lt Richard Green's T2065 (with Plt Off. Anthony Browne and RAAF Sgt Norman Wilson, an Australian from Wagga Wagga) had been shot down into the sea, followed by V5510 (19-year-old Lt Stan Forrester SAAF, with Sgt Wilf Fretwell and Flt Sgt Ron Hall) and T2003 flown by another South African, Sgt Harold Jeudwine (with Flt Sgt Henry Young and Flt Sgt Norman Lake); all nine crewmen perished. Two of the Blenheims fell to Uffz Rudolf Schmidt of 5 Staffel, the other being shot down by Uffz Herbert Horstmann of 6 Staffel. It would appear that return fire from the gunners struck the Messerschmitt flown by the Gruppe's long-serving Kommandeur, six-victory ace Hptm Helmut Henz, who was killed when his aircraft crashed into the sea off Antikythera Island during this combat. Lt Eric Lewis, SAAF pilot with 14 Squadron recalled:

> We took a beating over there so lost a good number of old faces, including my oppo Stan Forrester. I was lucky, in that after being briefed for a Crete raid, I threw stones for our flight dog to chase, and put my back out. I could hardly walk, let alone fly. I was damn lucky. No one came back from that raid. I had to go to hospital in Alex for treatment.[5]

Three 55 Squadron Blenheims, which arrived shortly afterwards, escaped interception and returned unscathed. They were followed during the afternoon by yet another four Blenheims of 45 Squadron, but three turned back with minor defects, leaving Lt Enock Jones SAAF (with Plt Off. Lawrence Bourke RNZAF and Sgt Ben Whiteley) to bomb alone. They reported near misses with their 20 lb bombs. The final strike of the day against Maleme was made by three Marylands and two Hurricanes. One Maryland and both Hurricanes were shot down.

The Royal Navy's First Battle Squadron departed Alexandria at midday for operations around Crete. On this occasion the battleships *Queen Elizabeth* and *Barham* accompanied the carrier *Formidable*, as well as eight destroyers. The carrier carried a dozen Fulmars and a mixed strike force of 15 Albacores and Swordfish. The Air Group's first task was to be a dawn raid on Scarpanto, since it was obvious that the island's airfield was being extensively used for operations against Herkalion and south coast ports. The subsequent strike was considered successful but the carrier was soon to be located and bombed by Ju 87s, forcing the Battle Squadron to return to Alexandria. Having called for aid during the Stuka attack, a lone Blenheim IVF from 45 Squadron was despatched from Fuka, followed shortly thereafter at intervals by three sections of Hurricanes.

Throughout **26 May**, aircraft of 204 Group once more became very active, the first strike of the day being made by six Marylands. Four of these were to bomb and strafe Maleme, while the other two were to drop medical supplies and ammunition to the garrison at Retimo. One of the supply-droppers, flown by an all-French crew, was shot down. The pilot was killed but his crew survived to be taken prisoner. Three of six Hurricanes sent of at intervals were also shot down. One of the survivors of the Maryland recalled vividly the moment the aircraft was shot down, similar to that experienced by many of the Blenheim crews:

> We noticed Canea on the way in and then arrived at Maleme; there was a crowd on the beach. The pilot sprayed the Ju 52s with his machine-guns and I joined in with my two machine-guns in turn. The reaction soon came—tracers arrived from all sides—above, below, right, left. The other gunner stated later that a German fighter had been attacking us. Brutally the plane side-slipped. I fell and the gunner fell from his turret, landing on me with his knees in my back. In falling he pulled out his intercom wire; there was total silence and we became entangled in our parachute harnesses. The plane flew on but through the machine-gun holes I saw the ground rapidly approaching. I waited for the crash and I braced myself, then … a void. On touching the ground the barrel of my machine-guns had pivoted on their axis and the sight had hit me on the head. When I regained my senses I saw that the plane was resting on its belly along a ditch, broken by the banking—an incredible chance. The engines were on fire and the heat revived me. No question of escaping from below so I detached my parachute and the gunner struggled to free the hatch near the turret. I helped pull him out but the moment we reached the ground a patrol of Austrian mountain troops appeared and captured us. I tried to indicate by gestures that there had been four of us in the burning plane [the pilot was killed].[6]

Six Blenheims of 45 Squadron were briefed to make a dusk attack on Maleme, but just prior to their take-off at 17:00, two more Hurricanes were sent off to strafe the airfield. Both returned safely, but the defences were now on full alert, and the Blenheims led by Sqn Ldr Willis were caught by patrolling Bf 109s of 6./JG77. The Messerschmitt leader, Oblt Walter Höckner, engaged Sgt Neville Thomas' T2339 and shot it down in flames with the loss of the crew, Sgt Geoffrey Adams and Flt Sgt George Grainger: their bodies were recovered and buried at Suda Bay. Höckner then attacked the leader, Flg Off. Tom Churcher's V5592, and severely damaged it. The crew baled out over land, Churcher and his observer Plt Off. Roderic May being captured at once, but the gunner Sgt Harry Langrish, a Canadian, was more fortunate in that he evaded capture and wandered for two days and three nights until he reached the south coast, where he was rescued by the destroyer HMS *Kandahar*.

Oblt Höckner claimed another Blenheim shot down, his second victim presumably T2350 flown by Plt Off. 'John Robinson' (in fact Plt Off. Désiré Celestin Guillaune Verbraecke, a Belgian RAF pilot using a *nom-de-plume*). Having become separated from his colleagues, Verbraecke suddenly found two Messerschmitts were overtaking from 600 yards astern. Undeterred, he flew straight on to Maleme, where the fires started by the other two were seen, and dropped his bombs before taking evasive action. Meanwhile, the Blenheim had taken several hits but Verbraecke managed to evade further attacks and turned for home. After two hours flying, he found himself in darkness and with only ten gallons of fuel in the tank, but overland, he ordered the crew to able out. With pilot and observer gone, air-gunner Sgt *Bing* Crosby found that his hatch would not open and it was some moments before he could get out. Then, fearing that the aircraft was too near to the ground, he pulled the release handle immediately. He came down on his back with such force that for 24 hours he was partially paralysed, and only able to crawl. Dragging himself along for about three miles over the salt flats, he found a rock under which to shelter for the night.

Next morning, Sgt Crosby sighted a figure some distance away. He waved his scarf and shouted for some time until he was able to attract his attention. It was Plt Off. Verbraecke. As soon as they joined forces, Sgt Wilf Longstaff, the observer, was then found. The three men took stock of their position. They had no water, no maps and no food. Southwards stretched nothing but flat salty desert, to the north a chain of mountains running east to west. After some discussion it was agreed that Crosby should rest in a nearby cave, while Verbraecke would search for the water bottle he had dropped on baling out, and Longstaff would search for the crashed aircraft. Both returned without success. But then Longstaff mentioned a flashing beacon he had seen to the north-east when he had baled out, and believed they should now search that area, but, as Verbraecke later explained:

I had seen a rather peculiar phenomenon of scintillation [atmospheric effects that influence astronomical observations] caused by the stars: if I placed myself in a certain position, I could see the glare of a particular star circling around the hilltops. This glare—which became strong as a beacon—enabled me to see my shadow in its light. This is evidently what he had seen. I therefore forbade him to look for it.[7]

However, Longstaff insisted he was going to search for the believed beacon and despite much opposition from Verbraecke and Crosby, set off on his quest at midday in searing heat. He was never seen again.

Meanwhile, Verbraecke and Crosby continued searching for the crashed Blenheim and eventually found the wreck at the bottom of a 1,000 feet gorge. It was totally smashed and partly burnt: and there was no trace of water. At 03:00

on the morning of the 27th, they set off again, skirting the mountain towards the east, which Longstaff had set out to climb, hoping they might find him. Six hours later they came across a small valley, where after failing to find water and eating some aloe berries, they found a cave in which to rest. Verbraecke's report continued:

It was then that the idea occurred to me that these mountains were not of the usual type; all the peaks were of same height, and reminded one of the cliffs that border certain seas. I presumed that we were in a depression and that above, there was a plateau, which constituted the normal level of the desert. Hence there was no hope of circling round the escarpment; the cliff had to be climbed. To make a success of the climb this time, I decided to spend the first half of the night resting.[8]

That evening, however, while looking for berries, they came across traces of their missing companion Sgt Longstaff, in the shape of what they described as 'tired footprints' and set out to look for him. In spite of their searching for some eight hours, they were unable to find him and concluded that he must have dragged himself into a cave in his last despairing efforts. The following day at dawn they set out to climb the mountain while they still had enough strength, and after four-and-a-half hours of struggle they reached the top, with a view of limitless desert stretching in front of them to the north.

Having now roughly plotted their position they decided to aim for their base, Fuka, on the coast. Walking slowly, they rested for half an hour every hour, seeking shelter from the blistering sun. After three days their small supply of berries had run out, but then Plt Off. Verbraecke found some small shells on the ground, as Sgt Crosby recalled:

He broke them with his teeth, and then seemed to suck something out of the shell. He told me it was good, so I straightaway picked up a shell and put it to my nose. The smell was putrid and I brought up in an instant the little I had in my stomach. Early next morning there seemed to be nothing else but these shells on the ground which I discovered were snails. I was absolutely dry by then and decided to try one.

I found that they had a very minute quantity of water and that after sucking about 30 of them, which was a very disgusting operation, one felt refreshed for about one hour—and so it went on until 31 May, when the snails ran out. There were just the empty shells. It seems that the birds were a little ahead of us.

Anyway, that particular morning I had a very strong feeling that we would strike something or other, and told the pilot about it, but he did not believe or trust my intuition, so I kept it to myself with the thought that at the first opportunity I would prove myself right or wrong. I had not long to wait, as my pilot asked me if I would like to walk another mile or two and see if there were any more snails, while he looked for shelter.

I immediately got up and set off at a pace which surprised me, and after about 2½ miles I did manage to pick up a few that had been left by the birds. I signalled to my pilot to come, and then carried on due north by means of the sun. After walking another 5½ miles, I struck a camp which had just been made a Forced Landing Ground. After having some water and something to eat, I accompanied the MO in an ambulance to where I had left my pilot.[9]

So, after five days of almost super-human endurance, the two airmen were flown back to their unit, and from there to hospital. The remains of Sgt Longstaff were never found.

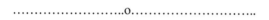

Despite the approaching evacuation, Air Commodore Collishaw considered 204 Group should continue to do what it could to frustrate the German advance—but the next 24 hours were to prove more costly than effective. Some unanticipated help came from an unexpected quarter during the early afternoon of **26 May**, when Do 17s subjected elements of the 85th Mountain Regiment to a heavy bombardment commencing at 13:00. This, in spite of swastika flags in evidence and the firing of white flares. The attack continued until 14:00 and inflicted a number of casualties and also had a very detrimental effect on troops' morale.

During the night of **26/27 May**, six Wellingtons again raided Maleme. At 03:00, three Blenheims of 45 Squadron prepared to take-off from Fuka to repeat the attack, but the leading aircraft—V5896—crashed and burst into flames. Flg Off. Norman Pinnington and his observer Plt Off. Howard Irving RNZAF were killed; the gunner Sgt Richard Martin was thrown clear, though badly burned, and succumbed to his injuries three weeks later. The operation, during which spikes and small bombs were to be dropped, was cancelled.

Early on the morning of **27 May**, while two Marylands were out making recces along the coastline of Crete, at their bases in Egypt, Blenheims were being prepared for yet a further attack on Maleme. 14 Squadron at Quotaifia landing ground (near el Daba) could make available just three aircraft, 55 Squadron at Ma'aten Bagush managed to assemble six. Just after 14:30, the first Blenheims began lifting off the latter base. The first pair collided as they became airborne, Flg Off. John Harris managing to belly-land with only minor injuries to himself and crew, but Sgt Bill Martin's aircraft T2051 spun in with loss of all aboard (the others being Sgt Eric Martin and Sgt Keith Bamber). The other four got off and raided Maleme successfully, believing that many of the Ju 52/3ms seen on the ground were probably destroyed by their bombing.

In rapidly failing light the Blenheims became separated during the return flight and only two landed back at base. The other two had become lost over the desert, both crashing. The wreck of T2175 and the bodies of the crew (former Halton Apprentice Sgt John Chesman, Sgt Doug Callender RNZAF and Sgt Ray Lyle) were found by a searching Lysander. The skipper of the other missing Blenheim (L9319), Sgt Richard Bale RNZAF (from Manawatu) had ordered his crew (Sgt Alf Wiles DFM and Sgt John Rigby) to bale out when their fuel was exhausted; all three arrived back at their base two days later.

The 14 Squadron section fared no better. One aircraft returned early with engine trouble, while the other two, which were to bomb troop concentrations between Maleme and Suda Bay, could not find their target so bombed the airfield instead. On return, in darkness, they became separated, both becoming lost and also crashing in the desert. V5593 came down 30 miles south-west of Mersa Matruh. The French-Canadian pilot Flg Off. Jean Le Cavalier ordered bale-out, though only the observer Sgt Len Page survived, Sgt Charles Bury's body being found beside the aircraft. The pilot was found dead at the controls. Sgt Page walked across the desert to Mersa Matruh. The Blenheim strike had achieved little. Six of the nine participating bombers had been totally lost—none to enemy action—while nine crew members had perished. 204 Group's Blenheim Wing could ill-afford such a rate of attrition.

The final operation of the day was launched at 15:30, when two Hurricanes rendezvoused with Blenheim T2243 of 45 Squadron flown by Lt D. Thorne SAAF, directed to attempt further interception of the Ju 52/3m air convoy still streaming in to Maleme. As the trio headed towards the south coast of Crete however, they encountered six Ju 88s of II/LG1 and attacked at once. Lt Thorne made a port beam attack on one low-flying bomber, the crew claiming that considerable damage had been inflicted and believed it was probably destroyed. Both Hurricane pilots also engaged, each believing that they had shot one down; indeed, the Blenheim crew reported seeing one Ju 88 falling in flames, and believed two others hit the sea. In fact, only one was lost, Ltn Hans-Georg Freysoldt and his crew (Uffz Paul Schnalke, Gfr Erwin Schäfer and Uffz Erwin Kreter) perishing in L1+EW. Presumably all three fighters had attacked the same aircraft, each unaware of the others' involvement. The Hurricanes flew onwards to Crete, landing at Heraklion following an uneventful patrol, while the Blenheim returned to base.

One 14 Squadron Blenheim was still unaccounted for—T2338 that had crash-landed 60 miles south of el Daba, the pilot Flg Off. Murray MacKenzie—a New Zealander in the RAF —having ordered a bale-out as the aircraft ran out of fuel:

Sgts [Bob] Fearn and [Jack] McConnell[10] drifted down on their parachutes … at a distance of about half a mile apart. They could see nothing above and nothing below. Naturally, they could not see each other, nor had they any

means of knowing whether their pilot had baled out or not. Then the worst
happened. There was a sudden violent explosion from below. For one instant
both saw a mass of wreckage as the aircraft they had left crashed headlong into
the scrub … the crash did not catch fire … after that one explosion the darkness
closed in like velvet.

When each man had dropped into the sand, released himself from his
parachute, and then got up, there was nothing whatever to give him an idea
as to which way to walk. The two sergeants tried shouting and hallooing …
and then listening breathlessly. But they were too far apart to hear each other.
Added to this, the stars were obscured and, until the early glow of the sun
heralded the dawn, they had no idea of north, south, east or west. Their only
hope was that they were already overdue at their home base and a search would
be laid on for them pretty soon.

Searching aircraft were despatched at dawn, but by noon they returned
reporting no sign of either crash or survivors in spite of an intensive low-
level quartering of the ground all about the area. Group HQ was notified and
therefore a big Bombay troop-carrier set out to take over the rescue attempt
[flown by Flg Off. George Allcock, also a New Zealander in the RAF]. For the
next two days the Bombay searched from dawn to dusk. Towards the end of
the third day MacKenzie's Blenheim was found near the edge of the Qattarra
Depression. The Bombay came down to land … the members of the search
party tumbled out and examined the crash carefully in the blazing heat of the
sun. But they found none of the crew, living or dead. But what they did find
… not far away from a rough desert track … was a parachute laying in the
sand. To their astonishment they saw the cords of the parachute had been cut
clean through, obviously by a knife. A little further away was a broken stick. A
careful examination showed that what seemed like half-obliterated footprints
of a lame man led from the scene of the crash to where the parachute and the
cut cords were lying. Other than these extraordinary clues there was nothing to
show what had happened to any of the men who had been flying the aircraft.

The search all over the crash area was then intensified, but it was not until
the sixth day that the first survivor was sighted. He was staggering drunkenly
across the desert, miles to the north of where the aircraft had gone in. His
face and his body were so hideously covered with insect bites that at first he
was unrecognisable, but in a croaking voice he was able to give his name …
Sergeant Fearn, the observer. At once he was hurried into the shade beneath
the wing of the Bombay, washed down and attended to by the doctor who was
with the search party, and then loaded on board and was taken back to base.[11]

Sgt Fearn, also a New Zealander (from Invercargill), was able to tell his
rescuers that in his search for water he had dug, with his bare hands, into the

sand beneath scrub patches. When he found water he filled his Mae West. During the fierce heat of the day he had lain hidden in the scrub, getting what shade he could. By night he had walked northwards, taking his course by the Pole Star, and knowing that if he could only keep going he must eventually reach the coast road. The Bombay pilot, Flg Off. Allcock, recalled:

In the afternoon I went out again and found the second member of the crew, the wireless-operator Sergeant McConnell. When I saw him he was crawling, too weak to stand. His chest was shrivelled. We doused him under the wing of our aircraft and the water disappeared into his skin like drips on a hot stove. He was also allowed a little water by mouth and some gentle feeding. The doctors said that he would have died next day.[12]

In spite of a continuing air and ground search, no sign of the missing pilot was found. Whatever happened to 27-year-old Murray MacKenzie from Canterbury, New Zealand, he could not have walked more than a mile or two from the crash site. And therefore his fate remains a mystery.

Following the latest heavy losses, few sorties were made by 204 Group on **28 May**, only two Blenheims of 55 Squadron making a strike on Maleme. Later, patrols were carried out by two 45 Squadron Blenheims escorted by Hurricanes but saw no enemy activity. With daylight on 29 May, came further aerial threats against the departure ships but just a single Ju 88 dropped bombs close to one of the warships. Apart from this isolated attack, the passage to Alexandria remained unhindered, however, although a solitary Ju 88 was seen approaching at 6,000 feet shortly after 13:00. This was at once engaged by an escorting Blenheim, T2252 of 45 Squadron flown by Sgt Eric McClelland, who made a quick frontal attack which he believed had caused severe damage, possibly bringing this aircraft down.

Apart from the occasional patrol with Hurricanes over the sea lanes during the next few days, the Blenheims role in the defence of Crete was over. During the twelve-day battle, 204 Group had suffered fourteen Blenheim losses, plus two Marylands and seven Wellingtons—and 23 Hurricanes. On 30 May, Air Chief Marshal Sir Arthur Longmore sent a long cable to the Chief of the Air Staff in London, which included the following extract:

Have held stocktaking over Crete. Sorry to say that though effort has had some valuable results the cost has been very heavy in relation to strength. Especially in Blenheims—Blenheim dawn and dusk raids in particular have been expensive, both in Crete and on return to the Desert. No doubt I am to blame in not keeping a tighter rein on Collishaw … stopped all day action over Crete other than recco on 28th.[13]

Cretan Epitaph

Fifty years on from the battle, 11 Squadron's Marcel Comeau MM, who retrained as a pilot, revisted Crete:

I have revisited Maleme, climbed Kavkazia Hill again and stood up on the iron bridge over the Tavronitis once more. On the slopes of Suda Bay lies the British War Cemetery, a beautiful place of flowering shrubs and perfumed foliage … The RAF are there also; flyers lying in crews, comrades in life and death. No one could visit this hallowed place without shedding a tear for its exquisite beauty.

On the bald hilltop of Kavkazia stands the German Cemetery where no fewer than 6,000 Germans, mostly young, lie buried two to a grave. Row upon row of regimented slaps stretch to the horizon in every direction. There is a feeling of endlessness.[14]

Appendix 1
Blenheim Losses

Though they were few, too few, who fought in Greece,
They waged a constant fight;
A new mythology of glorious deeds
Their mountain tombstones write;
So tell their lasting honour to the world.
And keep their torch alight![1]

The RAF Narrative of the Greek campaign records that the Blenheim bomber squadrons lost 91 aircraft, of which 61 were lost in battle; plus fourteen more operating over Crete during May.

RAF Blenheim Losses/Crew Casualties—Greece 1940-1941

7 Nov	K7103	30 Sqn	Sgt G. W. Ratlidge Sgt Walker †Sgt J. Merifield	damaged by CR.42
14 Nov	L1389	84 Sqn	†Flt Lt A. F. Mudie †Flt Sgt E. Hibbard-Lord †LAC W. J. S. Chick	crashed into mountain
	L1378	84 Sqn	†Sgt W. F. Sidaway †Sgt C. P. Hoare †Sgt A. J. W. Friend	crashed into mountain
15 Nov	L1120	30 Sqn	†Sgt E.B. Childs †Sgt J. D. Stewart †LAC D. Stott	s/d by CR.42
20 Nov	L1166	30 Sqn	Flg Off. C. de W. Richardson (Can) and crew	f/l on beach

24 Nov	L1539	211 Sqn	Flg Off. K. V. Dundas (Can) and crew	belly-landed G.50
	L1481	211 Sqn	Sgt J. R. Marshall and crew	f/l by G.50 Larissa
	L8411	211 Sqn	Sqn Ldr J. R. Gordon-Finlayson Plt Off. G. Davies Plt Off. A. C. Geary	s/d by AA f/l Corfu
28 Nov	L1385	84 Sqn	Plt Off. D. R. Bird Sgt S. Davis Sgt R. E. Scott	c/l by G.50 PoW
1 Dec	K7103	30 Sqn	Sgt G. W. Ratlidge and crew	f/l—icing salvaged
2 Dec	L8466	211 Sqn	Flg Off. P. B. Pickersgill Sgt H. Taylor Sgt P. Duffy	f/l—salvaged
6 Dec	K7100	30 Sqn	Flg Off. H. P. G. Blackmore (NZ) Plt Off. R. K. Crowther	f/l by AA salvaged
	L1097	30 Sqn	Plt Off. J. A. Attwell Sgt M. J. S. Walsh	f/l by AA salvaged
7 Dec	L4926	211 Sqn	†Flg Off. P. B. Pickersgill †Sgt H. Taylor †Sgt N. A. Hallett	crashed—icing
	L1535	211 Sqn	†Plt Off. G. I. Jerdein †Sgt J. E. Barber †Sgt J. Munro	crashed—icing
	L1381	211 Sqn	Flg Off. K. Linton (Can) Plt Off. A. C. Dunn Sgt R. L. Crowe	f/l by CR.42 salvaged
	L8455	84 Sqn	†Flt Lt L. P. Cattell †Sgt H. A. E. Taylor †Sgt F. L. Carter	s/d by CR.42

	L8457	84 Sqn	†Sgt M. P. Cazalet	s/d by CR.42
			†Sgt K. J. Ridgewell	
			Sgt C. R. Forster	POW
14 Dec	L8514	211 Sqn	Flt Lt L. B. Buchanan (NZ)	f/l—abandoned
			Sgt W. B. Stack	
			Sgt G. Pattison	
15 Dec	L6670	211 Sqn	Plt Off. R. V. Herbert	f/l—icing
				salvaged;
			Sgt P. Duffy	frostbite
18 Dec	L8462	30 Sqn	†Plt Off. S. Paget	s/d by G.50
			†Sgt G. Sigsworth	
			†Sgt W. Tubberdy	
22 Dec	L8471	84 Sqn	†Flg Off. P. F. Miles	s/d by G.50
			†Sgt F. G. Moir	
			†Sgt B. A. C. Brooker	
	L8374	84 Sqn	Flg Off. J. F. Evans	wounded—b/o ret'd
			Sgt H. B. Offord	b/o—returned;
			†Sgt A. L. Sargeant	s/d by G.50
	L4818	84 Sqn	Flt Sgt A. Gordon	damaged by G.50
			Sgt F. Levitt	
			Sgt G. Furney	wounded
26 Dec	L1482	211 Sqn	Plt Off. R. V. Herbert	c/l by CR.42
			Sgt J. Dunnet	DBR
			Sgt W. N. J. Young	
29 Dec	K7104	30 Sqn	†Flt Lt H. D. Card (Can)	s/d by G.50
			†Sgt F. Pease	b/o (killed)
			Sgt G. E. Bygrave	b/o (killed)
	L6672	30 Sqn	Plt Off. A. G. Crockett	f/l by G.50
			and crew	
30 Dec	L8466	30 Sqn	Sqn Ldr U. Y. Shannon (NZ)	combat with
			†Sgt F. Goulding (AG)	Z.506; DoW

31 Dec	L1540	211 Sqn	†Sgt S. L. Bennett †Sgt W. H. Tunstall †Sgt L. R. France	s/d by G.50
6 Jan 1941	L8536	211 Sqn	†Flg Off. L. S. Delaney †Sgt V. Pollard †Sgt T. A. McCord	s/d by G.50
	L8541	211 Sqn	Flt Lt G. B. Doudney and crew	c/l by G.50
	L1487	211 Sqn	Flg Off. R. D. Campbell (NZ) Sgt J. H. Beharrell Sgt R. Appleyard	s/d by G.50 all PoW
10 Jan	L8501	84 Sqn	Plt Off. I. P. C. Goudge Sgt I. B. Croker Sgt J. Wright	c/l Araxos abandoned
22 Jan	L8449	30 Sqn	Plt Off. R. W. Pearson Sgt G. J. Riddle Sgt G. Chignall	badly damaged by G.50
	L1528	211 Sqn	Plt Off. J. C. Cox Plt Off. E. Bevington-Smith	c/l engine fire injured
25 Jan	L8443	30 Sqn	Sgt L. W. Stammers Plt Off. Carter Sgt W. S. Akeroyd	damaged by G.50 wounded wounded
2 Feb	T2235	11 Sqn	†Sgt D. G. Strachan †Sgt G. Date †Sgt R. E. G. Clift †AC1 E. Bradbury	lost on ferry flight
	N3580	11 Sqn	Sgt E. H. J. Thornton Sgt F. T. Manly Sgt Brown	f/l—bad weather
5 Feb	L4833	84 Sqn	†Flt Lt R. A. Towgood Sgt R. F. Somerville Sgt P. F. Atherton	crashed on landing

6 Feb	L1393	84 Sqn	Flg Off. A. N. N. Nicholson †Plt Off. R. G. C. Day †Sgt A. J. Hollist	ditched in bad weather
13 Feb	L8541	211 Sqn	Flt Lt L. B. Buchanan (NZ) Sgt G. Pattison	damaged by G.50; c/landed
	T2237	11 Sqn	†Plt Off. J. Hutchison Sgt S. D. Whiles †Sgt W. T. Jackson	s/d by G.50 b/o—returned
	T2166	11 Sqn	Sgt L. Williams †Sgt O. L. G. Traherne †Sgt J. F. Adamson	b/o—POW; s/d by G.50 b/o—killed
	T2347	11 Sqn	Flg Off. J. V. Berggren Sgt N. R. Powell Sgt H. Murphy	f/l—G.50
	T2388	11 Sqn	Plt Off. A. D. P. Hewison Sgt D. Fisher Sgt P. Griffiths	damaged by G.50 wounded slightly wounded
18 Feb	L6662	211 Sqn	Flg Off. K. Linton (Can) and crew	u/c collapsed abandoned
20 Feb	L8542	211 Sqn	Plt Off. J. C. Cox Sgt W. B. Stack Sgt Martin	damaged by G.50 DBR
21 Feb	L1379	84 Sqn	Sgt N. A. Thomas Sgt E. Oliver Plt Off. T. G. Corner	crashed on t/off; abandoned
23 Feb	T2388	11 Sqn	†Plt Off. A. D. P. Hewison †Sgt J. S. Dukes †LAC G. Bevan LAC G. W. Causer AC1 J. H. McQueen Cpl McCrae	crashed on ferry flight—bad weather injured injured

27 Feb	T2399	11 Sqn	Unknown crew	c/l by CR.42; DBR no injuries
	N3579	11 Sqn	Unknown crew	c/l by CR.42: DBR no injuries
8 Mar	L1392	84 Sqn	Sgt A. Gordon Sgt F. Levitt	u/c collapsed; abandoned
26 Mar	N5910	211 Sqn	†Sqn Ldr R. J. C. Nedwill (NZ)	flying accident/ shot down in Gladiator
29 Mar	R2780	11 Sqn	Plt Off. P. Montague-Bates and crew	u/c collapsed; abandoned
30 Mar	L1390	84 Sqn	Sgt J. M. Hutcheson Sgt K. J. Irwin Sgt J. Webb	c/l by AA; blew up crew unhurt
1 Apr	T2382	84 Sqn	†Flt Lt D. G. Boehm (Aus) †Sgt K. G. Lee †LAC H. Jackson	crashed—accident
6 Apr	L9338	113 Sqn	Sgt V. F. McPherson and crew	f/l by AA; abandoned
	T2168	113 Sqn	Sgt K. R. Price Sgt J. D. Woodcock Sgt J. Rooney	f/l by AA; abandoned
8 Apr	Z5897	84 Sqn	Sqn Ldr H. D. Jones Flg Off. R. Trevor-Roper Sgt H. Keen	f/l weather; all slightly injured; abandoned.
	T2247	11 Sqn	Plt Off. R. J. Coombs Sgt C. H. Randall Sgt L. C. Macey	seriously injured; injured; a/c crashed on take-off
10 Apr	T2164	84 Sqn	Plt Off. J. C. Eldred Sgt A. L. Loudon Sgt A. J. Acres Greek General	f/l weather injured injured

11 Apr	L8612	84 Sqn	†Sgt L. Nuttall †Flt Sgt A. J. Neal †Sgt G. R. Thistle	s/d by AA
11/12 Apr	K7095	30 Sqn	Sqn Ldr R. A. Milward †Sgt J. Crooks	s/d by Ju 88
13 Apr	L8478	211 Sqn	†Sqn Ldr A. T. Irvine †Plt Off. G. Davies †Plt Off. A. C. Geary	s/d by Bf 109
	L8449	211 Sqn	Flg Off. A. C. Godfrey †Sgt J. B. T. O'Neill †Flt Sgt J. Wainhouse	s/d by Bf 109
	L1434	211 Sqn	†Flt Lt L. B. Buchanan (NZ) †Sqn Ldr L. E. Cryer †Sgt G. Pattison	s/d by Bf 109
	L8664	211 Sqn	†Flg Off. C. E. V. Thompson †Plt Off. P. Hogarth †Sgt W. Arscott	s/d by Bf 109
	L4819	211 Sqn	†Plt Off. Off R. V. Herbert †Wg Cdr P. B. Coote †Sgt W. N. Young	s/d by Bf 109
	L1539	211 Sqn	Flt Sgt A. G. James †Flt Sgt A. Bryce †Sgt A. J. Waring	s/d by Bf 109
14 Apr	T2177	113 Sqn	Flg Off. G. E. P. Green Sgt W. B. Gingell Sgt K. A. Jamieson	damaged by friendly AA; abandoned
15 Apr		211 Sqn	Flg Off. A. C. Godfrey †Flt Sgt A. G. James	wounded by Bf 109 killed by Bf 109; aboard Lysanders
18 Apr	L1391	84 Sqn	†Sqn Ldr H. D. Jones †Sgt H. Keen †Flt Sgt J. Webb	s/d by Bf 110

T2348	11 Sqn	†Plt Off. P. Montague-Bates	s/d by Bf 109
		Plt Off. H. R. Edge	b/o—returned
		†Sgt H. Murphy	

Blenheim Losses/Crew Casualties—Crete Ops April-May 1941

21 April	N3560	11 Sqn	Plt Off. A. T. Darling (inj)	tyre burst landing,
			passengers	swung and DBR
22 April	L1481	11 Sqn	Sgt V. G. Hudson	s/d by CR.42s,
				ditched
23 April	?L8444	113 Sqn	Unknown pilot	DBR on landing
			passengers	
27 April	L2937	203 Sqn	†Flt Lt J. C. Whittall (Aus)	s/d by Bf 110
			†Sgt S. O'Connor	
			†Sgt T. J. Air	
	K7177	30 Sqn	Flt Sgt D. Innes-Smith	hit by HMS *Defender*; DBR
28 April	L9044	203 Sqn	Flg Off. P. N. Gordon-Hall	damaged by RN
			Sgt C. Poole	ship and ditched
			Sgt I. B. Oultram	
23 May	V5624	45 Sqn	†Plt Off. P. J. Vincent	s/d by Bf 109
			†Plt Off. S. C. Niven RNZAF	
			†Flt Sgt O. B. Thompson	
24 May	V5766	45 Sqn	Sgt E. W. McClelland	engine cut—DBR
			Sgt H. Vipond	
			Sgt J. McGurk	
25 May	T2065	14 Sqn	†Flt Lt R. A. Green	s/d by Bf 109
			†Plt Off. A. D. Browne	
			†Sgt N. P. McK. Wilson	
	V5510	14 Sqn	†Lt S. R. E. Forrester SAAF	s/d by Bf 109
			†Sgt W. A. J. Fretwell	
			†Flt Sgt R. F. Hall	

	T2003	14 Sqn	†Sgt H. P. Jeudwine (SA)	s/d by Bf 109
			†Flt Sgt H. Young	
			†Flt Sgt N.B. Lake	

26 May	T2339	45 Sqn	†Sgt N. H. Thomas	s/d by Bf 109
			†Sgt G. R. Adams	
			†Flt Sgt G. R. Grainger	

	V5592	45 Sqn	Flg Off. T. F. C. Churcher	s/d by Bf 109 PoW
			Plt Off. R. D. May	PoW
			Sgt H. G. Langrish (Can)	Evaded

	T2350	45 Sqn	Plt Off. D. C. G.	b/o—returned
			Verbraecke (Bel)	
			†Sgt W. B. Longstaff	b/o—died
			Sgt A. F. Crosby	b/o—returned
26/27 May	V5896	45 Sqn	†Flg Off. N. W. Pinnington	crashed on take-off
			†Plt Off. H. F. Irving RNZAF	
			†Sgt R. J. R. Martin	died 3 weeks later

27 May	T2051	55 Sqn	†Sgt W. L. Martin	take-off collision
			†Sgt E. A. Martin	
			†Sgt K. Bamber	

	T2175	55 Sqn	†Sgt J. H. Chesman,	crashed in desert
			†Sgt D. G. Callender RNZAF	
			†Sgt R. F. Lyle	

	L9319	55 Sqn	Sgt R. B. Bale RNZAF	b/o—returned
			Sgt A. F. Wiles DFM	b/o—returned
			Sgt J. Rigby	b/o—returned

	V5593	14 Sqn	†Flg Off. J. B. Le Cavalier (Can)	crashed in desert
			Sgt L. Page	b/o—returned
			†Sgt C. P. A. Bury	b/o—killed

	T2338	14 Sqn	†Flg Off. M. MacKenzie (NZ)	crashed in desert
			Sgt M. B. Fearn RNZAF	b/o—returned
			Sgt W. J. McConnell	b/o—returned

Blenheims destroyed/written off during ground strafes, or otherwise abandoned

22 March 1941: L1490, L8531, L8533 (all 211 Sqn) destroyed on ground at Paramythia during Mc.200 strafe.

26 March 1941: L8466 (211 Sqn) possibly destroyed Paramythia.

15 April 1941: T2054, T2069, T2169, T2182, T2186, T2216 (all 113 Sqn) destroyed on ground at Niamata by Bf 109/Bf 110 strafe.

20 April 1941: T2341, Z5769, Z5885 (all 11 Sqn), K7096 (30 Sqn) and possibly V5372 (211 Sqn) destroyed on ground at Menidi by Bf 109 strafe.

6 May 1941: N3558, V5425 recorded as 'lost in Greece'.

7 May 1941: L8444 (113 Sqn) recorded as 'lost in Greece'.

30 May 1941: N3560, T2342 (11 Sqn), V7177 (30 Sqn DBR 27 April), T2183 (113 Sqn) abandoned in Crete.

30 May 1941: L8461, T2238, T2248 (all 113 Sqn), L1388 (84 Sqn) all recorded as 'lost in Greece', together with L9300, L9310, L9342, R3918, T2390, T2391, V5424 (unallocated).

32 Mira RHAF Blenheim Losses/Crew Casualties— Greece 1940-1941

2 Nov	B260	Unidentified crew	f/l AA, no injuries
8/9 Nov	B2??	Capt. L. Kousigiannis	crashed in darkness on return from op—broke back; others unhurt
11 Nov	B2??	†Lt P. Maravelias †Lt Y. Kapsampelis †Sgt Sivropoulos	s/d by G.50s
14 Nov	B254	†Capt. D. Papageorgiou †Capt. S. Charalambous †Sgt K. Koulis	s/d by AA

14 Nov	B253	Capt. P. Orphanidis Sgt Sotiriadis	AA/CR.42 wounded
27 Nov	B256	†1/Lt A. Malakis †Sgt A. Liapis †Sgt C. Filippidis	s/d by AA
30 Dec	B252	†Capt. P. Orphanidis †1/Lt M. Anastasakis †Sgt D. Gkikas	crashed on t/off
31 Dec	B260	†Lt K. Chatziioannou †Sgt Arabatzis †Sgt Sotiriadis	s/d by CR.42s
18 Feb	B2??	Flt Sgt E. Tzovlas	c/l in swamp –all OK
6 March	B2??	1/Lt H. Papatheou	damaged by Gladiators crew unhurt
11 March	B263	Flt Sgt E. Tzovlas †Sgt M. Tsolakidis †Sgt S. Mavromatidis	b/o—s/d by G.50s

Most of the remaining RHAF Blenheims were destroyed/damaged (including B253 and B255) on the ground at Eleusis on 20 April, although B268 was captured intact by the Germans.

RYAF Blenheim Losses/Crew Casualties, April 1941

6 April

3523	11 Ind Grupa	†W/Off. Obrad Milićević †2/Lt Sreten Glišović †Sgt Krsta Đukić	s/d by Bf 109—all killed
352?	11 Ind Grupa	†W/Off. Todor Radović †Lt Slavko Zelenika †Sgt Blagoje Bakić	s/d by Yugo AA—all k'd

| 35?? | 11 Ind Grupa | †Kapt. Milovanović
†Lt Kusovac
†Sgt Nikodijević | crashed—AA
damage/or fighters |

7 April

3544	201 Esk	W/Off. Branislav Majstorović Sgt Rokić Milan Sgt Grubović Vojislav	AA damaged, forced-landed at Davidovac; crew unhurt
35??	203 Esk	Sgt Živan Jovanović Lt Branko Glumac Sgt Bogdan Zečević	AA damaged; forced-landed at Bijeljina; crew unhurt
35??	204 Esk	†Kapt. Nikola Ivančević †Lt Vladimir Kink †Sgt Stjepan Jurković	s/d by AA; —all killed
35??	204 Esk	Sgt Đuro Ratković 2/Lt Hugo Vanjek Sgt Pavlović	wounded; AA damaged, crash- landed
35??	204 Esk	Sgt Dragonslav Ilic 2/Lt Milosev Unknown gunner	wounded; AA c/landed
35??	68 Grupa	†Maj. Lazar Donović †Lt Ivan Pandža †Sgt Dragutin Veselko	s/d by Bf 109 —all killed
35??	215 Esk	†Kapt. Vladimir Jovičić †Lt Mirko Jovanović †Sgt Marko Tošković	s/d by AA —all killed
35??	215 Esk.	†Sgt Viktor Grdović †2/Lt Dragomir Pavlović †Sgt Milisav Raković	s/d by Bf 110 —all killed

3525	215 Esk	Sgt Dragisa Baralic Lt Ivan Miklaveć Sgt Velimir Grdovic	s/d by AA/Bf 109; all POW
35??	216 Esk	†Kapt. Sergije Vojinov †Lt Petar Kukić †Sgt Ilija Mraković	s/d by Bf 109 —all killed
35??	216 Esk	†Lt Radomir Lazarević †Lt Andrija Pozder †Sgt Ilija Mićković	s/d by Bf 109 —all killed
3505	69 Grupa	†Maj. Dobrasav Tešić †Lt Milutin Petrović †Sgt Dragoljub Černe †Lt Dragutin Karner	s/d by Bf 109 —all killed
35??	218 Esk.	†Sgt Vladimir Ferant †Kapt. Rudolf Kobal †Sgt Ivan Čubrilović	s/d by Bf 109 Sgt Ferant believed died 13 April

8 April

35??	1 Bomb Puk	†Sgt Živan Jovanović †Col. Ferdo Gradišnik Sgt Dobrilo Terzić	s/d by AA—killed killed injured—POW
3547	21 Esk	†Kapt. Živomir Petrović †Lt Branko Novović †Sgt Branko Jelić	s/d by AA —all killed
3510	?? Esk	†W/Off. Vasilije Mirović †Lt Đorđe Stevanović †Sgt Slobodan Đorđević	s/d by AA —all killed

10 April

35??	11 Ind Grupa	†Lt Jmićije Korać †Lt Dragomir Dobrović †F/Sgt Dušan Vukčević, †Sgt Medveščak (mechanic)	crashed on take-off

12 April

3533	1 Bomb. Puk	Sgt Danilo Dejić (pilot)	Attempting escape;
		Sgt Dušan Jovanović (pilot)	no casualties
			Overflew RN warships
			at Preveza, hit by
			gunfire and crash-landed
			near Yannina

3550	11 Ind Grupa	Sgt Ilija Ivanović	Escaped to Montenegro;
		2/Lt Radovan Dačić	shot down/strafed by
		Sgt Žarko Sabljar (mechanic)	Mc.200s; no casualties
		Sgt Dobrijević (mechanic)	

35??	11 Ind Grupa	Unknown crew	Escaped as above;
			strafed by Mc.200s,
			no crew casualties.

Both above crews were ordered off to make their escape to Sokolac airfield in Bosnia, but were strafed by MC.200s of 359ª Squadriglia, 22°Gruppo whilst landing at Podgorica airfield in Montenegro.

35??	217 Esk	Kapt. Đorđe Putica	Escaped to Croat
		Lt Ivan Salević	territory
		unknown gunner	

| 35?? | 218 Esk | Kapt. Matija Petrović | Escaped to Croat |
| | | crew unknown | territory |

Both above machines landed at Croat territory. According to Lt Salević they experienced trouble with fuel gauges and short of fuel landed at corn field near Auguštinovac, while Petrović landed close to Zagreb, most probably at Borongaj airfield. Both aircraft were pressed into service with Croats.

3516	22 Esk	Sgt Stjepan Rudić	Escaped to Hungary
		Sgt Sava Šuković (mechanic)	
		Sgt Vladimir Molnar (mechanic)	

As Croat nationals, Rudić and Molnar were, in line with their own wishes, released from internment and they approached newly founded ZNDH (Independent Croatia Air Force). The destiny of Serbian national Sgt Šuković remains unknown.

Appendix 2
A Blenheim Wop/AG

Sgt Herbert Lord, better known as Bert or *Lofty*, arrived at RAF Habbaniya (formerlyDhibban) in May 1938 to join 30 Squadron which had recently become the first overseas squadron to receive the Blenheim MkI. It was here that *Lofty* would strike up a life-long friendship with another new recruit to the Squadron, Sgt Johnny Vellacott.

Lofty was assigned to C Flight as a Wireless Operator/Air-gunner (Wop/AG). His first taste of flying in the Blenheim came on 7 September 1938. *Lofty's* pilot was Sgt Wilson and the aircraft K7098. Before the month was through 30 Squadron was mobilised due to the Munich crisis and flew to Heliopolis. *Lofty* had completed less than 14 hours of flying.

After the excitement of the Munich crisis and the Squadron's subsequent recall to Habbaniya, *Lofty* settled down into day-to-day life. The next few months meant training, training and more training in the Blenheim. Such training included bombing practice, photography, radio telephony (R/T), wireless telegraphy (W/T), directional finding (D/F), rear camera-gun, night flying, camera obscura, local and cross country flying. By September 1939, *Lofty* had over 187 hours flying under his belt. It was time to put his experience into practice.

At the outbreak of war 30 Squadron had already arrived at its war station, Ismailia, Egypt. Despite being at war activities remained much the same—training. However, the emphasis now was on formation flying, bombing practice and gun practice. On Christmas Day of 1939, the Squadron began operational patrols over the Gulf of Suez. The first of these patrols was carried out in a Blenheim piloted by C Flight's commander Flt Lt Frank Marlow, with *Lofty* as Wop/AG. These patrols were to become a daily occurrence with *Lofty* taking part in his fair share.

With Italy entering the war on 10 June 1940, all the bombing practice was finally going to be put to good use. However B and C Flights were immediately ordered to convert their Blenheim bombers to fighter configuation by having a gunpack fitted to the bomb bay in place of the bomb cradles. Flt Lt Marlow and *Lofty* took two of the Squadron's Blenheims to the maintenance unit at Aboukir to carry out the conversion.

A day later Flt Lt Marlow and *Lofty* were part of a detachment of two Blenheims that flew to Qasaba to commence reconnaissance flights and offensive fighter patrols over the Libyan border. Several patrols were flown by the Blenheims in the ensuing days but with no enemy aircraft seen. The detachment was relieved by three aircraft of A Flight on the 25 June, whereupon the two fighter crews returned to Ismailia for a much deserved rest. For *Lofty* the nine-day detachment was a draining experience as can be seen from the comments in his logbook, they progress from 'very tired', 'again tired' to 'still tired' and finally 'fed up'!

Shortly after the detachment returned to Ismailia the Squadron was ordered to move to Ikingi Mariut, a desert landing ground in the Western Desert. They had been tasked with the Air Defence of Alexandria approximately 20km away. The Blenheims arrived at Ikingi on the 8th July and their first op was as a fighter escort for the Navy on the 12th with *Lofty* in K7177 with Flt Lt Marlow. Next day he was airborne once more in K7177, again as Naval fighter escort with a further two Blenheims from the Squadron. On this occasion his pilot was Flg Off. Ronald Le Dieu. The other Blenheims were piloted by Plt Off. Derryk Lea and Flt Lt Al Bocking. When the three Blenheims made contact with the naval fleet they immediately spotted three SM.79 bombers preparing to attack. Bocking's aircraft remained over the fleet while Le Dieu and Lea engaged the enemy.

Le Dieu attacked No. 3 of the enemy formation and the SM.79 was seen to dive away with smoke trailing from its starboard wing. Le Dieu then turned his attention to the leader of the enemy aircraft and a burst of fire silenced the rear-gunner. Lea's Blenheim, K7181, made a stern attack on the No. 2 aircraft but was caught by a burst of fire from the rear firing belly guns. He managed to parachute from the stricken aircraft just as it burst into flames but the Wop/AG, Sgt Christopher Burt, went down with the aircraft. Le Dieu, his ammunition exhausted, broke off the engagement and went down to see if he could throw a dinghy to Lea but he could not locate him. Attempts were made to contact the fleet by wireless but without success so the aircraft returned to base. Plt Off. Lea's body was never recovered. This action saw 30 Squadron's first victory and *Lofty's* first taste of combat, but was overshadowed by first loss of the war.

The remainder of July was spent carrying out standing patrols over Alexandria but without sighting any enemy aircraft. These patrols continued throughout August with *Lofty* pairing up with Frank Marlow for every patrol he undertook. Each patrol was maintained at 18,000 feet and lasted anything up to two hours although nothing in the way of opposition was encountered. The second year of the war started quietly for *Lofty* with only one standing patrol over Alexandria and an hour of formation flying in the first nine days of September. This was soon to change as Flt Lt Marlow (with *Lofty*) took K7096 to Ma'aten Bagush as part of a two aircraft detachment to 202 Group. They were tasked with carrying out protective standing patrols over Mersa Matruh, the first of which they carried out on the morning of 10 September. Their second patrol of the day took place early afternoon and no sooner as they had reached their patrol height of 18,000 feet they spotted a formation of six SM.79s approaching Mersa Matruh from the north-east at around 16,000 feet. The Italian aircraft, flying in two vic formations of three, were attacked by Gladiators and Hurricanes with the leading aircraft of the second formation being shot down. K7096 then attacked the starboard aircraft of the stragglers in the second formation from dead astern, a blind spot on the SM.79, opening fire from around 330–400 yards, closing to 100 yards, putting the enemy top gunner out of action. Fire was sustained in short bursts until flames emitted from under the port side of the aircraft whereupon the SM.79 fell into a steep right hand spiral dive and crashed into the sea. The Marlow/*Lofty* Lord team had accounted for their second air victory.

Further patrols were carried out over Mersa Matruh during the next few days by the same crews but without coming into contact with the enemy, however a change of patrol area on the 15th yielded instant results. Marlow and *Lofty*, again in K7096, in partnership with K7105 piloted by Plt Off. John Jarvis with Sgt George Sigsworth as his gunner took off from Ma'aten Bagush around 13:00 to patrol Sidi Barrani. Around an hour into the patrol a stick of bombs were dropped to the east of Sidi Barrani followed shortly after by another salvo to the west of the town. The aircraft guilty of this attack, a formation of four SM.79s, were spotted by *Lofty* heading out to sea and the chase ensued. The enemy aircraft were diving from a height of 10,000 feet down to sea level so it took 25 minutes for the Blenheims to overhaul them.

K7096 attacked a straggler from 150 yards and pieces of the aircraft were seen to be flying off but the wounded aircraft immediately closed into a tight vic formation. The combined firepower of the enemy aircraft forced the Blenheim to increase its range to 300 yards but they continued to press home their attack. K7105 attempted to silence the rear-gunners in the remaining aircraft before concentrating their fire on two of the SM.79s claiming damage to both of them. The attack was broken off due to all ammunition being expended and a course was set for base; however, *Lofty* reported that the aircraft that they had attacked was losing formation as if crippled. It was later confirmed that this aircraft had indeed failed to reach its base. Flt Lt Marlow was thus credited with his second kill in just five days, *Lofty's* share now being three confirmed.

Lofty spent the remainder of September and October carrying out patrols over Alexandria harbour with no enemy opposition encountered. One thing of note during October was the posting of *Lofty's* long term pilot, Flt Lt Marlow to HQ 202 Group. *Lofty* had flown with C Flight's commander on over 170 occasions.

November 1940 would see a drastic change of scenery and weather for *Lofty* and the other members of 30 Squadron. Due to the Italian invasion of Greece by way of Albania the Squadron was ordered to move to Greece.

.....................o.....................

On 5 April 1941, with the Greek campaign coming to its conclusion and the expected German intervention in the Balkans, *Lofty* returned to Crete, sooner than hoped, when six 30 Squadron Blenheims were ordered to move to Maleme, Crete to carry out convoy escort duties. With the Germans entering the war against Greece the very next day, *Lofty* carried out his escort duties and offensive patrols (or as he described them 'looking for trouble flights'). He made several flights at the end of April covering the evacuation of troops form Greece enduring heavy fire from Royal Naval ships on more than one occasion.

Lofty was one of the lucky airmen to leave Crete for the relative safety of Egypt prior to the island being besieged by the might of the German Luftwaffe. Five of the Squadron's aircraft were ordered to return to Egypt for complete overhaul as they were operationally unfit. He took off from the island for the last time on 7 May and made his last flight in a Blenheim, K7099, later the same day. *Lofty's* time on 30 Squadron had seen him fly with 41 different pilots, on a total of 493 flights in Blenheims, in a little over two and a half years.

After 30 Squadron, *Lofty* joined 12 Squadron SAAF flying Marylands on bombing missions in support of the North African campaign. He was severely injured on one such mission on 27 September 1941 and returned to England to recover from his injuries at the end of that year. A spell as an instructor on Blenheims with 13 OTU at Bicester followed before he joined 224 Squadron, Coastal Command, flying in Liberators on anti U-boat patrols over the Bay of Biscay. He was involved in several attacks on U-boats resulting in the sinking of one such vessel.

Lofty was commisioned in 1943 and awarded the DFC in July 1944 citing 'his excellent record of operational flying' and his 'keenness to engage the enemy'. He finally flew his last offensive sortie in early 1945 before being seconded to *BOAC*. His civilian career in aviation continued after the war, with *BOAC, British Eagle* and finally *Caledonian Airways*. He retired from flying in 1973 and emigrated to Australia some years later where he died in 1987. Herbert *Lofty* Lord was my Grandfather. I could not be any more proud of him.

Simon Lord

Appendix 3
Ian Carter's Visit to Greece 2001

Ian Carter is a luminary of the Blenheim Society, and is editor of its Journal. He and his father Bill have been, and still are, instrumental in keeping 211 Squadron's history alive (together with Don Clark in Australia), and were both heavily involved in the production of the late James Dunnet's *Blenheim over the Balkans*. 60 years after 211 Squadron's fateful raid on 13 April 1941, Ian found himself flying to Greece to pay homage to the fallen. He recalled:

I flew into Athens on the 11 April 2001, and was met by Maria Petroulaki who had agreed to take me around her country. Maria was a translator for the Greek air force and had corresponded with James [Dunnet] when his letters to the Greek air force had been passed to her for translatation; as it happened, James lived in Llandudno and Maria had spent time there. They became friends and Maria offered to help me make the trip, so on 11 April, we departed Athens. We journeyed westward in Maria's Citroën past the Corinth Canal, and crossed the Gulf of Corinth on a ferry. As soon as we reached the other side and started to follow the road as it wound its way around the side of the Gulf, the scene was very reminiscent of several photographs I had seen from late 1940. Paramythia is a village at the head of a valley in a mountainous area of Greece south, towards the Albanian border south of Yannina

As we got closer to Paramythia, approaching from the east, the weather was not at its best, in fact a little light rain was forthcoming and hence the cloud was just on the mountain tops at its highest point 5,000 feet at the western end of the ridge. However as Maria and I travelled into the valley I realised it looked familiar and then I saw the strange mark on the hillside, and the ridge line looked so familiar, it was an extraordinary feeling to be present in the valley, known as the 'Valley of Fairy Tales'.

We had been travelling for a number of hours and we still had some way to travel to make Yannina, our overnight stop, if we were to make the Florina Valley and the Prespa lakes, to coincide with the 60th Anniversary. So, in the late afternoon, we with a long way to go, jumped back into the little car and headed away. It was a long time before I could stop looking back at that beautiful valley;

I just couldn't get out of my mind how, all those years earlier, that the once-famous 211 Squadron and all the young men, flew into the annals of RAF history, their sacrifices and last resting places largely forgotten, until recent years.

Having over-nighted in Yannina we set of on the 13 April for the lake at Mikroprespa, and the hamlet of Mikrolimni. We crossed the mountains passing through Kastoria, and with a lot of (not by design!) dead reckoning navigation arrived into the valley that travels from Florina down to Lake Prespa, in perfect time. So, 60 years to the day and the time—when the Blenheims were being shot down, two into the lake we were beside—we sat and drank wine, and toasted their memories, in one of the most beautiful places in the world, in bright sunshine. Quite a moment. It was while sat here deep in thought it suddenly dawned on me that although I thought I knew where the Blenheims fell, as I surveyed the surroundings I realised a challenge lay ahead!

The two aircraft that we were confident that we knew where they fell were Buck Buchanan's and the CO's. From the first hand accounts it would seem that Buck and his crew were taken to an Albanian Hospital, in Koritza, and this was confirmed (with Maria translating) by John Constantinithis, who helped with the recovery of their aircraft, L1434 (which now lies in the Hellenic Air Force Museum at Tatoi). John also confirmed the aircraft was on fire, and ditched with the top hatch open. The crew have no known last resting place, as what happened to them after they were taken to Albania is unknown. Munitions were found which goes against the original accounts that 211 bombed their target. The one aircraft that did not have bombs on board was the CO's which crashed into Tumbitsa Mountain behind the village of Alona. This is the second of the six we can be reasonably sure of having identified; as it was the only aircraft with three officers on board, and eyewitness accounts confirm this, hence this aircraft was L8478.

The second aircraft from eyewitness accounts we knew had fallen into the lake at a location named Silka meaning (cave), and it was reported as have been recovered; however as we chatted or rather Maria translated in the café at Karie, it turned out that this was an Italian aircraft which crashed into Prespa at Pili, in late 1940, before the Germans arrived, and recovered by the villager sat behind me! This was quite a crucial discovery as it meant that the second Blenheim still lay in Mikroprespa and it was subsequently confirmed that it lies about a mile behind Buck's aircraft. Shortly before departing we were told that parts of this aircraft could be seen in the water.

Maria and I were then taken to a field outside of the village, and shown the crash locations of two aircraft. One in a field, the original crater having recently been filled; the other several miles away across the valley from the field we were stood in between two small ridge lines. I was advised not to go looking in this area as it was not safe to do so, due to the proximity of the Albanian border; regretfully (as I feel it was a site that may have helped identify another aircraft)

I heeded the advice, and left a poppy in the field at Karie. The likely Blenheim at this site in the field is either Alan Godfrey's L8449 or Tommy Thompson's L8664 as both these aircraft were Rootes-built. We know this as a plate located at the crater in 1979 by *Jock* Bryce when he was trying to locate the grave of his brother, confirms a Rootes-built aircraft, and this points to these two aircraft as the others were built by Bristol. *Jock* was an ex-Vickers test pilot and brother of Andy Bryce, Andy who James remembered well, was in *Jimmy* James' Blenheim L1539.

We visited Trigonon and were lucky that a farmer we met was able to take us to the crash location, where they showed us what was purported to be a bomb from the aircraft. It certainly looked like the back of a bomb, and not wishing to disturb it, had a look around but I was unable to find any fragments or burnt patches that would confirm an aircraft. This is thought to be James's crew, in which was the Wing Commander *Paddy* Coote the Western Wing Commander who wished to look at the German advance. The crew that James had shared so many operations with plus the flight out from England, Herby the pilot who was the last of three brothers to die in the RAF and *Jock* Young a fellow Scott. I left poppies; and Maria and I drove away. On our return to Mikrolimni conditions were still unsuitable for going out on the lake but the boatman again confirmed there was a second aircraft on the Greek side a mile or so behind L1434 and reasonably close to Mikrolimni.

We moved on from our hotel in Pisoderi, to Alona to try and locate the last crash location, the one of the CO, in L8478, talking to the villagers Pantlis Alexciou and Constantine Marcos, who was an 18-year-old at the time, they reported seeing a single aircraft not damaged by the 109s coming up the valley very low. The aircraft lifted up over the balcony that Constantine was stood on and went between it and the trees, clipping the trees with one wing. The aircraft did not clear the Mountain Tumbitsa at the head of the valley crashing into the side of the hill, the reports from the time would indicate that the CO had seen the mountain, but too late, although mist and fog were present, as the aircraft was reasonably intact when the villagers went up the next day, where they removed the pilot and observer from the cockpit without trouble but the gunner they had difficulty as he was trapped in the wreckage; they then buried them in shallow graves. The following day the Germans went up on a motorcycle to see the site and stopped the locals attending. Unfortunately, when we were there we had quite a fall of snow and it wasn't possible to go up the mountain to try and find the crash site. However this was the last of the six and I now had a good idea of the locations.

What really brought things home to me was, as people gathered around Maria and me, two ladies (delete who) came and sat on a small wall and joined in the conversation. I realised as we chatted one of them was crying, and later I asked Maria why. She said a large number of the men from the village had been rounded up by the Germans and taken away, including her family, never to be seen again. The people of Northern Greece are just wonderful, they made me very welcome, were very helpful and kind, they also live in a beautiful part of the world. The area around Lake Prespa is now a nature reserve and it is quite strange to see a pelican fly by.

There are many questions unanswered. The CO, according to accounts, broke away from the other five when they dived, and does not appear to have been noticed by the German fighter leader from his account, neither did he have bombs on board, when all the other aircraft appeared to do so. What made the CO dive when he saw the Germans below is unknown, with a height advantage of several thousand feet they could have flown back into the cloud and history would have been different. The loyalty of the other crews was total, as they must have known at that moment, as they followed the CO down; with a 100mph speed advantage the fighters would catch them. Whatever the answer, and we will never know, other than the outcome was tragic. I still have work to do and hopefully will return one day to try and identify the Blenheim in the lake and the other opposite the field in Karie.

To the fallen of 211, in that most beautiful of places, so far away from home, I say to you what some of the Greek people said to me, "We still have a duty". You are not forgotten.

In memory of James and Helene Dunnet, and all of 211 Squadron lost in Greece.

Ian Carter
January 2014

Bibliography

A Don at War by David Hunt (Routledge 1990)

Air War for Yugoslavia, Greece & Crete by Chris Shores & Brian Cull with Nicola Malizia (Grub Street 1987)

Alfie's War by Richard Pike (Grub Street 2012)

An Elephant on My Wing by Peter Wright (Woodfield 2011)

Blenheim over the Balkans by James Dunnet (Pentland 2001)

British Naval Aviation by Ray Sturtivant (Arms & Armour 1990)

Desert Prelude: Early Clashes by Hakan Gustavsson & Ludovico Slongo (Stratus 2010)

Flat Out by John F. Hamlin (Air Britain 2002)

From Sea to Sky by Sir Arthur Longmore (Bles 1946)

Gladiator Ace by Brian Cull (Haynes 2010)

Jump For It! by Gerald Bowman (Evans 1955)

Memories of a Lifetime by Ch. Potamianos (via Themis Serbis)

New Zealanders in the RAF by H. L. Thompson (Dept of Internal Affairs, NZ 1959)

On Spartan Wings by John Carr (Pen & Sword 2012)

Operation Mercury by Marcel Comeau (Kimber 1961)

RAF Bomber Losses in the Middle East & Mediterranean by David Gunby & Pelham Temple (Midland 2006)

Scorpions Sting by Don Neate (Air Britain 1994)

Skozi deset taborišč (Through Ten Prison Camps) by Ivan Miklavec

The Bristol Blenheim by Graham Warner (Crecy 2005)

The Diary of an Aviator (1937–42) by Georgios Sakkis (Athens 2009)

The Price of Surrender by Ernest Walker (Blandford 1992)

War in a Stringbag by Charles Lamb (Cassell 1977)

Winged Promises by Vincent Orange (RAF Benevolent Fund Enterprises 1996)

Wings over Olympus by Sqn Ldr T. H. Wisdom (Allen & Unwin 1942)

The London Gazette AVM D'Albiac Report

FlyPast December 2000: James Dunnet article

Volare March 2009: Mirko Molteni article
War diary of Sminagos Despotides (via Themis Serbis)
Report of Archisminias Georgios Sakkis (via Themis Serbis)
John Vellacott Memoirs (30 Squadron Archives)
Greek Aircraft of WW2 (Aviation Publications, via Themis Serbis)
The Air War over Greece (Periscopio Publications 2010, via Themis Serbis)
The Blenheim Society: courtesy of Ian Carter
113 Squadron website (unable to contact owners)
D. Clark 211 Squadron RAF www.211squadron.org courtesy of Don Clark

11 Squadron ORB
14 Squadron ORB
30 Squadron ORB
45 Squadron ORB
55 Squadron ORB

84 Squadron ORB
113 Squadron ORB
203 Squadron ORB
211 Squadron ORB

Acknowledgements

First and foremost my sincere thanks go to my wife Val, almost a perpetual grass-widow—even though I'm usually only a few feet away in my office. Her patience, tolerance and understanding know no bounds.

Acknowledgements to my main contributors, Simon, Themis, Aleks, Ludovico, Ian and Don are expressed in the Introduction, but I wish to emphasise that without their respective contributions the story of the Blenheims in the Greek war could not have been told in its entirety. Hopefully that is our achievement.

Our thanks are extended to the members of Ruy Horta's *Twelve O'Clock High* website, while Themis wishes to acknowledge assistance he has received from Philip Daskas, Maria Sakkis, Andrea Babuin, John Battersby, and the Historical Section of the Hellenic Air Force; Ludovico thanks Giovanni Massimello and Roberto Gentilli; and I wish to thank the staff of the National Archives for their usual courtesy and assistance, as ever.

Last but not least, Alan Sutton, Jay Slater and their team at Fonthill Media are thanked for producing this book.

Endnotes

Preamble

1   Report of Archisminias Georgios Sakkis (via Themis Serbis).
2   *Ibid.*

Chapter 1

1   30 Squadron Archives (Simon Lord).
2   Wg Cdr Lord Arthur Forbes, a pre-war civil pilot (and later the 9th Earl of Granard) had been Air Attaché in Bucharest. In Greece, flying his personal Percival Q.6 G-AFMV, he undertook a number of 'unusual and hazardous tasks' for which he was awarded an Air Force Cross.

Chapter 2

1   see Al Bocking Memoirs: *RCAF Roundel.*
2   *Lofty* Lord memoirs (Simon Lord).
3   see Al Bocking Memoirs: *RCAF Roundel.*
4   War diary of Sminagos Despotides (via Themis Serbis).
5   *The Times* November 1940.
6   see Al Bocking Memoirs: *RCAF Roundel.*
7   *Ibid.*
8   30 Squadron ORB.
9   *The London Gazette* AVM D'Albiac Report.
10 see *From Sea to Sky* by Sir Arthur Longmore.
11 see *Wings over Olympus* by Sqn Ldr T. H. Wisdom.
12 *Ibid.*

Chapter 3

1   see Al Bocking Memoirs: *RCAF Roundel.*
2   211 Squadron ORB.
3   see Al Bocking Memoirs: *RCAF Roundel.*
4   211 Squadron ORB.
5   *Wings over Olympus.*
6   D. Clark 211 Squadron RAF www.211squadron.org
7   see *Scorpions Sting by Don Neate.*
8   211 Squadron ORB.
9   Flg Off. Alonzo Barnes was a trained fighter pilot but became involved in a series of silly pranks, which included stalking the orderly officer with a shotgun! Hence the name *Buckshot!* He was grounded and posted to the role of transport officer.
10 see *Scorpions Sting.*
11 see *Wings over Olympus.*
12 see *Scorpions Sting.*
13 211 Squadron ORB.

14   correspondence with the author.
15   see *Blenheim over the Balkans* by James Dunnet.
16   see *Wings over Olympus.*
17   *Memories of a Lifetime* by Ch. Potamianos, via Themis Serbis.
18   *The London Gazette* AVM D'Albiac Report.

Chapter 4

1   see *From Sea to Sky.*
2   *Volare* March 2009: Mirko Molteni article via Ludovico Slongo.
3   via Ian Carter.
4   see *An Elephant on my Wing.*
5   see *Blenheim over the Balkans.*
6   see *Wings over Olympus.*
7   211 Squadron ORB.
8   D. Clark 211 Squadron RAF www.211squadron.org.
9   see *Wings over Olympus.*
10   *Ibid.*
11   see *Flat Out.*
12   30 Squadron Archives.
13   see *Blenheim over the Balkans.*
14   D. Clark 211 Squadron RAF www.211squadron.org.
15   correspondence with the author.
16   D. Clark 211 Squadron RAF www.211squadron.org.
17   30 Squadron Archives.
18   *The London Gazette* AVM D'Albiac Report.
19   see *Operation Mercury.*
20   Report of Archisminias Georgios Sakkis (via Themis Serbis).
21   11 Squadron ORB.
22   see *Blenheim over the Balkans.*
23   *New Zealanders in the RAF* by H. L. Thompson RNZAF history.
24   see *Wings over Olympus.*
25   *Ibid.*
26   D. Clark 211 Squadron RAF www.211squadron.org.
27   211 Squadron ORB.
28   Sgt George Fridd, finding his slit trench nearly overrun, ordered his party to retire to the New Zealand lines, and was killed giving them covering fire.
29   30 Squadron Archives.
30   see *Al Bocking Memoirs: RCAF Roundel.*
31   *Volare* March 2009: Mirko Molteni article via Ludovico Slongo.
32   211 Squadron ORB.
33   see *Wings over Olympus.*
34   *Ibid.*
35   see *From Sea to Sky.*
36   see *Operation Mercury.*
37   211 Squadron ORB.
38   *Ibid.*
39   see *From Sea to Sky.*
40   211 Squadron ORB.
41   see *Wings over Olympus.*
42   *Ibid.*
43   see *Operation Mercury.*

Chapter 5

1   D. Clark 211 Squadron RAF www.211squadron.org.
2   11 Squadron ORB.
3   via Simon Lord.

4   see *Wings over Olympus.*
5   *Ibid.*
6   see *Scorpions Sting.*
7   D. Clark 211 Squadron RAF www.211squadron.org.
8   see *Blenheim over the Balkans.*
9   30 Squadron Archives.
10 30 Squadron ORB.
11 Errol Martyn, the leading authority on New Zealanders in the RAF and RNZAF, wrote in *For Your Tomorrow*:
    [Sqn Ldr Nedwill] took off from Paramythia at 17:20 to relieve another pilot on defensive patrol. The patrol was instructed to land 30 minutes later, at which Nedwill broke off independently at 20,000 feet and dived to 12,000 feet. The Gladiator then entered another dive and made an aileron turn before coming straight down to crash near the airfield perimeter. Nedwill, who it was thought had blacked out during the dive, was killed [or was he a victim of the Macchis?].
12 see *Blenheim over the Balkans.*
13 113 Squadron website.
14 see *Scorpions Sting.*
15 *Ibid.*
16 *Ibid.*
17 D. Clark 211 Squadron RAF www.211squadron.org.
18 Ludovico Slongo's granddad Ruggero was born on 28 February 1901 and enlisted in the Italian Royal Navy (*Regia Marina*) as a volunteer at the age of 16 in 1917. At the age of 18, he completed the School for Navy Mechanics at Castellammare di Stabia (near the local shipyards). His first enrolment ended after nine years. During this period, in 1922-33, he took part in the survey campaign of the Red Sea in the hydrographic survey ship *Ammiraglio Magnaghi*. He left the Navy with the rank of Petty Officer. He was called again in active service in 1935, because of the international crisis that followed the attack on Ethiopia and embarked in the minesweeper and colonial ship *Legnano*. He was released one year later, in 1936, with the rank of Chief Petty Officer.
    He started to work for the National Railways (*Ferrovie di Stato*) as a driver of steam locomotives, but in 1939 the war in Europe started and the Navy called him again. His age and his occupation in the civil life would have normally avoided him to be recalled in active service, as the railway system was considered of strategical relevance for the country, but Italy in the 1940s still suffered a pervasive shortage of technical talent among its population, and a Chief Petty Officer (Mechanic) was the kind of figure which its Navy could not easily give up.
    Ruggero Slongo, at the age of 38, was just given the chance of choosing the ship where he had to serve and he chose the cruiser *Fiume* assuming that a big ship had less risk of being sunk than a smaller one. On the night of 28 March 1941, he had just started his shift in one of the engine rooms of the cruiser when it was hit (at 22:30) by the guns of HMS *Warspite*, or not, there are little chances that he was able to abandon the ship when it finally sank at 23:15.
19 30 Squadron Archives.
20 see forthcoming *Marylands over Malta.*
21 see *Scorpions Sting.*
22 113 Squadron website.

Chapter 6

1   In the period the Ju 52 detachment operated, the transports made 1,665 troop-carrying and 2,363 supply sorties from Foggia to Albania, carrying across 30,000 men and 4,700 tons of supplies whilst bringing back some 10,000 wounded and sick.
2   correspondence with author.
3   see *British Naval Aviation* by Ray Sturtivant.
4   correspondence with author.
5   see *War in a Stringbag* by Charles Lamb.
6   correspondence with author.
7   see *War in a Stringbag.*
8   *Ibid.*
9   see *British Naval Aviation.*

10   correspondence with author.
11   *Ibid.*
12   *Ibid.*
13   *Ibid.*

Chapter 7

1   see *Skozi deset taborišč (Through Ten Prison Camps)* by Ivan Miklavec.
2   see *Air War for Yugoslavia, Greece & Crete* by Chris Shores & Brian Cull with Nicola Malizia.
3   see *Skozi deset taborišč (Through Ten Prison Camps).*
4   *Ibid.*
5   Blenheim 3505 was modified at the Ikarus factory to include a Teleoptik SP-40 hydraulic turret fitted with a SAFAT MC.12.17 machine-gun, while a 12.7mm calibre was mounted in the rear and the fuselage was fitted with an additional M.30 Sent-Etien Darn 7.7mm machine-gun, which resulted in the increase of the crew by another machine-gunner. Furthermore, additional M.38 FN Browning 7.99mm machine-gun was installed in the modified front starboard cabin windshield, which could be used by the observer or pilot.

Chapter 8

1   Plt Off. Bill Winsland of 33 Squadron (correspondence with author).
2   A. L. Loudon website.
3   30 Squadron Archives.
4   *Ibid.*
5   see *Blenheim over the Balkans.*
6   see *Out of the Blue* by Laddie Lucas.
7   20-year-old Richard Herbert, first of three brothers killed flying with the RAF. His older brother Philip was killed in January 1942, flying with 1 PRU, while younger brother Gerald was killed with 158 Squadron in February 1943.
8   see *Blenheim over the Balkans.*
9   *Ibid.*
10   see Gerlach report in *Blenheim over the Balkans.*
11   see *Blenheim over the Balkans.*
12   *Ibid.*
13   correspondence with author.
14   see *Alfie's War* by Richard Pike.
15   *Ibid.*
16   D. Clark 211 Squadron RAF www.211squadron.org.
17   30 Squadron Archives.
18   correspondence with author.
19   see *Blenheim over the Balkans.*
20   *Ibid.*
21   113 Squadron website.
22   *Ibid.*
23   correspondence with author.
24   113 Squadron website.
25   *Ibid.*
26   D. Clark 211 Squadron RAF www.211squadron.org.
27   *Ibid.*
28   see *Operation Mercury.*
29   30 Squadron Archives.
30   D. Clark 211 Squadron RAF www.211squadron.org.
31   see *Operation Mercury.*
32   30 Squadron Archives.
33   *Ibid.*
34   see *Air War for Yugoslavia, Greece & Crete.*
35   30 Squadron Archives.
36   *Ibid.*

37 Report of Archisminias Georgios Sakkis (via Themis Serbis).
38 see *Blenheim over the Balkans.*
39 correspondence with author.
40 see *Don at War.*
41 see *First of the Few* by Brian Cull.
42 see *Don at War.*
43 Lucky Hudson had a further lucky escape following his return from Crete. On 17 June, during operations against Syria, his Blenheim struck an object on take-off, caught fire and was destroyed when the bombs exploded. It was thought that the crew were killed but all three were later found wandering around the airfield in a dazed state; Hudson and his observer received injuries but survived.
44 see *Scorpions Sting.*
45 113 Squadron website.
46 see *Operation Mercury.*
47 Lord Forbes' Q.6 later reappeared in Cairo and was transferred to the RAF as HK838 but there is no record of it being flown from Greece/Crete to Egypt. Presumably Lord Forbes had flown it back to Egypt and then returned to Greece aboard another aircraft, or alternatively, it was dismantled and shipped to Egypt before the fall of Greece.
48 see *Don at War.*
49 see *Wings over Olympus.*

Chapter 9

1 D. Clark 211 Squadron RAF www.211squadron.org.
2 30 Squadron Archives.
3 see *Wings over Olympus.*
4 30 Squadron Archives.
5 Courtesy of Chris Goss.
6 *Ibid.*
7 see *Wings over Olympus.*
8 Plt Off. Bill Vale DFC – see *Gladiator Pilot* by Brian Cull.
9 correspondence with author.
10 *Ibid.*
11 *Flg Off.* Bud Richardson made his first flight in Hurricane V7181 on 9 May. On returning to Egypt, 30 Squadron re-equipped with Hurricanes. Some of the former Blenheim fighter pilots re-trained, including Richardson, Flt Lt Bob Davidson, Flg Off. John Jarvis, Flg Off. Andy Smith, Flg Off. Lawrence Basan, Plt Off. Travers Allison, Flt Lt *Jock* Ratlidge, and Sgt Tony Ovens, while Sqn Ldr *Percy* Milward was posted to Burma as CO of 67 Buffalo Squadron. *Jock* Ratlidge was particularly successful in the Desert, shooting down two Ju 88s before he collided with a Ju 52 he was attacking, and was killed. Another 30 Squadron pilot, Sgt Les Stammers, was posted to 33 Squadron following conversion to Hurricanes and shot down an 11 Squadron Blenheim in mistake for a Ju 88 on 21 November 1941. The pilot was the Belgian Plt Off. Désiré Verbraecke, who had survived the desert ordeal at the end of May (see Chapter XI). The observer was Sgt James Dunnet, formerly of 211 Squadron. The damaged Blenheim carried out a forced-landing without injury to the crew, but then a Ju 88 arrived on the scene and bombed the exposed aircraft, the explosion killing Plt Off. Verbraecke.
 30 Squadron was posted to Ceylon in March 1942, in time to help defend the island against Japanese carrier attacks the following month, only to suffer five of its pilots killed/died as a result. These included Flt Sgt Tony Ovens, while Flg Off. Pee-Wee Allison was wounded in the neck, but survived (only to be killed in a postwar air liner crash). On the credit side Flt Lt Bob Davidson was credited with shooting down two Japanese aircraft. He would later be credited with two German aircraft, and postwar claimed two MiGs damaged in Korea. This gave him shares in eight enemy aircraft – two Italian, two Japanese, two German and two Russian/Chinese! A unique record.
 Other 30 Squadron Greece veterans included Flt Lt Derek Walker who was given command of 260 Squadron, with which he shot down two Bf 109s but was also wounded. He received a DFC and later commanded a Typhoon squadron, before promotion to Wing Leader of 16/124 Wing. He married the beautiful ATA pilot Diana Barnato in May 1944, but was killed in a flying accident the following year, shortly after war's end.

12 On 28 May, Air Vice-Marshal D'Albiac had a lucky escape when aboard a 203 Squadron Blenheim as a passenger *en route* to the Transjordan. The Blenheim swung on take-off at Lydda, hitting a steamroller and killing an Arab workman.

13 see 30 Squadron Archives.

14 via Simon Lord.

15 *The London Gazette* AVM D'Albiac Report.

Chapter 10

1 see *Operation Mercury.*

2 30 Squadron Archives.

3 *Ibid.*

4 see *Alfie's War.*

5 see *Flat Out.*

6 see *The Price of Surrender* by Ernest Walker.

7 see *Operation Mercury.*

8 see *Flat Out.*

9 *Ibid.*

10 30 Squadron Archives.

Chapter 11

1 see *From Sea to Sky.*

2 The parents of Lt Enock Jones SAAF lived in Cardigan, Wales.

3 see *Winged Promises* by Vincent Orange.

4 see *The Price of Surrender.*

5 see *Winged Promises.*

6 see *Air War for Yugoslavia, Greece & Crete.*

7 see James Dunnet's article in *FlyPast* December 2000.

8 *Ibid.*

9 *Ibid.*

10 Sgt Jack McConnell was erroneously confused by the compiler of the official RNZAF history (New Zealanders in the RAF published in 1959) with New Zealander Sgt John McConnell, a Spitfire pilot who was killed at Malta on 15 June 1942 (see *Spitfires over Malta* by Brian Cull and Frederick Galea).

11 see *Jump For It!*

12 see *New Zealanders in the RAF.*

13 see *From Sea to Sky.*

14 see *Operation Mercury.*

Appendix 1

1 Air Vice-Marshal James Gordon-Finlayson.

Index